poetic designs

an introduction to
meters
verse forms
and figures of speech

poetic designs

an introduction to

meters

verse forms

and figures of speech

stephen j. adams

broadview press

Canadian Cataloguing in Publication Data

Adams, Stephen, 1945-
    Poetic designs : an introduction to meters, verse
forms, and figures of speech

Includes index.
    ISBN 1–55111–129–2

    1. English language   Versification.   2. Poetics. I. Title.

    PE1505.A32 1997   821.009   C97-930475-X

Broadview Press gratefully acknowledges the financial support of the Book Publishing
Industry Development Progam, Ministry of Canadian Heritage, Government of Canada.

Broadview Press Ltd. is an independent, international publishing house,
incorporated in 1985

North America:
Post Office 1243, Peterborough, Ontario, Canada K9J 7H5
3576 California Road, Orchard Park, NY, USA 14127
TEL: (705) 743-8990; FAX: (705) 743-8353;
E-mail: customerservice@broadviewpress.com

UK and Europe:
Turpin Distribution Services Ltd., Blackhorse Rd., Letchworth, Hertforshire SG6 3HN
TEL: (1462) 672555; FAX (1462) 480947; E-mail: turpin@rsc.org

Australia:
St. Clair Press, Post Office Box 287, Rozelle, NSW 2039
TEL: (02) 818 1942; FAX (02) 418 1923

www.broadviewpress.com

PRINTED IN CANADA

For Ruth

Verse, as a form, is artificial. Poetry is not a form, but rather a result.

—Amiri Baraka

There is no escape from meter; there is only mastery.

—T.S. Eliot

Contents

Acknowledgements

Many individuals have contributed expert advice and encouragement to this project. Without implicating any of them in the shortcomings of my book, I thank my colleagues at the University of Western Ontario, especially Peter Auksi, James Crimmins, Patrick Deane, Stan Dragland, Minnette Gaudet, Allan Gedalof, Alison Lee, Michael O'Driscoll, Richard Stingle, Jane Toswell, and Nicholas Watson.

Beyond Western, I have benefitted from the acute critiques of Annie Finch, Don McKay, Theodore J. Sherman, and Demetres Tryphonopoulos, and a memorable day of conversation with Marjorie Perloff.

In another sort of community, I have gleaned much material from several who might be surprised to find their names here—especially Michel Delville, David Rothman, Thomas Kirby-Smith, and Steven Willett—whose e-mail postings and exchanges over the past year have been a source of insight and exhilaration.

For technical assistance within the university, I am grateful to James Good, for time and support in the office of the Dean of Arts, as well as Connie Mabb, Lynn Larmour, and above all, Elly Pakalnis.

At Broadview, I am supremely grateful to Terry Teskey, for her patient editing, and for coping with the vagaries of scansion by word processor; to Anne Hodgetts for cover design; to Michael Harrison for his faith in this project; and to Don LePan, president of Broadview Press, for his generosity. This last repeats a debt of gratitude I owe Don LePan's father, Douglas LePan, for support and many kindnesses when I was a graduate student.

BETJEMAN, JOHN: Excerpt from "False Security" from *Collected Poems* by John Betjeman. By permission of the author and John Murray (Publishers) Ltd.

BIRNEY, EARLE: "Bushed" and excerpts from "Anglo-Saxon Street" and "trawna tuh bellul by knayjin psifik" from *Selected Poems of Earle Birney* by Earle Birney. Used by permission of McLelland & Stewart, Inc., Toronto, *The Canadian Publishers.*

BRIDGES, ROBERT: Excerpt from "London Snow" from *Poetical Works of Robert Bridges* (Oxford University Press, 1936) by permission of Oxford University Press.

CAGE, JOHN: Excerpt from "Anarchy" by John Cage, from *John Cage at Seventy Five*, ed. R. Fleming and W. Duckworth. Bucknell University Press, 1989. By permission of Associated University Presses.

COOK, ALBERT: Excerpts from Homer, *The Odyssey*, a new verse translation by Albert Cook, W.W. Norton & Co., Inc., copyright © 1967 by Albert Cook.

CRANE, HART: Excerpts from "To Brooklyn Bridge," "Cutty Sark," and "Voyages" from *The Poems of Hart Crane*, edited by Marc Simon, copyright © 1986, Marc Simon and Liveright Publishing Corporation.

CULLEN, COUNTEE: Excerpt from "Only the Polished Skeleton," in *The Medea and Some Poems*, published by Harper & Brothers (1935). Copyright held by the Amistad Research Center, renewed 1962 by Ida Cullen, administered by permission of Thompson and Thompson, New York, N.Y.

CUMMINGS, E.E.: "l(a," "r-p-o-p-h-e-s-s-a-g-r," "o//the round," and lines from "anyone lived in a pretty how town" and "as freedom is a breakfast food," from *Complete Poems 1904–1962* by E.E. Cummings, edited by George J. Firmage. Copyright 1923, 1925, 1926, 1931, 1935, 1938, 1939, 1940, 1944, 1945, 1946, 1947, 1948, 1949, 1950, 1951, 1952, 1953, 1954, © 1955, 1956, 1957, 1958, 1959, 1960, 1961, 1962, 1963, 1966, 1967, 1968, 1972, 1973, 1974, 1975, 1976, 1977, 1978, 1979, 1980, 1981, 1982, 1983, 1984, 1985, 1986, 1987, 1988, 1989, 1990, 1991 by the Trustees for the E.E. Cummings Trust. Copyright © 1973, 1976, 1978, 1979, 1981, 1983, 1985, 1991 by George James Firmage. Reprinted by permission of Liveright Publishing Corporation.

DABYDEEN, DAVID: "Coolie Son" from *Coolie Odyssey*, © 1990, Dangaroo Press.

DAY LEWIS, C.: Excerpt from "Do Not Expect Again a Phoenix Hour," from *The Complete Poems* by C. Day Lewis, published by Sinclair-Stevenson (1992), in the estate of C. Day Lewis, by permission of Reed International Books Ltd.

DOOLITTLE, HILDA: "Oread" and lines from *The Walls Do Not Fall*, from *Collected Poems 1912–1944*, New Directions Publishing Corporation. Copyright © 1982 the Estate of Hilda Doolittle.

ELIOT, T.S.: Excerpts from "The Love Song of J. Alfred Prufrock," "Gerontion" and "The Waste Land" in *Collected Poems 1909–1962* by T.S. Eliot, copyright 1936 by Harcourt, Brace & Company, copyright © 1964, 1963 by T.S. Eliot, reprinted by permission of the publisher. Excerpt from "The Dry Salvages" in *Four Quartets*, copyright 1941 by T.S. Eliot and renewed 1969 by Esme Valerie Eliot, reprinted by permission of Harcourt, Brace & Company. Excerpt from "Little Gidding" in *Four Quartets*, copyright 1943 by T.S. Eliot and renewed 1971 by Esme Valerie Eliot, reprinted by permission of Harcourt, Brace & Company, and by Faber and Faber.

FORREST-THOMSON, VERONICA: Found poem from Veronica Forrest-Thomson, *Poetic Artifice: A Theory of Twentieth-Century Poetry* (Manchester: Manchester Univ. Press, 1978), reprinted by permission of the publisher.

FROST, ROBERT: Excerpts from "Birches," "Spring Pools," "The Old Man's Winter Night," "Design," "Once by the Pacific," and "The Cow in Apple Time" from *The Poetry of Robert Frost*, edited by Edward Connery Lathem. Copyright 1923, 1930, 1939, © 1969 by Henry Hold and Company, Inc. Copyright 1936, 1942, 1944, © 1951, © 1958 by Robert Frost. Copyright © 1964, 1967, 1970 by Lesley Frost Ballantyne.

GUNN, THOM: "Considering the Snail" from *My Sad Captains* by Thom Gunn. Copyright © 1961 and copyright renewed © 1989 by Thom Gunn. By permission of Farrar, Straus & Giroux, Inc., and Faber and Faber Ltd.

HACKER, MARILYN: Excerpt from "The Last April Interval" from *Going Back to the River* by Marilyn Hacker, Random House, Inc., Vintage Books, 1990.

HARDY, THOMAS: "The Coquette, and After" and excerpt from "The Respectable Burgher on Higher Criticism" in *The Complete Poems of Thomas Hardy* reprinted by permission of Macmillan General Books and Papermac.

HAVEL, VÁCLAV: "Estrangement" by Václav Havel reprinted by MODULO by permission of Václav Havel and Grove Press, Inc.

HUGHES, LANGSTON: Excerpts from "Widow Woman" and "Harlem Sweeties" from *Collected Poems* by Langston Hughes, copyright © 1994 by the Estate of Langston Hughes. Reprinted by permission of Alfred A. Knopf, Inc., and by permission of Harold Ober Associates, Inc., © 1994 by the estate of Langston Hughes.

KIPLING, RUDYARD: "Sestina of the Tramp Royale" reprinted by permission of Bantam Doubleday Dell Publishing Group, copyright © A.P. Watt, Ltd.

LAYTON, IRVING: Excerpt from "To the Girls of My Graduating Class" from *A Wild Peculiar Joy* by Irving Layton. Used by permission of McClelland & Stewart, Inc., Toronto, *The Canadian Publishers.*

LEPAN, DOUGLAS: Excerpt from "Elegy in the Romagna" from *Weathering It* by Douglas LePan. Used by permission of McClelland & Stewart, Inc., Toronto, *The Canadian Publishers.*

LORDE, AUDRE: "A Small Slaughter" from *The Black Unicorn,* Poems by Audre Lorde, W.W. Norton & Company, Inc., New York. Copyright © 1978 by Audre Lorde.

LOWELL, ROBERT: Excerpt from "In Memory of Arthur Winslow" in *Lord Weary's Castle,* copyright 1946 and renewed 1974 by Robert Lowell, by permission of Harcourt, Brace & Company. Excerpt from "Skunk Hour" from *Life Studies* by Robert Lowell. Copyright © 1956, 1959 by Robert Lowell. By permission of Farrar, Straus & Giroux, Inc., and by Faber and Faber.

MACLEISH, ARCHIBALD: Excerpts from "The End of the World" and "Ars Poetica," in *Collected Poems 1917-1982* by Archibald MacLeish. Copyright © 1985 by The Estate of Archibald MacLeish. Reprinted by permission of Houghton Mifflin Co. All rights reserved.

MACPHERSON, JAY: Stanza from "A Lost Soul" from *Poems Twice Told* by Jay Macpherson. By permission of Oxford University Press Canada.

MCKAY, DON: "Softball" from *Sanding Down This Rocking Chair on a Windy Day* by Don McKay. Used by permission of McClelland & Stewart, Inc., Toronto, *The Canadian Publishers.*

MERWIN, W.S.: Excerpt from "Odysseus" in *The Drunk in the Furnace* by W.S. Merwin, © 1956, 1957, 1958, 1959, 1960, by permission of Georges Borchardt, Inc.

MIDDLETON, CHRISTOPHER: "The Child at the Piano" © Christopher Middleton, reprinted by permission of the author.

MILLAY, EDNA ST. VINCENT: Excerpts from "Oh, think not I am faithful to a vow!", "What lips my lips have kissed," and "I, being born a woman and distressed" by Edna St. Vincent Millay. From *Collected Poems,* HarperCollins. Copyright 1921, 1923, 1948, 1951 by Edna St. Vincent Millay and Norma Millay Ellis. All rights reserved. Reprinted by permission of Elizabeth Barnett, literary executor.

MOORE, MARIANNE: Excerpts from "The Fish" and "Silence" from *Collected Poems of Marianne Moore,* copyright © 1935 by Marianne Moore, renewed 1963 by Marianne Moore and T.S. Eliot. Reprinted by permission of Simon & Schuster, and by Faber and Faber.

NASH, OGDEN: Excerpt from "The Rhinoceros" in *Verses 1929 On* by Ogden Nash. By permission of Little, Brown and Company.

OLSON, CHARLES: Excerpt from "The Distances" from *Selected Poems of Charles Olson,* edited by Robert Creeley, copyright © 1993 Regents of the University of California, © 1987 Estate of Charles Olson and the University of Connecticut, reprinted by permission of the University of California Press.

PEACOCK, MOLLY: "Little Miracle" from *Original Love* by Molly Peacock, W.W. Norton & Company, Inc., 1995, reprinted by permission of the author.

PLATH, SYLVIA: Excerpt from "Lady Lazarus" from *Ariel* by Sylvia Plath. Copyright (©) 1963 by Ted Hughes. Reprinted by permission of Faber and Faber Ltd., and HarperCollins Publishers, Inc.

POUND, EZRA: "The Return," and excerpts form "The Seafarer," "Apparuit," "The River Merchant's Wife: A Letter," "Homage to Sextus Propertius," "Hugh Selwyn Mauberley," and Canto 20, from *Personae,* copyright 1926 by Ezra Pound, and *The Cantos of Ezra Pound,* copyright 1934, 1948 by Ezra Pound, published by New Directions Publishing Corporation and Faber & Faber.

PRINCE, F.T.: Excerpt from "Soldiers Bathing" from *Collected Poems* by F.T. Prince. Reprinted by permission of Sheep Meadow Press.

RANSOM, JOHN CROWE: Excerpts from "Here Lies a Lady" and "Dead Boy" from *Selected Poems* by John Crowe Ransom, copyright © 1969 by Alfred A. Knopf, Inc. Reprinted by permission of the publisher.

ROBINSON, EDWIN ARLINGTON: Excerpt from "Miniver Cheevy" from *The Collected Poems of Edwin Arlington Robinson* (New York: Macmillan, 1961) reprinted with the permission of Simon & Schuster.

ROETHKE, THEODORE: Excerpt from "To a Young Wife" from *The Collected Poems of Theodore Roethke,* Bantam Doubleday Dell Publishing Group.

SANDBURG, CARL: Excerpt from "Chicago" in *Chicago Poems* by Carl Sandburg, copyright 1916 by Hold, Rinehart and Winston, Inc., and renewed 1944 by Carl Sandburg, and excerpt from "Love in Labrador" in *Good Morning, America,* copyright 1928 and renewed 1956 by Carl Sandburg, reprinted by permission of Harcourt, Brace & Company.

SCOTT, F.R.: Excerpt from "W.L.M.K." from *The Collected Poems of F.R. Scott.* Used by permission of McLelland & Stewart, Inc., Toronto, *The Canadian Publishers.*

SERVICE, ROBERT: Excerpt from "Only a Boche" from *Rhymes of a Red Cross Man* by Robert Service. Copyright © by Robert Service. Published by Putnam Publishing Group.

SMITH, STEVIE: Excerpt from "For Karl" from *The Collected Poems of Stevie Smith,* Allen Lane, Penguin Books Ltd. Copyright © Stevie Smith 1975. Reprinted by permission of New Directions Publishing Corporation.

SOLT, MARY ELLEN: "Forsythia" reprinted by permission of the author.

STARBUCK, GEORGE: "A Tapestry for Bayeux" from *The Argot Merchant Disaster: New and Selected Poems,* © 1982, Atlantic/Little, Brown & Co.

STEVENS, WALLACE: Excerpts from "Sunday Morning," "The Idea of Order at Key West," and "A High-Toned Old Christian Woman" from *Collected Poems* by Wallace Stevens, copyright 1954 by Wallace Stevens. Reprinted by permission of Alfred A. Knopf, Inc., and by Faber and Faber.

SYMONS, ARTHUR: Excerpt from "The Opium Smoker" by Arthur Symons. By permission of Brian Read, M.A. (Oxon), literary executor.

THOMAS, DYLAN: Excerpt from "Do Not Go Gentle into That Good Night," "Altarwise by Owl Light," "When All My Five and Country Senses See," "A Process in the Weather of the Heart," and "Vision and Prayer" reprinted by permission of David Higham Associates.

TRINIDAD, DAVID: Excerpt from "Movin' with Nancy" from *Hand over Heart: Poems 1981–1988,* Serpent's Tail Press, 1991. Copyright 1991 by David Trinidad. Reprinted by permission of the author.

WALCOTT, DEREK: Excerpt from "The Gulf" from *The Gulf and Other Poems* by Derek Walcott. Copyright © by Derek Walcott. Excerpt from "The Hotel Normandie Pool" from *The Fortunate Traveller* by Derek Walcott. Copyright © 1982 by Derek Walcott. By permission of Farrar, Straus & Giroux, Inc.

WALDROP, ROSEMARIE: Excerpt from *Inserting the Mirror,* from *The Reproduction of Profiles,* New Directions Publishing Corportion, copyright © 1987 by Rosemarie Waldrop.

WILBUR, RICHARD: Excerpt from "Junk" in *Advice to a Prophet and Other Poems,* copyright © 1961 and renewed 1989 by Richard Wilbur, and excerpt from "Love Calls Us to the Things of this World" in *Things of This World,* copyright © 1956 and renewed 1984 by Richard Wilbur, reprinted by permission of Harcourt, Brace & Company.

WILKINSON, ANNE: Excerpt from "Lens" from *The Collected Poems of Anne Wildinson and a Prose Memoir,* edited by A.J.M. Smith, © Macmillan of Canada, 1968, and Dr. Alan G. Wilkinson, literary executor.

WILLIAMS, WILLIAM CARLOS: "The Rose," "Poem," "The Locust Tree in Flower," and excerpts from "At the Ball Game," "To a Poor Old Woman," and "Smell!" from *Collected Poems of William Carlos Williams 1909–1939,* volume 1. Copyright © 1938 by New Directions Publishing Corporation.

WRIGHT, JUDITH: Excerpt from "Woman to Child" by Judith Wright from *A Human Pattern: Selected Poems* (ETT Imprint, Watsons Bay, Australia 1996), reprinted by permission of the publisher.

YEATS, WILLIAM BUTLER: "No Second Troy" and excerpts from "Among School Children," "Lapis Lazuli," "Easter 1916," "The Second Coming," "Two songs from a Play," and "In Memory of Major Robert Gregory" from *The Collected Poems of W.B. Yeats* reprinted by permission of A.P. Watt, Ltd., on behalf of Michael Yeats. Excerpts from "Leda and the Swan," "Among School Children," "Lapis Lazuli," "Easter 1916," "The Second Coming," and "Two Songs from a Play" from *The Collected Poems of W.B. Yeats,* Volume 1: The Poems, revised and edited by Richard J. Finneran. Copyright 1924 by Macmillan Publishing Company; copyright renewed © 1968 by Bertha Georgie Yeats. Excerpts from "The Second Coming" and "Easter 1916" copyright 1924 by Macmillan Publishing Company; copyright renewed © 1952 by Bertha Georgie Yeats. Excerpt from "Lapis Lazuli" copyright 1940 by Georgie Yeats; copyright renewed © 1968 by Bertha Georgie Yeats, Michael Yeats, and Anne Yeats.

Meter and Rhythm

The study of *prosody*[1] is not an end in itself, but a means to an end. Although it can easily degenerate into a set of dry technical terms and rules—and I won't pretend to have entirely avoided this snare—its ultimate goal is to heighten the experience of poetry. Some teachers evidently think it possible to evoke this experience on the spot, bypassing the snarls of prosodic terminology and understanding and instead attempting to convey a personal enthusiasm for a poem through a mixture of oohs and ahs, nods and winks, and personal charisma. The student may be temporarily persuaded into some kind of experience of the poem, but is left with little or nothing to help in understanding the next poem, for he or she remains ignorant of how effects have been achieved.

The Importance of Prosody

The effects of poetry are to a great extent induced via *meter* and *form,* the two elements that most obviously distinguish poetry from prose, and the bona fide student of poetry must acquire an intellectual understanding of them.

The most difficult part of this more demanding process, perhaps, is keeping the ultimate goal in mind. A student of botany, for example, struggling with an enormous catalogue of Latin- and Greek-derived terms, may well wonder what they have to do with an enthusiasm for roses; and the literary student struggling with a first attempt at *scansion*[2] may think it impossible that such an apparently mechanical procedure can ever yield insight. An experienced reader of poetry, on the other hand, recognizes the "fingering" of an iambic pentameter line as inwardly, as instinctively and unconsciously, as the average pianist knows the

---

[1] *Prosody* is the general term that encompasses all aspects of poetic meter and form. Technical terms are italicized upon first appearance in the text and defined, where necessary, in a note.

[2] *Scansion* is a visual code for marking meter and rhythm.

C-major scale. This analogy with music is suggestive. Learning to scan "Was this the face that launch'd a thousand ships" is like learning to play a simple scale. I like to think of all the labours of poetic analysis—including scansion and prosodic analysis—as rehearsal for a performance. They are not the performance itself; but without them the performance, the experience of the art, will be lacking.

No one reads the rules for the game of, say, hockey for pleasure; yet no one can possibly understand the game without knowing the meaning of "icing the puck" or "offside." Without this understanding, the game is a meaningless blur. Only with it does the game begin to "make sense." But prosody, like the rules of hockey, is not simply a body of information that one learns and then "applies." The truly informed fan *sees* the offside happen before the whistle blows, experiences it in the stir of action. In poetry as in sport, the observer's eyes—and ears—must be educated to this same point of instinctive understanding.

At the same time, even the best referee in the NHL is not the equal of a Gretzky. Knowledge of the rules of prosody may create an informed critic or skilled versifier, but not a poet. As the poet Amiri Baraka rightly says, "verse, as a form, is artificial. Poetry is not a form, but rather a result." Still, a Gretzky ignorant of the rules is not much use to anybody. The aspiring poet remains ignorant of the principles of prosody at his or her peril.

The Sound of Meter

The metrical "sound" of a poem can be understood as an interplay of five elements: meaning, voice, rhythm, meter, and syntax. Although the first two will not be considered further here, they are just as vital as the rest. Every "reading" of a poem—whether aloud or silent, whether dramatic soliloquy or private lyric—is a performance. In it, the reader adopts a character or impersonates a voice constructed from the text. The character, or voice—as any actor knows—comprises a multitude of inflections, hesitations, body language, knowing smiles—that constitute the "meaning" of the speech as much as its rational content. The trained Shakespearean actor acquires an understanding of prosody in order to speak the lines correctly, but will not be curbed by prosodic rules when the passion of the moment demands breaking the meter. Although these dramatic dimensions of poetry are fundamental, their understanding falls outside the strict realm of prosody.

In prosody, the first key concepts are *rhythm* and *meter*. What is the difference between the two? "Meter" refers to the abstract model for poetic measure, "rhythm" to the actual sound and inflection of the words, the free give-and-take of accents, inflections, and pauses within a line. Thus the "meter" of *every* line of a poem "in" iambic pentameter is *the same*, regardless of its "metrical variations":

Meter: ˘ ˘ | ˘ ´ | ˘ ´ | ˘ ´ | ˘ ´
Rhythm: ´ ˘ | ˘ ´ ‖ ˘ ´ | ˘ ´ | ˘ ´
              Passions of rain, or moods in falling snow

This line is in iambic pentameter, even though at the beginning the rhythm de-
parts momentarily from the regular metrical pattern. As we shall see, English
iambic pentameter is so flexible that one can even, in theory, have a whole line
(a very unusual one) without a single iamb in it:

Meter: ˘ ´ | ˘ ´ | ˘ ´ | ˘ ´ | ˘ ´
Rhythm: ´ ˘ | ´ ´ ‖ ˘ ˘ ´ | ´ ˘ ‖ ´ ´
              Shouting "Bang bang" with a toy rifle, "Bang bang!"

But even in such an extreme case, the *meter* of the line remains iambic penta-
meter. It is quite wrong to say that the poet has departed from iambic penta-
meter; she has just stretched its resources to the limits.

Different Metrical Systems and Their Histories

Not every English poem is written in iambic pentameter. The English language
has become exceptionally rich in metrical possibilities, and the student should
be aware from the start that there are now not only many meters to choose
from, but five completely different *systems* of meter, each with its own rules and
its own expressive possibilities. Determining, at first encounter with any particu-
lar poem, which system applies is one of the most sophisticated and perplexing
challenges facing the beginning student of poetry.[3] This chapter will concentrate
on the system that includes iambic pentameter, the accentual-syllabic system,
leaving the rest for Chapter 2. But they are all described briefly here. They are:

1. Pure *accentual* meter. In this system, only the number of *accented syllables*
    is counted in each line; the commonest version is a line of four accented
    (and an undetermined number of unaccented) syllables.[4] This is the earliest
    system in the English language, and remains second in importance after the
    accentual-syllabic.

---

[3] The reader coming to this section with no previous knowledge of poetic form, or with
little knowledge of literary history, may find parts of it hard to follow; but the broad his-
torical outline is needed from the beginning, I think, to make sense of the full variety of
English meters. Those who find this material difficult at first should return to it after
reading the first two chapters.

[4] English words are compounded of *syllables,* each of which has one vowel sound that
may or may not be bounded by consonants. Students who have difficulty determining the
number of syllables in a given word, or finding the accents, may benefit by practising
on individual words (checking the results in a dictionary) before moving on to scansion.

2. Pure *syllabic* meter. In this system, only the number of syllables, regardless of accentuation, is counted in each line.
3. *Accentual-syllabic* meter. In this system, both the number of syllables and the number of accents are counted, and the rhythm results from interplay between the two. This is the most complex and the most subtly expressive of the metrical systems, and the one that constitutes the main tradition of English literary poetry from the mid-sixteenth century to the present. The commonest version of this system is iambic pentameter.
4. *Quantitative* meter. This is an attempt to reproduce the effects of Greek and Latin meters in English. These meters are determined not by accent but by patterns made by "quantity"—that is, by long and short syllables. Since speakers of English normally pay little attention to quantity, these meters have remained rare, isolated experiments by individual, classically educated poets, and they assume a classically educated readership.
5. *Free verse.* This "system" is really an absence of system: anything goes. Free verse is infinite in its varieties, but no version of it takes a regular count of syllables, accents, or any other feature of the language. Rare before 1900, free verse has become dominant in this century. Free verse still has "form," but analysis of it requires *ad hoc* adaptations of the principles that operate in metered verse; this topic will be discussed in Chapter 5.

Fortunately for the student, the metrical system appropriate for bodies of poetry of earlier than the twentieth century is usually predictable from its historical context, as Table 1 indicates.

Linguists divide all languages into two general types: the syllable-timed and the accent-timed. Some languages, like French or Greek, are syllable-timed: speakers of these languages—quite unconsciously—try to equalize the span of time allotted to each syllable, ignoring accent. Languages like English and German, however, are accent-timed: speakers quite unconsciously try to equalize the time span between primary accents, regardless of the number of syllables. The most natural meter for English, then, is an accentual meter, with a greater or lesser degree of regulation of the number of syllables between accents. (The consequences of this observation will be more fully explored in Chapter 2.)

English poetry thus began in a pure accentual meter: the standard line of verse through the Old English period is a line of four accents, with a medial *caesura,* bound together in a pattern of *alliteration* in the two halves of the line.[5] The number of unaccented syllables is left unpatterned. Here are lines

---

[5] My account of Old English alliterative meter is deliberately simplified. The issue has been complex and controversial ever since Sievers introduced his line "types" at the end of the nineteenth century, but fuller treatment is best left to specialized courses. The historical connection between the Old English line and its fourteenth-century revival is likewise a matter of controversy.

TABLE 1: METRICAL PERIODS

Old & Middle English	Accentual meter patterned with alliteration. Accentual rhymed lyrics arise in the twelfth century
14th to mid-16th centuries	Chaucer practices a meter that approximates accentual-syllabic; period of language change and metrical confusion
Mid-16th through 17th centuries	Regulation of line to equal numbers of syllables; stabilization and development of accentual-syllabic meter in verse drama by Marlowe and Shakespeare, in *epic* by Milton
Late 17th through 18th centuries	Dominance of iambic pentameter in *heroic couplet* and post-Miltonic *blank verse*
19th century	Continued refinement and exploration of accentual-syllabic meters; gradual emergence of accentual meters; Whitman introduces free verse
20th century	Free verse of various types gradually gains ascendance over metrical verse; metrical options expand to include accentual, syllabic, and accentual-syllabic types; many experimental developments

from the Old English poem "The Seafarer" (circa ninth century), first in the original and then as translated by Ezra Pound in a way that approximates the verse form:

Nap nihtscua,   norþan sniwde,

hrim hrusan band;   hægl feol on eorþan,

corna caldast.   Forþ cnyssaþ nu

heortan geþohtas,   þæt ic hean streamas,

sealtyþa gelac   sylf cunnige

Neareth nightshade, snoweth from north,

Frost froze the land, hail fell on earth then,

Corn of the coldest. Nathless there knocketh now

The heart's thought that I on high streams

The salt-wavy tumult traverse alone.

Some modern poets have written a meter that reproduces the effects of Old English alliterative verse:

> An axe angles
> > from my neighbor's ashcan;
> It is hell's handiwork,
> > the wood not hickory.
> The flow of the grain
> > not faithfully followed.
>
> Dawndrizzle ended   dampness steams from
> blotching brick and   blank plasterwaste
> Faded housepatterns hoary and finicky
> Unfold stuttering   stick like a phonograph

Various types of accentual meter dominate the earliest English poetry from its beginnings up to the fourteenth century, the time of Chaucer, the first major author to practice something that approximates accentual-syllabic meter in our language. Eventually, Chaucer's line, further refined and regularized, became the dominant mode in the literary tradition; but pure accentual meters remain evident in certain non-literary kinds of verse such as nursery rhymes and ballads. Accentual meters then began to re-emerge in the nineteenth century, most notably in Coleridge's experimental poem "Christabel":[6]

> 'Twas the middle of night by the castle clock
>
> And the owls have awakened the crowing cock,
>
> Tu---whit!---Tu---whoo!
>
> And hark, again! The crowing cock
>
> How drowsily it crew. (´)

Subsequently, accentual meters show up in the mid-nineteenth century in certain poems of Tennyson and in the so-called sprung rhythm of Gerard Manley Hopkins, and become freely available to poets writing in the twentieth century.

After Chaucer in the fourteenth century, the English language itself underwent rapid major changes (by no means limited to the loss of the pronounced final *e*); the metrical practices during the next 150 years were confused and remain the subject of controversy among specialists. Few authors of this period tend to be included in non-specialized anthologies of poetry, apart from John

---

[6] The scansion of the last line is explained in the discussion of accentual meters in Chap. 2.

Skelton (whose unique "Skeltonics" are a surviving version of accentual meter) and Sir Thomas Wyatt (whose meter remains a subject of dispute).

Then in the middle of the sixteenth century, English poets, attempting to stabilize English meter, used (as Chaucer before them had done) the strict syllabic meters of Italian and French as a model. They tried to regularize the number of syllables per line—lines of eight or ten syllables being favoured—and, as well, tried to regularize the alternation of accented and unaccented syllables. Sir Thomas Wyatt's most famous poem was written before 1536, before the time of this regularization:

> They flee from me that sometime did me seek,
> With naked foot stalking in my chamber.
> I have seen them gentle, tame and meek,
> That now are wild, and do not remember
> That sometime they put themselves in danger
> To take bread at my hand ...

When it was first printed in 1557, however, Tottel, the editor of the famous *Tottel's Miscellany*, felt the need to make Wyatt's lines conform to the newly discovered regularity. Below, Wyatt's original appears beneath Tottel's regularization; the alterations are most instructive.

> With naked foot stalking within my chamber
> With naked foot stalking   in my chamber

> Once have I seen them gentle, tame and meek,
> I have   seen them gentle, tame and meek,

> That now are wild, and do not once remember
> That now are wild, and do not   remember

> That sometime they have put themselves in danger
> That sometime they   put themselves in danger

The added syllables make all the difference—and debate still lingers whether the voice of the poem is more convincing in its original or its Tottelized version.

This period also produced the first piece of English blank verse, that is, unrhymed iambic pentameter—Surrey's translation of part of Virgil's *Aeneid*:

> With this the sky gan whirl about the sphere:
> The cloudy night gan thicken from the sea,
> With mantles spread that cloakèd earth and skies,

And eke the treason of the Greekish guile.
The watchmen lay disperst, to take their rest ...

This verse strikes the contemporary ear as very stiff, but its invention prepared the medium which, just one generation later, produced Marlowe and Shakespeare, and the great flowering of Elizabethan poetic drama. Its principle is essentially a strict syllabic count, with a care for alternating unaccented and accented syllables; in the words of the poet George Gascoigne (1575), "we use none other but a foote of two sillables, whereof the first is depressed or made short, and the second is elevate or made long."[7] To these poets and their successors, the art of versification was known as the art of "*numbers.*"

But a strictly syllabic meter (because English is not syllable-timed) could not prevail: ways had to be found to give it more variety, and the dominating power of English accentuation quickly asserted itself. The accentual-syllabic system basically evolved as a compromise between the syllabic regularity imported from the continent and the native accentuation of our language. This evolution is striking in the development of Shakespeare himself: the early plays are quite metrically and syllabically regular, but the later plays become gradually more free both in their syllable count and their treatment of accent and enjambment. After Jonson, Donne, Milton, and others firmly established this accentual-syllabic system—whether rhymed in couplets and in a dazzling variety of lyric stanzas, or unrhymed as blank verse—this system became the dominant meter in the literary tradition that extends through the great Augustan, Romantic, and Victorian periods and on into the present century. The student can therefore trust that, with rare exceptions, poetry of this long period, from the mid-sixteenth century into the late nineteenth and early twentieth, can be understood metrically using the accentual-syllabic procedures described below.

Exceptions, however, became more and more frequent through this time. Nineteenth-century poets became interested in formal experimentation such as, within the accentual-syllabic system, *triple meters* (meters, primarily anapestic, having not one but two slack syllables between accents). Uncommon though by no means unknown in the seventeenth and eighteenth centuries, triple meters appeared more and more frequently through the nineteenth, and so did more exotic types, like *trochaic octameter.* In other systems accentual meters, as I have said, began to re-emerge after Coleridge's "Christabel." And then, in the year 1855, a startling innovation occurred in the United States, at that time a new English-speaking country devoted to individual liberty and the questioning of Old World traditions: Walt Whitman, reading in Emerson that "it is not meters, but a meter-making argument, that makes a poem,"[8] launched the first full-length poetic career in free verse. Followers were few at first, but before the twentieth

---

[7] Quoted in John Thompson, *The Founding of English Metre* (London: Routledge, 1961), p. 71.

[8] Ralph Waldo Emerson, "The Poet," in *Essays: Second Series* (1844).

century had passed two decades, free verse had perhaps equalled or surpassed metrical verse, at least in volume of production.

The experimentation has not stopped. Forms were imported from foreign languages: *sestinas* and *villanelles* from France, the *haiku* from Japan, more recently *ghazals* from Arabic and Persian. A new type of pure syllabic meter appeared in poems by Robert Bridges and Marianne Moore. Typographic experimentation has been tried by E.E. Cummings and others. The margins of poetry itself have been stretched and sometimes crossed by *prose poems, concrete poems,* and *sound poems.* Free verse itself has taken an amazing variety of developments.

The result for the poet is an unprecedented array of choices, each with its own expressive potential. But for the student, the result is a bewildering dilemma. Encountering a twentieth-century poem for the first time, she may have little to tell her whether the poem is free verse, or metrical, or almost metrical, or syllabic—or whatever. English verse form has become a true embarrassment of riches.

The Meaning of Meter

The study of meter demands attention to minute details of language that escape ordinary notice. This is one of its virtues. But the student should be braced for the quantity of minute detail to follow. The suppleness, subtlety, and variety of English meters cannot be understood without painstaking observation of detail and attentive listening. Still, meter and form have dimensions of meaning that do not depend solely on the sensitivity of one's ears.

The historical dimension is one of these. A poet's choice of meter and form is conscious and deliberate: one does not write dactylic hexameter by accident. In making this choice, the poet places his work in relation to all the rest of English poetry, both past and present. A modern poet choosing to write in blank verse is, simply by that choice, rejecting the free forms that dominate contemporary poetry and placing the poem in relation to the literary tradition that stretches back through the great Romantics and Milton to Shakespeare. An eighteenth-century writer choosing heroic couplets is accepting the dominant meter of the day; but a twentieth-century writer making the same choice is necessarily evoking the Augustan period. Dactylic hexameter has never been common in English; but any poet using it, as Longfellow does in "Evangeline," can only be placing his work in relation to the epics of Homer and Virgil, which (in Greek and Latin) use that meter. The stanzas associated with particular poets (the Burns stanza, the Spenserian) or particular poems (the "In Memoriam" stanza, the "elegiac quatrain" used by Gray) will always carry traces of their history, just as the ballad stanza will always seem folksy. Many formal inventions in poetry have, on the other hand, had their origins in a poet's desire to shed the clichés of the present or the associations of the past. Such points require little subtlety of observation, but they remain integral to the meaning of formal choices.

Beyond this historical element, there is another, more general one: the poet's choice of meter establishes, to borrow a metaphor introduced by John Hollander,[9] a kind of contract with the reader, assuring her that every syllable in the poem has been duly weighed and measured, that the language has been written with full attention not only to its content, but to its expressiveness as language, even to the physical accidents of language. This contract creates a kind of aesthetic distance, a kind of reading with a heightened awareness of the language as language. The existence and perception of meter depends on this aesthetic awareness of language on the part of the reader. Even in oral and folk poetry, the presence of meter sets the language apart as distinct from ordinary speech. The meter says that a poem must be heard as a poem.

Both the aesthetic distance created by metrical contract and the historical associations of the form exist in any poem as an ever-present background. Where the meter is smooth, conventional, or unremarkable, it tends to remain background; where the meter is rough, unconventional, or insistent, it fore-grounds itself and forces a more self-conscious awareness. Elizabethan writers drew a distinction between "smooth song" and "strong lined" poetry that is still valid today. In strong lined poetry—of whatever period—the poetic rhythms create meaning through the intricacies of their play with the metrical frame. In general, a crowding of accented syllables suggests the slow, the emphatic, or the difficult. A grouping of unaccented syllables suggests speed, lightness, and ease. A sudden rhythmic reversal often accompanies a surprise, a turn of thought, a new *tone* of voice, an intensification of some kind. But the perception of such effects—not to mention their analysis—requires an educated ear.

The Accentual-Syllabic System

To explain what happens in a line of iambic pentameter, an array of terms is necessary. The foot,[10] to begin with, is a basic unit of rhythm within the line, a kind of interchangeable rhythmic module. There are six kinds of metrical feet commonly used in English scansion, four of which can serve as the metrical base:

---

[9] "Blake and the Metrical Contract," in F.W. Hilles and Harold Bloom, eds., *From Sensibility to Romanticism* (London: Oxford Univ. Press, 1965).

[10] I find the foot useful as a teaching aid, even though many linguists deny its existence, and I have grave doubts myself. Nonetheless, it is a useful fiction, and countless poets have themselves undoubtedly thought of their lines in terms of feet. For a strong—but decidedly not conclusive—argument against the foot system, see the first chapter of Derek Attridge's *The Rhythms of English Poetry* (London: Longman, 1982).

˘ ´   *iamb* (iambic)
´ ˘   *trochee* (trochaic)
˘ ˘ ´   *anapest* (anapestic)
´ ˘ ˘   *dactyl* (dactylic)

Two others can serve only as rhythmic variations within the line:

´ ´   *spondee* (spondaic)
˘ ˘   *pyrrhic* (pyrrhic)[11]

In addition, lines can be different lengths, from one foot to eight:

monometer	=	one-foot line
dimeter	=	two-foot line
trimeter	=	three-foot line
tetrameter	=	four-foot line
pentameter	=	five-foot line
hexameter	=	six-foot line
heptameter[12]	=	seven-foot line
octameter	=	eight-foot line

These sets of terms are used in combination. Thus, a poem in "trochaic trimeter" uses a line made up of three trochees:

´ ˘ | ´ ˘ | ´ ˘

The process of gaining rhythmic variety through substitution may be explained very simply: the iambic line consists of five iambs, that is, five iambic feet:

˘ ´ | ˘ ´ | ˘ ´ | ˘ ´ | ˘ ´

Theoretically, any one of these feet can be replaced by a foot of any other kind, *without altering the meter of the poem*, a procedure known as *metrical substitution*. Try these out loud:

´ ˘ | ˘ ´ | ˘ ´ | ˘ ´ | ˘ ´

˘ ´ | ˘ ˘ ´ | ˘ ´ | ˘ ´ | ˘ ´

---

[11] For reasons explained below, I use the pyrrhic foot *only* in combination with the spondee, thus: ˘ ˘ ´ ´. I also ignore as unnecessary the amphibrach (˘ ´ ˘) and amphimacer (´ ˘ ´) used in some other methods.

[12] Please, *not* "diameter," "triameter," "quatrameter," or "septameter."

˘ ´ | ˘ ´ | ´ ´ | ˘ ˘ ´ | ˘ ´

˘ ´ | ˘ ´ | ´ ˘ ˘ | ´ ´ | ˘ ´

The iambic pentameter paradigm remains in the reader's ear as a *measure* (which is what "meter" literally means) of the actual rhythm in the words, indicated by the scansion. It is kept in the reader's ear by two forces: one is the expectancy built up by the repetition of mostly iambic units in five-foot line lengths; the other, perhaps more important, is the learned convention based on the reader's previous experience of the meter in poetry. The free play of rhythms in the actual line creates a kind of tension against this unchanging metronomic ticking in the reader's ear. Obviously, then, the conventional pattern of iambic pentameter is an essential component of the metrical experience of poetry. This book hopes, with the reader's cooperation, to encourage and reinforce that experience.

This explanation is, of course, oversimplified. In practice, substitution is much more controlled; some feet (especially the trochaic) act as substitutions routinely, while others (like the dactylic) hardly ever appear. Every poet has his or her own limits of tolerance, some, like Shelley, freely allowing anapestic substitution and others, like Milton, avoiding it almost altogether. Some poets stick close to the paradigm, writing mainly in smooth, regular lines, while others depart from it excitedly. These variations, however minute they may seem, add up to the individual poet's metrical style, an essential element of the poet's personal voice.

The scansion itself is merely a kind of shorthand, a way of making the rhythm visible, objectifying it so that it can be talked about. Many methods of scansion have been developed, ranging from the fairly simple and traditional one described here to highly elaborate codes that try to account for a legion of linguistic features. As a rule, the more elaborate the code, the harder it is to use and interpret. Long and often silly arguments have been printed over which code of scansion is best. I use the method described here not because it is the "right" one, but because it employs the most widely recognized terms and symbols in a simple and practical way.

The student should also understand from the beginning that every line of poetry is, within limits, susceptible to several more or less plausible correct scansions. We all read lines with slight differences of emphasis, and we sometimes even read them differently from one day to another. Each alternative scansion represents a different accommodation between the performed rhythm and the metrical paradigm. This does *not* mean that there are no incorrect scansions, however, or that (as students idly claim) "it's all subjective." Different plausible scansions, just like any other kinds of critical interpretation, can be debated as more or less satisfying.

Wrong scansions arise from two circumstances: first, when the marking is impossible to the ear:

˘ ´ ˘

syllable

´ ˘

erupting

The word "syllable" cannot be pronounced with the accent on the second syllable; the word "erupting" has three syllables, not two. (There are some words that can be pronounced with different numbers of syllables, but this is not one of them.) Secondly, wrong scansions occur when the marking is untrue to the rules of the metrical system, that is, when the pentameter does not add up to five feet, or the feet diverge from the recognized types, or (in the system I present here) when there are three or more unaccented syllables in succession.[13]

Finally, five terms with relation to the line as a whole must be introduced here:

	end-stop	=	the line pauses at its end
→	*enjambment*	=	the line pushes ahead to the next
‖	*caesura*	=	the line pauses in the middle
	one-syllable ending (also "one-syllable rhyme")		
	extra-syllable ending (also "extra-syllable rhyme")[14]		

The last two terms need further explanation. Most lines of iambic pentameter end on the accented syllable; but poets have the option of adding one extra, unaccented syllable at the end of the line:

˘ ´ | ˘ ´ | ˘   ´ | ˘   ´ | ˘   ´ (˘)

to watch the soundless waltzers dart and swivel

The extra syllable often gives the line an extra lift, a lightness; but it does not enter into the patterning of the metrical feet. Thus, a unit like this:

´ ´ ˘

is not a recognized foot in the system presented here, but such a unit might occur at the end of a line with a spondee plus extra-syllable ending. For scansion, I like to indicate it with parentheses, as above.

Very rarely, a double extra-syllable ending may appear:

---

[13] Every one of these rules in fact has exceptions, but when they occur, they should be treated as rare and exceptional. They may be extraordinary effects, or possibly just artistic lapses on the poet's part.

[14] This terminology is adopted in preference to the traditional terms "masculine" and "feminine" endings, which have come to appear sexist. One sometimes finds the more unwieldy terms "hypermetrical" or "hypercatalectic."

˘ ´ | ˘   ´ |˘ ´ |˘ ´ |˘ ´ (˘ ˘)
The Gods make this a happy day to Antony!

Such cases call on the reader's judgment whether to read—that is, scan and pronounce—the line as a double extra-syllable ending, or as a normal extra-syllable ending (if *elision,* or the slurring of a syllable, is possible):

˘ ´ | ˘   ´ |˘ ´ |˘ ´ |˘ ´ (˘)
The Gods make this a happy day to Ant'ny!

or as an iambic hexameter (an *alexandrine*):

˘ ´ | ˘   ´ |˘ ´ |˘ ´ |˘ ´ |˘ ˘
The Gods make this a happy day to Antony!

The Regular Iambic Pentameter Line

In reading the following account of iambic pentameter and the system of scansion used here, the reader should go slowly, pausing over every example, sounding it aloud, attempting to internalize the rhythmic patterns. With care and sensitivity, this procedure should begin to develop a feeling for the subtly expressive rhythms possible in English verse. *I cannot emphasize too much the benefit of sounding out the examples aloud, slowly.* If the student's reading of these pages is successful, she should be able to set her internal clock in motion.

By far the greatest number of lines in iambic pentameter are perfectly regular. This is important to keep in mind, since we will be looking at so many departures from the basic paradigm, and at illustrations of truly exceptional and uncommon effects. But in the process of formal scansion, as in the act of reading, the reader should begin with an expectation of regularity such as in these lines:

˘ ´ | ˘ ´ | ˘ ´ |˘ ´ |˘   ´
Was this the face that launch'd a thousand ships

˘ ´|˘ ´ |˘ ´ |˘   ´|˘ ˘
The holy hush of ancient sacrifice

˘ ´ |˘ ´ | ˘ ´|˘ ´ |˘ ´
Remember me when I am gone away

˘   ´ |˘ ˘ ´ |˘ ´ |˘ ´ |˘ ´
And swims or sinks, or wades, or creeps, or flies

Every one of these lines is a construct of five smooth iambs.

Notice in the first example above the apostrophe in "launch'd." This mark (whether provided by poet or editor) is a guarantee that the word is to be pronounced as one syllable, not as two—"launchèd." The apostrophes that sprinkle pages of poetry, especially sixteenth- to eighteenth-century poetry, are metrical guides; but whenever the "-ed" is printed, unmarked, the reader must then decide by ear on metrical grounds whether to pronounce it—whether the syllable is required to fill out the ten-syllable meter or not. This is an especially important principle for actors to understand. Notice also that the foot divisions, as in the second example here, may fall anywhere, even dividing single words.

The following examples illustrate metrically regular lines that feature caesura, natural pauses of syntax:

Nor can I, like that fluent sweet tongue'd Greek

I found a dimpled spider, fat and white

The caesura is a free variable: it may fall anywhere in the line without affecting the metrical pattern, even, as in the second example, in the middle of a foot. It may occur—with notable effect—even at the extremities of the line:

O good but most unwise patricians! Why→

Line ends and caesuras constitute part of the syntactic rhythm of a poem, overlaid over the meter.

Variation 1: Reversal of Accent (Trochaic Substitution)

The commonest of all departures from the iambic paradigm is the trochaic substitution. But this common variation has a variety of possible effects, partly depending on where it occurs in the line. Frequently it occurs at the beginning of the line, where it sounds so fluid and natural that the metrical disturbance may be slight, the merest ripple:

Passions of rain, or moods in falling snow

Poets make pets of pretty, docile words

Drove them before him thunder-struck, pursu'd

Notice in these examples that the iambic movement of the line rights itself immediately. The student, on finding a trochee at the beginning of a line, should quickly learn by ear to expect this smooth return to the iambic feeling. Beginners often forget, and, without listening, lunge forward mechanically into an absurd, unpronounceable scansion:

> ´ ˘ | ´ ˘ | ´   ˘ | ´ ˘ | ´   ˘
> Passions of rain, or moods in falling snow

The beginner at scansion, however, *should always approach each line as a whole,* as a unit, pronouncing it against the background of this steady, familiar beat. Any attempt to learn scansion by proceeding one syllable at a time is doomed to failure.

The student may wonder at this point why this same line could not be scanned like this:

> ´ ˘   ˘ | ´ ˘ | ´   ˘ | ´ ˘ | ´
> Passions of rain, or moods in falling snow

Nothing is altered in the actual sound of the line—only the imaginary foot divisions, which convert the line into a trochaic (or dactylic) meter. But this makes no sense at all as an explanation of the line in an iambic context, which in the correct scansion reasserts itself immediately. The foot divisions are, indeed, imaginary, part of the explanation of the line rather than the actual sound. But as explanations, they should be kept as simple and rational as possible, or else they lose the power to explain. Scansion, therefore, is determined not by the sound of the line alone, but *by the sound of the line as understood against its metrical frame.* (This scansion that is wrong in iambic pentameter would be correct in the context of the rare trochaic pentameter; see "Trochaic Meters" in Chapter 2.) As a general rule for iambic meters, though, any initial dactyl is likely to be wrong.

After a caesura, a similar pattern of trochaic substitution often appears, just as at the beginning of a line:

> ˘ ´ | ˘ ´ | ˘ ´ ‖ ´ ˘ | ˘ ´
> Her lips suck forth my soul: See where it flies!

> ´ ˘ | ˘ ´ | ˘ ´ ‖ ´ ˘ | ˘ ´
> Better it is to die, better to starve

> ´ ˘ | ˘ ´ ‖ ´ ˘ | ˘ ´ | ˘ ´
> Tears then for babes, blows and revenge for me

The same principle applies: the initial trochee creates a rhythmic throb, then returns smoothly and immediately to the iambic base.

The impact of trochaic reversal is much greater if it follows enjambment, the two effects combining with redoubled force, as in these passages from *Paradise Lost* which describe the fallen angels plummeting from the heavens:

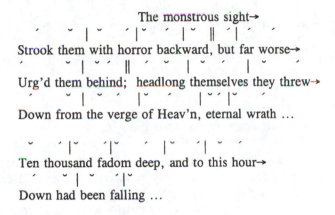

The monstrous sight→

Strook them with horror backward, but far worse→

Urg'd them behind; headlong themselves they threw→

Down from the verge of Heav'n, eternal wrath ...

Ten thousand fadom deep, and to this hour→

Down had been falling ...

Milton is so fond of this effect that one unkind critic, F.R. Leavis, called it the "Miltonic thump." Incidentally, the word "heav'n" in the first example is marked to indicate that it is a monosyllable, but even without the apostrophe is usually so treated. It belongs to a small group of words which may be treated as having either one or two syllables, depending on the demands of the meter: "heaven," "seven," "tower," "power," "flower."

Trochaic substitutions in the middle of a line, with no preparation, can have great power:

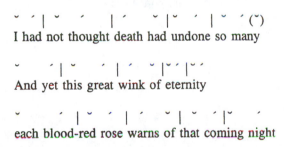

I had not thought death had undone so many

And yet this great wink of eternity

each blood-red rose warns of that coming night

In the first example here, the metrical shudder on the word "death" is, I think, magnificently evocative; in the second, it firmly underscores the poet's daring paradox; in the third, it underscores the feeling of urgency.

Trochaic substitution occurs infrequently in the second position of the pentameter line, but when it does it seems to have the greatest disruptive power:

˘ ´ | ´ ˘ | ˘ ´ ‖ ´ ˘|˘ ´
In rage deaf as the sea, hasty as fire

The following example combines this uncommon effect with an equally unusual succession of two trochees in an iambic line:

˘ ´ | ´ ˘ | ´ ˘|˘ ` | ˘ ´
A gaze blank and pitiless as the sun

Trochaic substitution almost never occurs at the end of a line:

˘ ´|˘   ´ | ˘ ´|˘   ´   ‖ ´ ˘
Elations when the forest blooms; gusty→
Emotions on wet roads on autumn nights.

Poets almost without exception avoid this positioning of the trochee because it is so difficult to distinguish from an ordinary extra-syllable ending. Here, the unusual trochaic substitution is determined by the fact that the line has only ten syllables, not the eleventh required by the extra-syllable ending; the effect makes a remarkably sensitive metrical comment on the word "gusty."

Variation 2: The Principle of Relative Accent
(Spondaic and Pyrrhic Substitution)

In the regular alternation of the iambic pentameter line, any unaccented syllable may be strengthened, creating a spondaic substitution. The result is a heightening of emphasis, a feeling of urgency and condensation:

˘   ´|˘ ´ | ˘   ´|´   ´ |˘ ´
O'er bog or steep, through strait, rough, dense or rare,
˘   ´ | ´   ´ |˘ ´ |˘ ´|˘   ´
With head, hands, wings, or feet pursues his way

´   ´ |´ ´ |´ ´ |˘ ´ |˘ ´
Rocks, caves, lakes, fens, bogs, dens, and shades of death

These examples from *Paradise Lost* show Milton loading his lines with spondaic accentuation, an effect of ponderous emphasis; the last example is a celebrated metrical stunt, Milton loading his line about as heavily as practically possible. Spondaic substitution can be more subtle:

˘ ´ | ˘ ´ |˘ ˘ ‖ ´ ´ | ´ ˘ ˘ (˘)
The way to dusty death. Out, out, brief candle

´ ´ | ˘ ´ | ˘ ´ |˘ ´ | ˘ ˘
Men, monkeys, lap-dogs, parrots, perish all

On the other hand, any accented syllable may be weakened. Some metrists explain this as a "pyrrhic substitution":

´ ˘ | ˘ ´ ‖ ˘ ´ |˘ ˘ | ˘ ´
Law in his voice, and fortune in his hand

Such an explanation might seem perfectly logical, the converse of spondaic substitution. But to me the notion of a foot containing no accented syllable presents a theoretical quandary. English is an accent-timed language, and the purpose of accentual-syllabic meter is to regulate the pattern of syllables between accents. What happens in such lines is that in a series of three unaccented syllables (forbidden in the accentual-syllabic system), the middle syllable holds the position of an accented one. Therefore, I prefer to employ a separate metrical symbol for this case:

´ ˘ | ˘ ´ ‖ ˘ ` |˘ ˘ ` | ˘ ´
Law in his voice, and fortune in his hand

The *accent grave* over the word "in" signifies that the word is not accented, at least not strongly accented, but that it nevertheless holds a metrical position. When speaking such a line, I do give the word a slight accent and, more importantly, taking account of five full metrical feet, I measure out the time of speaking into five units—as I would not do if the line occurred in a passage of prose, where I would use only four equally timed accents and rush through the unaccented syllables, thus:

´   ´   ´   ´
Law in his | voice, and | fortune in his | hand.

The conventions of poetry demand that the reading, silent or aloud, maintain a deliberateness, a lingering that indicates consciousness of the five-beat metrical tick-tock in the background.[15]

---

[15] Students who find this discrimination confusing or difficult may mark the weakened accent with an ordinary accent mark:

´ ˘ | ˘ ´ ‖ ˘ ´ |˘ ´ | ˘ ´
Law in his voice, and fortune in his hand

To approach this problem from the other direction: one of Yeats's most out-rageous closing lines would, as prose, read with three primary accents:

Slouches | towards Beth | lehem to be born

Scansion is needed to space these syllables out against the underlying iambic pentameter frame:

Slouches towards Bethlehem to be born

The accents here are indeed difficult to hear—as accents—but as place-holders, they are essential to measure out the line, giving it, to my ear, a terrible inevita-bility.[16]

Any method of scansion limited solely to accented and unaccented syllables will often, as in this instance, have difficulty with secondary accents—with lev-els of accentuation that fall between the extremes. English speech, some linguists tell us, employs four discernible degrees of accentuation, and some complex codes of scansion have been devised that attempt to graph them. For ordinary purposes, this degree of detail is unnecessary. Yet there are some common cases, like the line from Yeats above, where it is helpful to indicate a secondary accent or a purely metrical or place-holding accent.

This symbol, besides reflecting subtle truths about the speaking of poetry, has another great advantage: using it, one finds that, with few exceptions, no line of iambic pentameter will contain more than two unaccented syllables in suc-cession. If, in scansion, one finds ˘ ˘ ˘, the line is either one of those rare excep-tions, or the meter is really accentual, or (most likely) the scansion is wrong. This weakened accent occurs most frequently on "little" words—prepositions, con-junctions, articles, and the like:

They are the lords and owners of their faces

Her udder shrivels and the milk runs dry

---

[16] The history of English prosody is marked by battles, often acrimonious, between "stressers" and "timers," who argue for the exclusive dominance of one or the other of those features of language. While stress seems more foregrounded in literary pentameter, and time in the ballad quatrain (see Chapter 2), both features, I think, play roles in all phases of English prosody.

The weakened accent can also appear in connection with *polysyllabic* words that have primary and secondary accents in themselves. In my experience, students have more difficulty scanning polysyllabic words than with any other of the problems they confront, so lines like the following may at first take careful listening:

Oh Earth, lie heavily upon her eyes

Easy my unpremeditated verse

In *Paradise Lost*, Satan, flying with great effort through Chaos, suddenly meets

A vast vacuity; all unawares

I have often puzzled how Milton, in the middle of the seventeenth century, knew about air pockets, for he has created one in the rhythm of this line brilliantly with the weakened accent plus cæsura.

The so-called pyrrhic substitution does appear in the system presented here, but only in one particular circumstance, namely in combination with the spondee, thus:

In my old griefs, and with my childhood's faith

The pyrrhic foot is balanced by the two accents in the spondee, almost as if the two adjacent syllables had changed places, disturbing neither the number of syllables nor the number of accents in the line. This rhythmic effect, a kind of emphatic underscoring of the phrase in which the spondaic heaviness is softened and thrown into relief by the pyrrhic, is by no means uncommon:

Alack, the night comes on, and the high winds

With the sweet silent hours of marriage joys

I walk through the long schoolroom questioning

This unit of four syllables, ˘ ˘ ´ ´, is sometimes called by its classical name, the *ionic foot* (actually a double foot). It occurs twice in the following examples (the first being tetrameter):

˘ ˘| ´   ´ |˘ ˘| ´   ´

Like a green thought in a green shade

˘ ˘| ´   ´ |˘ ˘| ´   ´ |˘ ´

As a calm darkens among water-lights

In the second example, Wallace Stevens' image of flickering lights on the water dying down to shadow is hauntingly captured in this unusual rhythmic pattern.

Having said this, I must insert a word of caution. Beginning students are apt to be overly impressed by such critical claims for pictorialism: the rhythm "reflects the shadows in the water." The claim in this case is justified, I think, but this is purely an act of critical judgment on my part. Metrical onomatopoeia as literal as this is rare; metrical variations far more frequently work by simple emphasis, or just for the sake of variety itself. In the first example here (an iambic tetrameter line), Andrew Marvell's use of the same unusual pattern simply underscores, incisively, his syntactic parallelism; the rhythmic effect is quite abstract, not pictorial at all. At the same time, the personal discovery of such onomatopoeia as Stevens' line is one of the satisfactions of sophisticated reading. The student is advised to make such claims infrequently and with caution.

The reverse pattern, spondee plus pyrrhic, is rare, for the same reason that dactylic substitution (see below) is rare:

´   ´ |˘ ˘|´ |˘ ‖ ´ | ´   ´ (˘)

Fight, gentlemen of England! Fight, bold yeomen!

Notice that in the iambic scheme this rhythm produces a rare instance of three successive unaccented syllables. This is the reason it is usually avoided, though in this particular example the agitation of feeling is revealed in the wildness of the almost unscannable rhythm.

Variation 3: Added Syllables (Anapestic and Dactylic Substitution)

Thus far we have considered variations possible within the ten-syllable frame of iambic pentameter (with the exception of extra-syllable endings). Even with the dullest ears, a beginner can achieve a degree of success scanning lines of this kind, if only by keeping count on his fingers. But the triple rhythm of anapestic substitution can be detected only by ear:

˘ ˘   ´|˘ ˘ `|˘ ´|˘ ´ |˘   ´

Being destin'd to a dryer death on shore

This is where it is particularly important in scansion to listen to the entire line as a whole, locating the primary accents before beginning to mark the line. That little anapestic ripple should quickly become familiar, but the student who cannot catch it by ear will inevitably produce prosodic absurdities like this:

⏑⏑ | ⏑ ′ | ⏑ ˋ | ⏑⏑ | ⏑   ′ (˘)
Being destin'd to a dryer death on shore

Sometimes the anapestic substitution occurs on the caesura, an effect rather like a mid-line extra-syllable ending:

⏑   ′|⏑ ‖ ⏑⏑ | ⏑   ′ | ⏑   ′ | ⏑   ′
Half flying; behoves him now both Oar and Sail

In earlier phases of the accentual-syllabic tradition, these triple rhythms were usually rationalized into the "numbers" of the ten-syllable line by an elaborate system of blurs and glides known as *elision*. I would probably scan the following line thus:

⏑   ′|⏑ ⏑ ′ |⏑   ′|⏑ ′ |⏑ ′
And given in earnest what I begged in jest

But the poet may well have understood the line as ten-syllables with an elision, like this:

⏑   ′ |⏑ ′ |⏑   ′|⏑ ′ |⏑ ′
And giv'n in earnest what I beg'd in jest

Since the word "given" can be elided to "giv'n," either of these scansions is acceptable.

Poets before the nineteenth century often seem reluctant to write anapestic substitutions that cannot be justified by elision, with syllables that cannot be gracefully slurred together. Robert Bridges' analysis of Milton, for example, which elaborates all the phonetic circumstances where elision is possible, claims there are no lines in *Paradise Lost* that are not decasyllabic (though he is forced by his theory into some cumbersome rationalizations). Only gradually did poets themselves become comfortable with a free use of the anapestic foot within the iambic frame: the turning point occurs approximately during the two Romantic generations at the beginning of the nineteenth century, in such lines as:

⏑   ′|⏑ ⏑   ′|⏑ ‖ ′ | ⏑   ′ | ⏑   ′
This populous village! Sea, and hill, and wood,

⏑   ′ | ⏑ ′ | ⏑ ⏑   ′|⏑ ′ |⏑ ′
With all the numberless goings on of life

Since that time, anapestic substitution has become more and more freely available. When Robert Frost remarked that for him the possible English meters are "virtually but two, strict iambic and loose iambic,"[17] he was essentially contrasting iambic meters that admit anapestic substitutions with those that don't.

Anapestic substitution usually has the effect of suggesting lightness and speed, sometimes a kind of looseness or informality. For Wallace Stevens, anapests express

> A jovial hullabaloo among the spheres

And John Crowe Ransom extracts rhythmic irony from them in an understated poem about death where the anapests seem perversely jolly:

> Of chills and fever she died, of fever and chills

Dactylic substitution in iambic meters is extremely rare in any period—logically so, because in the iambic frame it almost forces the forbidden three successive unaccented syllables:

> Victory and triumph to the Son of God

This scansion is possible, as is an alternative, trochee plus anapest (´ ˘ | ˘ ˘ ´), a combination that is likewise normally avoided. I have little doubt, however, that Milton rationalized his rhythm by an unmarked elision, like this:

> Vict'ry and triumph to the Son of God

This may be true even of the magically effective line in "Birches" where Frost captures the collapse of winter ice falling from the trees:

> Shattering and avalanching on the snow crust

"Shattering" is probably "shatt'ring"; even so, an exceptional line like this stretches iambic pentameter to its limits—but how knowingly, and with what graphic purpose.

---

[17] "The Figure a Poem Makes," in *Selected Prose of Robert Frost*, ed. Hyde Cox and Edward Connery Lathem (New York: Collier, 1966), pp. 17–18.

Variation 4: Omitted Syllables

This variation is included here for the sake of completeness and symmetry, but in practice (with one important historical qualification), syllables are virtually never dropped in iambic pentameter lines. My first example comes from King Lear's insane ranting against the elements—a measure of the kind of dramatic situation needed to elicit such rhythmic violence:

ˊ   ˊ | ˘   ˊ | ˘   ˊ ‖ (x)ˊ ‖ (x)ˊ

Blow, winds, and crack your cheeks! Rage! Blow!

˘   ˊ| ˘   ˊ |˘   ˊ|˘   ˘   ˊ | ˘   ˊ

What studied torments, tyrant, hast thou for me?

˘   ˊ ‖ (x)ˊ ‖ (x)ˊ ‖   ˘   ˊ|˘   ˊ (˘)

What wheels? Racks? Fires? What flaying? Boiling
In leads or oils.

The omitted syllables here, noted in parentheses, create monosyllabic feet, and push the lines in the direction of an accentual metric, a five-beat accentual line. They are metrically possible only because the metrical paradigm rides on the accents—and because the dramatic emotion is so intense.

The qualification that I mentioned takes us back to Chaucer, whose "iambic pentameter" line has the individual peculiarity that it often drops the initial syllable:

(x)ˊ | ˘   ˊ | ˘   ˋ | ˘   ˊ | ˘   ˊ (˘)

Whan that April, with his shoures soote

Chaucer's own understanding of meter remains the subject of scholarly debate.[18] Lines like this could indeed be interpreted as "trochaic" lines freely mingled with "iambic," or as a pure ten-syllable line. The simple fact remains that in Chaucer they occur regularly, and however he rationalized them, they represent a metrical option that he freely exercised, just as they also suggest the

---

[18] Chaucer's meter can easily be heard as iambic pentameter by modern ears trained on the accentual-syllabic system, and one authority, Paull F. Baum, asserts bluntly that "Chaucer's line is a series of five iambs" (*Chaucer's Verse* [Durham: Duke Univ. Press, 1961], p. 11). How Chaucer truly understood his own versification, however, is a subject still under debate by specialists. Some, assuming French influence, believe he wrote a syllabic line of ten syllables; see, for example, James I. Wimsatt, *Chaucer and His French Contemporaries: Natural Music in the Fourteenth Century* (Toronto: Univ. of Toronto Press, 1991). Issues are further clouded by such questions as contemporary pronunciation, manuscript transmission, and editing practices, modern texts often being "corrected" in order to regularize meter.

strongly accentual basis to his versification. Poets in the accentual-syllabic tradition from the mid-sixteenth century onward, however, systematically avoid this particular kind of line, with only occasional exceptions.

Syntactic Rhythm and the Line Unit

The accentual-syllabic system just described governs the patterning within an individual line of poetry; but poems are made of many lines, grouped either into *stanzas* (*stanzaic verse*) or into *continuous* forms like blank verse or heroic couplets (*stichic verse*) organized into *verse paragraphs*. Discussions of poetic rhythm are often guilty of focusing on the minutiae of syllable counts and forgetting the larger sweep of syntactic rhythm.

Syntactic rhythm exists in ordinary prose, of course, and when it is analyzed there, critics have available the vocabulary of grammatical analysis: the length or shortness of sentences and clauses, the use or avoidance of *parallel structures,* complication by subordinate clauses, syntactic *inversions,* delaying of the verb (as in the so-called periodic sentence), and so on. Syntactic rhythm in poetry, however, is governed by all of these features *plus* the structure of the printed line units (whether or not they are punctuated by rhyme).

Perhaps the most dramatic illustration of the force of syntactic rhythm is a comparison of the following passages of rhymed iambic pentameter side by side:

> Sol through white curtains shot a timorous ray,
> And op'd those eyes that must eclipse the day.
> Now lapdogs give themselves the rousing shake,
> And sleepless lovers just at twelve awake.
> Thrice rung the bell, the slipper knocked the ground,
> And the pressed watch returned a silver sound.
>
> That's my last duchess painted on the wall,
> Looking as though she were alive. I call
> That piece a wonder, now: Fra Pandolf's hands
> Worked busily a day, and there she stands,
> Will't please you to sit and look at her? I said
> "Fra Pandolf" by design, for never read
> Strangers like you that pictured countenance ...

In the first passage, Alexander Pope writes *closed couplets* (or heroic couplets): the lines are all end-stopped; there is no enjambment (or very slight) from one line to the next, even less from one couplet to the next; each line comes to rest on the rhyme, throwing it into relief. The effect is of neat, tensely coiled line units, crackling with energy and wit. In the second passage, on the other hand, Robert Browning uses iambic pentameter couplets rhymed in the identical way;

but these are *open couplets,* which make use of continuous enjambment. Browning conceals the rhymes so skillfully that, in an effective dramatic reading, the listener is scarcely aware of them; they exist as a kind of subliminal structure underlying the character's apparently casual speech.

A similar principle operates in blank verse, though the effect is more subtle because there is no help from rhyme. Early in the development of blank verse, Christopher Marlowe moves largely in end-stopped lines:

> Was this the face that launch'd a thousand ships,
> And burn'd the topless towers of Ilium?
> Sweet Helen, make me immortal with a kiss!
> Her lips suck forth my soul: see where it flies!
> Come, Helen, come, give me my soul again.
> Here will I dwell, for heaven is in these lips,
> And all is dross that is not Helena.

Variety in this highly regular and end-stopped blank verse is achieved by slight metrical variation plus shifting the position of the caesura. (This principle was articulated much later by Alexander Pope for the Augustan heroic couplet, where end-stopping is also the rule: no more than three lines in succession may have the caesura in the same position. Not all poets are this self-conscious, but the principle is a good one.)

The development of Shakespearean blank verse shows not only a rapid increase in metrical variety but also an increased freedom of enjambment. Early Shakespeare resembles Marlowe in its use of the end-stop:

> Was ever woman in this humour wooed?
> Was ever woman in this humour won?
> I'll have her, but I will not keep her long.
> What? I that killed her husband and his father
> To take her in her heart's extremest hate,
> With curses in her mouth, tears in her eyes,
> The bleeding witness of my hatred by,
> Having God, her conscience, and these bars against me,
> And I no friends to back my suit at all,
> But the plain devil, and dissembling looks?

By the end of his career, Shakespeare arrived at a suppleness of enjambment like this:

> Give me my robe, put on my crown, I have
> Immortal longings in me. Now no more
> The juice of Egypt's grape shall moist this lip.
> Yare, yare, good Iras; quick. Methinks I hear

> Antony call. I see him rouse himself
> To praise my noble act. I hear him mock
> The luck of Caesar, which the gods give men
> To excuse their after wrath. Husband, I come:
> Now to that name my courage prove my title.

It remained for Milton to apply these lessons to non-dramatic verse, developing in *Paradise Lost* a syntactic drive, building the line units into rhythmically coherent verse paragraphs in a way rarely equalled in our poetry:

> Descend from Heav'n, Urania, by that name
> If rightly thou art call'd, whose Voice divine
> Following, above the Olympian Hill I soar,
> Above the flight of Pegasean wing.
> The meaning, not the Name I call: for thou
> Nor of the Muses Nine, nor on the top
> Of old Olympus dwell'st, but Heav'nly born
> Before the Hills appeared, or Fountain flow'd,
> Thou with Eternal wisdom didst converse,
> Wisdom thy Sister, and with her didst play
> In presence of th'Almighty Father, pleas'd
> With thy celestial song.

Enjambment and caesura are sometimes confusing terms to students because both are relative, not absolute. If the end of a line of verse coincides with the end of a sentence, both being marked by a period, one is quite safe calling it an end-stopped line. Beyond that, however, there are greater and lesser degrees of end-stopping and enjambment. The enjambment is slight if the line coincides with the phrase boundaries of the syntax (whether or not marked by punctuation):

> I should prefer to have some boy bend them
> As he went out and in to fetch the cows—
> Some boy too far from town to learn baseball,
> Whose only play was what he found himself,
> Summer or winter, and could play alone.

Here, Robert Frost's sentence in "Birches" occupies five lines of blank verse, but each line—including the first—ends with a completed grammatical unit, so the feeling of the line unit remains strong, and enjambment relatively weak. But in lines describing the boy's careful climb up the tree, stronger enjambments suggest the precarious sense of containment, of barely controlled balance:

> He learned all there was
> To learn about not launching out too soon

> And so not carrying the tree away
> Clear to the ground. He always kept his poise
> To the top branches, climbing carefully
> With the same pains you use to fill a cup
> Up to the brim, and even above the brim.

Even this degree of enjambment, however, is significant not because it is unusual, but because it reflects the meaning, the arduous maintenance of poise, so intelligibly.

More radical effects of enjambment can occur not only between lines, but between stanzas. Emily Dickinson uses this device to suggest, in a poem that demonstrates her metrical savvy, the momentum of the railroad train:

> I like to see it lap the Miles—
> And lick the Valleys up—
> And stop to feed itself at Tanks—
> And then—prodigious step
>
> Around a Pile of Mountains—
> And supercilious peer
> In Shanties—by the sides of Roads—
> And then a Quarry pare
>
> To fit its sides
> And crawl between
> Complaining all the while
> In horrid—hooting stanza—
> Then chase itself down Hill—
>
> And neigh like Boanerges—
> Then—prompter than a star
> Stop—docile and omnipotent
> At its own stable door.

Ben Jonson, in his great "Ode to Cary and Morrison" early in the seventeenth century, produced daring effects of enjambment rarely matched until the twentieth century, splitting his own name across two stanzas, and then breaking a single word into two lines:

> And there he lives with memory, and Ben
>
> Jonson! who sung this of him, ere he went
> Himself to rest,
> Or taste a part of that full joy he meant

> To have expressed
> In this bright asterism;
> Where it were friendship's schism
> (Were not his Lucius long with us to tarry)
> To separate these twi-
> lights, the Dioscuri,
> And keep the one half from his Harry.
> But fate doth so altérnate the design,
> Whilst that in heaven, this light on earth must shine.

Caesura too is a relative matter, sometimes weaker, sometimes stronger, sometimes marked by punctuation, sometimes not, simply marking the ordinary phrase boundaries as the rhythmic voice of the poem unfolds. These pauses enter the constant play of the verse rhythm against the metrical paradigm, and a sensitive "performance" of the poem, aloud or silent, takes them naturally into account; but they are not usually foregrounded by critical attention unless they become, in some way, part of the meaning, as when Milton's Satan, noted above, meets

> A vast vacuity; all unawares …

Enjambment and caesura, then, are matters of degree: the question is usually not whether enjambment occurs, but how much?—and occasionally why.

Rhyme, Alliteration, Assonance and Onomatopoeia

Meter is the most complex and abstract element of prosody, the one that takes the most getting used to. The most conspicuous element, however, is rhyme, the chiming of similar sounds in a predictable pattern. To the naive reader, poetry cannot exist without rhyme. Sophisticated readers know better—but the gratification of rhyming remains an unfailing if primitive pleasure, and a plain test of the poet's care and skill. The discovery of pattern, of "meaning," within the arbitrary mix of sounds that create language somehow ensures that the poet is finding where the hidden meanings are. Alliteration and *assonance* belong with rhyme as accidental elements of physical language that can yield unexpected delight and meaning. Students are quick to seize on alliteration, because it is so often visible to the eye, but have difficulty recognizing its gentler but more pervasive sibling assonance. All of these features of verbal sound, however, share a range of possible effects within poetic systems.

Rhyme is, above all, a structuring agent.[19] The so-called *rhyme scheme* is

---

[19] Alliteration (occasionally called "head rhyme") can also appear as a structuring agent, as in the Old and Middle English alliterative line, with the same effect described here; assonance, for some reason, rarely enters into predictable patterns. An excellent study

often treated as a kind of numb blueprint for producing, say, a particular category of stanza or *sonnet*—and to some degree that is what it is. But rhyme is more important as a dynamic force operating within the form, within the reading experience. Consider this stanza from Coleridge's "Rime of the Ancient Mariner":

> Water, water, everywhere,
> And all the boards did shrink;
> Water, water, everywhere,
> Nor any drop to drink.

The first rhyme word, "shrink," sets up, within the familiar lilt of the ballad rhythm, an expectation: it punctuates the metrical end of the line, leaving its sound waiting in the ear. Another rhyme, we know, will follow, seven beats later. When the expected rhyme does arrive, with "drink," we know the pattern is complete, the stanza has reached a point of *closure*—it feels finished. The rhyming is not flashy; but the completed pattern—anticipation plus satisfaction—remains satisfying and memorable. This is the commonest effect.

But consider what happens in another stanza of the same poem:

> An orphan's curse would drag to hell
> A spirit from on high;
> But oh! more horrible than that
> Is the curse in a dead man's eye!
> Seven days, seven nights, I saw that curse,
> And yet I could not die.

The rhyme is satisfied as before, but the stanza unexpectedly plunges ahead, adding yet a third rhyme. The third rhyme is uncalled for, superfluous—a kind of excess. And this is the structuring principle of all rhyme: a pattern of anticipation, then of satisfaction (and possible closure), and then, if anything more, of saturation or excess. This dynamic structuring principle is the most important function of rhyme, and it will figure importantly in the next chapter's consideration of stanza and form. Beyond this structuring capability, however, rhyme, together with alliteration and assonance, largely determine the actual "sound" of the poem, the music of the poem as a field of *phonemes*.[20]

---

is Donald Wesling, *The Chances of Rhyme: Device and Modernity* (Berkeley: Univ. of California, 1980). On closure, see Barbara Herrnstein Smith, *Poetic Closure: A Study of How Poems End* (Chicago: Univ. of Chicago Press, 1968).

[20] A "phoneme" is the smallest unit of sound in a language that can create a difference of meaning. In this text I assume a standard pronunciation of English, knowing, of course, that pronunciation has altered over the centuries and today varies widely from place to place. Even so, while actual phonemes vary, I assume that the basic structure of the language, in its formation of phrases and sound patterns, maintains a coherent internal pattern of relationships.

These three related devices have three distinct functions within a poem. The first of these is simple emphasis: the words marked by rhyme (or alliteration or assonance) tend to be more prominent. Standard advice to the novice poet about rhyming is, "Be sure your rhyme words are the most important words." Though there are reasons why a poet may ignore this advice from time to time, the general principle is sound.

A second function of rhyme, alliteration, and assonance within a poem is one I call "semantic linkage." When two words are brought into relationship by an accidental similarity of sound, the meanings of those words also begin to engage with each other:

> Some are bewilder'd in the maze of schools,
> And some made coxcombs Nature meant but fools.
>
> And others whom I will not name,
> Each different, each the same

The rhyme of "schools" with "fools" raises, subliminally, an array of intriguing semantic relationships. What do "schools" have to do with "fools"? The relationship may be one of similarity, or *antithesis,* or any of a number of possibilities. The potential relationship brought to the surface by the foregrounded rhyme (or alliteration or assonance) can even create the risk of incongruity. Likewise, the linkage of "same" with "name" underscores the poet's inquiry into the question of individuality. I recall the words of a popular hymn which invariably make me wince when they rhyme the name "Jesus" with the word "diseases." Comic and ironic rhyming depend on this effect of semantic linkage:

> In the room the women come and go
> Talking of Michaelangelo.

A third function of rhyme, alliteration, and assonance is the most controversial. These sound effects may be described—with considerable circumspection— as having inherent qualities: some consonant sounds are soft, voiced, and sustained, like *m, n, v,* or the liquids *l* and *r;* others are hard, unvoiced, or plosive, like *k, p,* or *t.* Many linguists deny that verbal sounds have inherent properties, emphasizing the arbitrary relation between a word and its referent. But it is hard to deny that poets consistently foreground particular sound fields for particular contexts. The difficulty for students is that these relationships exist at a very high level of abstraction; the temptation is to concoct naive, literalistic claims for onomatopoeia. (I always think of a student who tried to persuade me that the repeated letter *w* in a particular line made it sound "like a field of wheat.") There is nothing about the letter *m* that makes it "sound like" *mud,* or *migraine,* or *madness*, just as there is nothing about the key of B flat that connects it with any particular kind of feeling. Usually the sound is simply neutral.

Literal onomatopoeia, like Tennyson's celebrated stunt

The murmuring of innumerable bees,

occurs in poetry far less frequently than youthful analysts suppose. Instead, this effect of sound, though real, tends to be elusive, and requires genuine critical tact, critical self-control, to describe. Consider this:

Ask me no more where Jove bestows,
When June is past, the fading rose;
For in your beauty's orient deep,
These flowers, as in their causes, sleep.

The beauty of Thomas Carew's anthology piece arises in part, certainly, from its beautifully modulated sound field. Assonance on the long *o* predominates, prolonging the speech, and the conspicuous consonants—*m*, *n*, and *r*—are soft, sustained, voiced sounds, while gutturals are largely avoided. The alliteration between "Jove" and "June" is difficult to characterize: it does *not* lie, I think, in any mystique about the letter *j*; it is perhaps simply a form of quiet emphasis.
But if one tries to alter the sounds:

Ask me no more where Zeus bestows

the result is catastrophic. Alexander Pope chose his words wisely when he wrote, "The sound must seem an echo to the sense." Not only is the relation between sound and sense a *seeming*, a kind of illusion, but it is also an *echo*—not a literal replication.
Discussions of consonant and vowel sounds in poetry can be assisted with some elementary phonetics. Only a few very obvious principles need to be made explicit. First, since the English alphabet contains only twenty-six letters and the language uses approximately forty-five phonemes, the letters and phonemes are bound to recur. The recurrence must be foregrounded, made more prevalent or prominent than random expectation, before it merits attention. Second, alliteration and assonance are foregrounded most conspicuously on accented, not unaccented, syllables. Third, spelling is not a reliable guide: alliteration may be claimed for "cool" and "kangaroo" but not (as some naive students submit) for "cool" and "cello"; likewise for assonance, "cool" and "threw" pass muster, "cool" and "cooperate" do not.
Alliteration can be taken to a finer point. Because the field of English phonemes is a structure of differentiated pairs, as shown in Table 2, a detailed examination of alliteration can take this fact into account. The phonemic pairings match voiced with unvoiced consonants (that is, the sounds *p* and *b* are produced by identical formations in the mouth; the only difference is the voicing of *b* by

Table 2: English Consonants

p, b	plosives: *pop, bib*
t, d	dentals: *tot, did*
ck, g	gutturals: *kick, gag*
ch, j	affricatives: *church, judge*
f, v	fricatives: *fife, verve*
th, th	dental fricatives: *thigh, they*
s, z	sibilants: *cease, zoos*
sh, zh	alveolar sibilants: *shush, azure*
l, r	liquids: *loyal, rarer*
m, n, ng	nasals: *mime, nine, singing*
y, w	vocalic glides: *yo-yo, wayward*
h	aspirate: *how*

the larynx). Thus, the relationship between the gutturals in "cool" and "God" may, in a given poetic context, make a meaningful alliteration.[21]

Vowel sounds require more complex phonetic analysis than seems practical here, but the simple distinction between long vowels and short is widely understood. One might claim a kind of assonance by noting that a passage employs mainly short vowels, shifting to deeper resonances on the emotively weighted words:

> There is a comfort in the strength of love
> 'Twill make a thing endurable, which else
> Would overset the brain, or break the heart.

Rhyme, too, has its further complexities. If the naive reader insists that poems must rhyme, he or she also insists that the rhymes be always perfect. Poets are not so pedantic. Especially in the twentieth century, poets have used a whole array of "imperfect" rhymes—"near" rhymes, "slant" rhymes, "eye" rhymes, "light" rhymes, "assonantal" rhymes, "apocopated" rhymes, and so on (see Appendix 1). The terminology is extensive—and not used by critics with notable consistency. For most purposes, a single general term, like "imperfect" rhyme, is sufficient. But the important point for the student is to get used to the idea that not every rhyme has to be obvious. As W.B. Yeats once remarked, "There comes a time in the career of a great poet when he ceases to take plea-

---

[21] Most of these terms have currency in critical practise, though some more than others; critics often speak of liquids, sibilants, or gutturals, but rarely distinguish, say, "dental" fricatives or "alveolar" sibilants.

sure in rhyming 'mountain' with 'fountain' and 'beauty' with 'duty.'"[22] Yeats himself was a master of imperfect rhyme:

> What youthful mother, a shape upon her lap
> Honey of generation had betrayed,
> And that must sleep, shriek, struggle to escape
> As recollection or the drug decide,
> Would think her son, did she but see that shape
> With sixty or more winters on its head,
> A compensation for the pang of his birth,
> Or the uncertainty of his setting forth?

The device obviously releases to the poet a much larger vocabulary available for each rhyme position; it also creates possible effects of rhyming sometimes less emphatically, sometimes more.

Facility

Finally, we return to the point where we started. The beginner, labouring with first attempts at scansion, may despair of ever achieving competence, much less rapid facility, just as the beginner at the piano keyboard, learning the first scales and arpeggios, may despair of ever performing Mozart or Liszt. Success in both cases demands a certain amount of confidence and practice—and self-education. It helps to keep goals in mind.

Detailed understanding of meter enters one's experience of poetry in different ways: while scansion is a tool for formal literary analysis, it is also a means of arriving at a sophisticated reading experience. The skill outlined above has practical uses in the academic analysis of poetry, and for this purpose it remains a highly deliberate, self-conscious task. (It has other practical uses as well, for the aspiring poet, actor, composer, editor, linguist, speech pathologist ...) But for the student of poetry, this understanding tends to be more unconscious, more instinctive. The reader, her ear educated to the cadences of the line, measuring it by instinct, experiences the metered rhythm as background, silently noting points where, straining against the paradigm, it emerges into the foreground. She is more likely simply to notice the effect with pleasure than to think quietly to herself, "That was a beautiful trochaic reversal in the second foot." Such self-consciousness belongs to formal analysis. But if the pleasurable effect is to be experienced, an understanding of meter has to be internalized. "Scansion" of this sort really occurs at exactly the speed of reading.

---

[22] Quoted in Ezra Pound, *The Spirit of Romance* (1910; New York: New Directions, 1968), p. 50.

Just so for the writer. In all fairness, very few poets (Pound and Auden come to mind) have aspired to equal mastery in all the English forms and meters; most cultivate one or a few small areas. Yet within his *métier,* a poet is likely to have passed through the phase of conscious technique to a stage of instinctive craftsmanship. Although surviving manuscripts of poets like Keats or Cummings reveal that they scanned their own lines carefully (if evidence were necessary), few poets, I suspect, have created their metrical effects by calculating, "Now, in this line I will create three anapests." More likely, the words and phrases form in the poet's mind, combining and recombining, until they "feel" right. This "feeling," however, is not a vague intuition. The lines feel right when they satisfy the poet's trained rhythmic instincts—and those instincts have been cultivated, self-taught, fully internalized, when the writer has fully mastered the principles of meter.

2

Beyond Iambic Pentameter

Iambic pentameter is the most pervasive literary meter in English poetry: it is the meter of Shakespeare's plays and the great tradition of Elizabethan drama, the meter of *Paradise Lost*, the meter of the Augustan heroic couplet, the meter of most sonnets, and the meter of the meditative blank verse tradition that continues into the twentieth century. Iambic pentameter is also the subtlest of English meters, the most difficult to come to grips with. It is, therefore, the usual focus of metrical study. But English poetry has far more to offer beyond iambic pentameter.

Given the four basic metrical feet and the practicable numbers of feet from one to eight in a line, one should be able, mathematically, to produce examples of all thirty-two possible varieties of the accentual-syllabic line. But many of these, dactylic trimeter for example, are hard to find, at least as continuous meters. Examples at extreme ends of the scale within the accentual-syllabic system are scarce: though iambic monometer has been spotted, one might read poetry for many years without ever encountering pure examples of trochaic monometer or dactylic octameter in the wild. But the reasons why some theoretically possible meters rarely surface are complex: they are related not only to the habits of poets, but to the perceptual psychology of the ear and problems of rhythmic *Gestalt*. This question brings us to those systems other than the accentual-syllabic present in English poetry, and to a very different way of thinking about meter.

Accentual Meters and the Ballad Stanza

The native Old English line is nothing like iambic pentameter. It is an accentual line of four beats with a caesura, bound together by alliteration (see Chapter 1). This line has an inescapable feeling of symmetry. The same symmetry is inherent in the human body, with its own bilateral structure: we have two feet, not one or three, and therefore the basic rhythm of the human body is a two-step. The four-beat line is an extension of this. The implications of this fact for poetic rhythm are immense, but for now I simply note that the even-numbered line lengths tend to feel more natural, while odd-numbered line lengths tend to be more artificial or self-conscious. The very reason "iambic pentameter" became the preferred literary meter of our language is that, as Derek Attridge observes, "it is the only simple metrical form of manageable length which *escapes* the elementary four-beat rhythm, with its insistence, its hierarchical structures, and its close relationship with the world of ballad and song."[1]

The native accentual four-beat line can still be heard in the tetrameter lines and in the ballad stanza described below. Tetrameter is overwhelmingly the preferred version of anapestic and trochaic meters, a sign of their closeness to natural symmetry and the native accentual line. Iambic tetrameter lines, often called "octosyllabics," are by far the commonest sustained meter in English poetry after the iambic pentameter. Often described simply as "lighter" than the iambic pentameter line, they seem so mainly because they reflect their folk origins.

At this point, it is helpful to consider the native meter in one of its most familiar forms, the ballad stanza. The rhymed quatrain, by far the commonest of the lyric stanzas in English, is a much more complex and various form than first appears. Here is a straightforward iambic tetrameter quatrain:

> ˘ ´ | ˘ ´| ˘   ´ | ˘ ´
> A frightful feeling, frenzy born,

> ˘ ´ |˘   ´ | ˘ ´ | ˘   ´
> I hurried down the dark oak stair

> ˘ ´ | ˘ ´ | ˘   ´ | ˘ ´
> I reached the door whose hinges torn

> ˘   ´ | ˘ ´ | ˘   ´ | ˘   ´
> Flung streaks of moonshine here and there.

Here, for comparison, is a so-called "ballad stanza," which alternates lines of iambic tetrameter and iambic trimeter (commonly with an *xaxa* rhyme scheme):

> ˘   ´ | ˘ ´ | ˘ ´ | ˘   ´
> There lived a wife at Usher's Well,

> ˘   ˘   ´ | ˘   ´ | ˘   ´ (´)
> And a wealthy wife was she;

> ˘ ´ | ˘   ˘   ´ | ˘   ´ | ˘   ´
> She had three stout and stalwart sons,

---

[1] Derek Attridge, *The Rhythms of English Poetry* (London: Longman, 1982), p. 124 [my emphasis].

And she sent them o'er the sea.

In reading this ballad stanza, the voice naturally pauses at the end of each trimeter line. This silent pause evens out the rhythm of the trimeter line so that it becomes, to that extent, equivalent to the tetrameter. The tetrameter and trimeter lines are equivalent to each other *in time*, even though the final "beat" in the trimeter line is realized only by a silent pause. The power of the four-beat line asserts itself to create a stable feeling of accentual symmetry, and in its traditional folk manifestations—in ballads, or hymns, or nursery songs—this rhythmic symmetry is often reinforced by the musical phrase. Another version of the ballad quatrain uses three trimeter lines, with silent pause, and only one line of tetrameter (with *abab* rhyme scheme):

We give thee but thine own,

Whate'er the gift may be;

All that we have is thine alone,

A trust, O Lord, from thee.

The single line of tetrameter is enough to confirm the presence of the pause in all the other lines.

It is useful to consider all three of these quatrains as versions of a single structure, a ballad quatrain with a number of options that give the simple basic form astonishing variety:

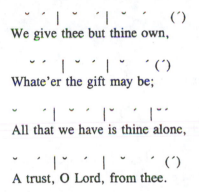

In any individual poem, the poet normally selects one of these metrical options and sticks with it: the full tetrameter version (*long meter*), the alternating tetrameter and trimeter (*common meter*), or the short three-trimeter version (*short meter*). Other combinations occasionally appear as well. Prosodic options also extend to other features, such as the rhyme scheme (*xaxa*, *abab*), or alternation of extra-syllable and one-syllable endings, or a pattern of internal rhymes in the tetrameter lines.

Furthermore, this structure easily adapts to other meters—trochaic or ana-
pestic—or, as in this example,[2] to pure accentual forms:

Hinx, minx, the old witch winks,

The fat begins to fry,

Nobody at home but Jumping Joan,

Father, Mother and I

One of the most familiar versions of this folk stanza sounds like this:

There was an old woman of Norwich,

Who lived upon nothing but porridge;

Parading the town, she turned cloak into gown—

The thrifty old woman of Norwich.

In the *limerick,* the short meter version of the stanza can clearly be heard
(though the third, tetrameter line is more usually printed as two short rhyming
dimeter lines). The limerick form also requires that the tetrameter line feature
caesura and internal rhyme, with the scheme *aabba;* it is usually, but not al-
ways, anapestic; and it often uses extra-syllable rhymes. Like much else in pro-
sody, spelling out the rules for the limerick sounds hopelessly complicated; but
nearly everyone who speaks English recognizes the form on first encounter, and
many people create limericks who could not describe what, metrically, they are

---

[2] As we proceed, I use different methods of marking scansion, as appropriate, sometimes
marking foot divisions, sometimes not; sometimes marking every syllable, sometimes
not. An alert student will see the rationale for this. As I have already remarked, there
is nothing authoritative about any one system for marking scansion.

doing. (Awkward limericks, on the other hand, can usually benefit from informed, presumably tactful, correction.)

The fact that all of these structures are variants of the same basic ballad stanza appears most convincingly, perhaps, in poems where different versions are used interchangeably. Many of Emily Dickinson's poems use the stanza this way (see, for example, "A narrow Fellow in the Grass," or study the variations in "I like to see it lap the Miles," chap. 1, p. 29). The power of accentual symmetry in the quatrain is demonstrated dramatically in an anonymous popular ballad called "The Bitter Withy":

> As it fell out on a holy day,
>
> The drops of rain did fall, did fall,
>
> Our Saviour asked leave of his mother Mary[3]
>
> If he might go play at ball.

Since this is unmistakably accentual verse, my scansion dispenses with the foot divisions of accentual-syllabic scansion and simply marks the accents (and pauses). This opening stanza, made of three four-beat lines plus one three-beat line, is followed by another using a different variant of the quatrain structure:

> To play at ball, my own dear son,
>
> It's time you was going or gone,
>
> But be sure let me hear no complain of you,
>
> At night when you do come home.

The accentual symmetry can still be heard in the final stanza, which repeats the pattern of the first, but with unaccented syllables crowding so fast that they stretch the line almost to the limit:

> Then he says to his mother, "Oh! the withy, oh! the withy,
>
> The bitter withy that causes me to smart, to smart,

---

[3] I have chosen to mark this line with the "wrenched" accent often found in oral ballads (see Appendix 1).

Oh! the withy, it shall be the very first tree

That perishes at the heart." (´)

The ballad quatrain, like the four-beat accentual line itself, lost its accentual wildness and was brought into the regularity of syllabic count by the mid-sixteenth century. This control of syllable count appears in literary lyrics since this period. It is a shaping feature of the hymns sung in Christian churches, largely to eliminate confusion when people are singing in groups; hymnody has in turn exerted a powerful formal influence on the literary lyric.

The commonest hymn stanzas are syllabically regular versions of the ballad stanza options (usually with *abab* rhyme schemes). Even today in Christian hymn books, the verses are often marked with numbers indicating the syllabic pattern, the syllables matching the tune note for note; thus, the full iambic tetrameter stanza, or long meter, is marked 8888, here rhymed in couplets:

> Eternal are thy mercies, Lord,
> Eternal truth attends thy word;
> Thy praise shall sound from shore to shore,
> Till suns shall rise and set no more.

The metrical indication in the hymn book enables the text to be sung interchangeably with any tune written in the same meter. The alternating tetrameter and trimeter stanza, 8686, is called common meter, here rhymed *abab:*

> Our God, our help in ages past,
> Our hope for years to come,
> Our shelter from the stormy blast,
> And our eternal home.

The three-trimeter version, 6686, is called short meter, here rhymed *abab:*

> We give thee but thine own,
> Whate'er the gift may be;
> All that we have is thine alone,
> A trust, O Lord, from thee.

Later, in the nineteenth century, when accentual rhythms began to reassert themselves and break free of syllabic regularity, the ballad quatrain likewise began to recover its origins in accentual symmetry. Coleridge's "Rime of the Ancient Mariner" reveals the author's thorough comprehension of the structure of the ballad stanza, using many variants of the structure interchangeably in the same poem. (A formal examination of the poem is recommended in this context.[4]) The formal experiments of Emily Dickinson are another case of this greater freedom. In this century, a familiar modernist ballad by E.E. Cummings supplies a particularly haunting example of the accentual quatrain:

> anyone lived in a pretty how town
>
> (with up so floating many bells down)
>
> spring summer autumn winter
>
> he sang his didn't he danced his did.
>
> Women and men (both little and small)
>
> cared for anyone not at all
>
> they sowed their isn't they reaped their same
>
> sun moon stars rain

The Accentual Meters

For the student first encountering this concept, perhaps the most difficult task is knowing how to recognize an accentual meter, how to distinguish it from the more usual accentual-syllabic. Historical context is useful: accentual meters fell into disuse about the beginning of the sixteenth century (at least in literary poetry) and began to emerge again, gradually, through the nineteenth. There is also some difference of tone, accentual meters being typically more folksy, more col-

---

[4] Coleridge's poem also illustrates several ways of extending the quatrain into stanzas of five or six lines, or even longer:

> With sloping masts and dipping prow,
> As who pursued with yell and blow
> Still treads the shadow of his foe,
> And forwards bends his head,
> The ship drove fast, loud roared the blast,
> And southward aye we fled.

Thus the power of four-beat accentual symmetry is not restricted solely to stanzas of four lines.

loquial. But aside from these signs, there are three other formal signs that the poet is thinking in accentual terms.

First and most obvious is the presence of isolated accented syllables, such as we have seen in several previous examples:

> Hinx, | minx, | the old | witch winks,
>
> The fat | begins | to fry,
>
> Nobo | dy at home | but Jump | ing Joan,
>
> Fa | ther, Mo | ther and I
>
> they sowed | their is | n't they reaped | their same
>
> sun | moon | stars | rain
>
> 'Twas the mid | dle of night | by the cast | le clock
>
> And the owls | have awa | kened the crow | ing cock,
>
> Tu— | —whit!— | —Tu— | —whoo!

Unfortunately for purposes of identification, this sure sign of accentual meter is not always present.

Somewhat more subtle is the presence of three or more unaccented syllables in succession.

> ˘ ˘ ´ | ˘ ˘ ˘ ˘ ˘ ´| ˘ ´
> I have heard that hysterical women say
>
> ˘ ˘ ´ |˘ ˘ ˘ ´|˘ ˘ ˘ ´ | ˘ ´
> They are sick of the palette and fiddle-bow,
>
> ˘ ´| ´| ˘ ´| ˘ ˘ ´
> Of poets that are always gay,
>
> ˘ ´| ˘(´) ˘ ˘ ´ |˘ ´ | ˘ ˘ ´
> For everybody knows, or else should know
>
> ´| ˘ ´| ˘ ´ |˘ ˘ ˘ ´
> That if nothing drastic is done
>
> ´ ˘| ˘ ˘ ´| ˘ ˘ ´ | ˘ ˘ ´
> Aeroplane and Zeppelin will come out,
>
> ´ ˘ | ˘ ´|˘ ´ | ˘ ˘ ´
> Pitch like King Billy bomb-balls in
>
> ˘ ˘ ´| ˘ ˘ ´| ˘ ´ | ˘ ´
> Until the town lie beaten flat.

This verse paragraph begins as if in a triple meter, anapestic tetrameter. The third line drops the triple meter, but without moving beyond the limits of substitution for anapestic tetrameter. Foot division is no guide. The fourth line, however, strays beyond the limits for unaccented syllables (even if the syllable count in "everybody" is reduced to four), while the fifth line veers dangerously toward a three-beat line:

$$\breve{} \; \breve{} \; \acute{} \mid \breve{} \quad \acute{} \mid \breve{} \; \breve{} \; \acute{}$$

> That if nothing drastic is done

But such a pronunciation would make little sense with the rest of the verses, while an end pause would make little sense given the pressure of enjambment. Here, the multiple unaccented syllables provide the main cue for a proper reading: the stable feature is the four-beat pattern. This test must be used with some caution, since there are rare occasions when accentual-syllabic meters admit three successive unaccented syllables, and there are other possible explanations as well (an unmarked elision, for example). But the presence of more than two unaccented syllables should always alert the reader to the likelihood of accentualism.

Finally, there is the simple inability of any recognizable accentual-syllabic pattern to account for a feeling of rhythmic regularity—in effect, accentual meter by default. The following passage is scanned as if in iambic tetrameter, but in fact no metrical foot succeeds in establishing a predictable pattern:

$$\breve{} \; \acute{} \mid \breve{} \quad \acute{} \parallel \acute{} \; \mid \breve{} \quad \acute{}$$

> This darksome burn, horseback brown,

$$\breve{} \; \acute{} \mid \breve{} \quad \acute{} \mid \breve{} \quad \acute{} \mid \breve{} \quad \acute{}$$

> His rollrock highroad roaring down,

$$\breve{} \; \acute{} \mid \breve{} \; \breve{} \; \acute{} \mid \breve{} \; \acute{} \mid \breve{} \; \breve{} \; \acute{}$$

> In coop and in comb the fleece of his foam

$$\acute{} \; \breve{} \mid \acute{} \; \breve{} \mid \breve{} \; \acute{} \mid \breve{} \quad \acute{}$$

> Flutes and low to the lake falls home.

$$\breve{} \; \acute{} \mid \breve{} \; \acute{} \mid \breve{} \; \breve{} \mid \acute{} \quad \acute{}$$

> A wind-puff bonnet of fáwn-fróth

$$\acute{} \; \breve{} \mid \acute{} \; \breve{} \mid \acute{} \; \breve{} \mid \breve{} \quad \acute{}$$

> Turns and twindles over the broth

$$\breve{} \; \breve{} \; \acute{} \mid \breve{} \; \acute{} \mid \breve{} \parallel \acute{} \mid \acute{} \quad \breve{}$$

> Of a pool so pitch-black, féll-frówning,

$$\breve{} \; \acute{} \mid \breve{} \quad \acute{} \mid \breve{} \; \acute{} \mid \breve{} \; \acute{} \quad \breve{}$$

> It rounds and rounds Despair to drowning.

Iambic tetrameter can be clearly heard in lines two and three; the first line, however, lacks a syllable, and the fourth contains two successive trochees—quite a rare combination in iambic meter. Perhaps the metrical base is trochaic? Well, only two of the six lines establish a trochaic pattern; line one still lacks a syllable (truncated, perhaps, at the caesura?), and line five (the accents specified by the poet) causes more serious problems. The simplest metrical explanation here is a four-beat accentual line—a possibility that conforms to the known metrical habits of its author, Gerard Manley Hopkins.

Such discriminations sometimes demand a high degree of sophistication and a well-trained metrical ear. Distinguishing a pure accentual pentameter (however rarely found) from a traditional accentual-syllabic iambic pentameter can be a close call. To some extent, of course, this is merely a matter of labelling: the ear still *hears* the beat. Yet there is also an issue of discerning the poem's underlying structure and the poet's intentions. The poet's choice of an accentual meter establishes a particular relation between the poem and its poetic tradition. The real nature of the meter ultimately matters. Still, the beginner struggling with the scansion of basic iambic pentameter will not be able to eliminate alternatives in these cases easily; she should try to improve elementary scansion, and the rhythmic sensitivities that go with it, before worrying overmuch about this problem.

On the other hand, once a meter is *determined* to be accentual, the scansion itself is easy, much easier than in accentual-syllabic meters. One simply marks the most prominent accents, preserving as far as possible a regular count. And principles like those in accentual-syllabic meters still prevail: the more crowded the accents, the stronger the feeling of emphasis and heaviness; the greater the number of unaccented syllables, the greater the feeling of lightness and speed. In practice, one rarely finds more than four or five unaccented syllables between beats—at that point, as in prose, secondary accents naturally begin to assert themselves and take part in the meter. Thus while it is true, as many metrists say, that the unaccented syllables do not enter into the *meter*, they certainly do enter into the *rhythmic* feeling.

By far the greatest number of poems in accentual meters, both folk and literary, use the four-beat line or a version of the ballad quatrain. But other accentual lines occur. Accentual dimeter and, less frequently, trimeter, are also known in the nursery:

> One, two,
> Buckle my shoe;
> Three, four,
> Knock at the door;
> Five, six,
> Pick up sticks;
> Seven, eight,
> Lay them straight,

Nine, ten,
A big fat hen;
Eleven, twelve,
Dig and delve;
Thirteen, fourteen,
Maids a-courting;
Fifteen, sixteen,
Maids in the kitchen;
Seventeen, eighteen,
Maids in waiting,
Nineteen, twenty,
My plate's empty.

Ding, dong, bell,
Pussy's in the well.
Who put her in?
Little Johnny Green.
Who pulled her out?
Little Tommy Stout.

One notices in these examples the isolated accents, with no slack syllables: "One, two," "Díng, dóng, béll." Also, there is no pattern that could clearly be called iambic or anapestic; the only regular feature is the number of accented syllables. The accentual trimeter of "Ding dong bell" also features a perceptible pause after each line.

The following literary versions of these meters are by Langston Hughes and W.B. Yeats:

Have you dug the spill

Of Sugar Hill?

Cast your gims

On this sepia thrill:

Brown sugar lassie,

Caramel treat,

Honey-gold baby

Sweet enough to eat.

This other man I had dreamed

A drunken, vainglorious lout,

He had done most bitter wrong

To some who are near my heart,

Yet I number him in the song;

He, too, has resigned his part

In the casual comedy;

He, too, has been changed in his turn,

Transformed utterly:

A terrible beauty is born.

The second passage, notice, could almost be rationalized as anapestic trimeter, except for the emphatic second-last line, "Transformed utterly"; but there are enough such lines in the poem as a whole, and enough indeterminacy about any basis in accentual-syllabic feet, to regard the poem as accentual. A well-known lyric of Tennyson uses accentual trimeter with an elegiac tone:

Break, break, break,

On thy cold grey stones, O Sea!

And I would that my tongue could utter

The thoughts that arise in me.

O well for the fisherman's boy,

That he shouts with his sister at play!

O well for the sailor lad,

That he sings in his boat on the bay!

But the last two stanzas reveal the real matrix of the stanza in the short meter accentual form of the ballad quatrain:

> And the stately ships go on
>
> To their haven under the hill,
>
> But O for the touch of a vanished hand,
>
> And the sound of a voice that is still!

> Break, break, break,
>
> At the foot of thy crags, O Sea!
>
> But the tender grace of a day that is dead
>
> Will never come back to me.

Like accentual trimeter, the accentual hexameter is uncommon; yet it has existed in the English language from its Old English origins, where it appears as an occasional alternative to the four-beat alliterative line, an extension for added gravity. Here is a Middle English example from the fourteenth century, exhibiting, like all longer forms of the accentual line, an invariable medial caesura:

> Child, thou nert a pilgrim bot an uncuthe guest:
>
> Thy dawes beth itold, thy jurneys beth icest.
>
> Whoder thou shalt wend, north other est,
>
> Deth thee shall betide with bitter bale in brest.

 ́   ́   ́ ‖   ́   ́   ́

Lollay, lollay, little child, this wo Adam thee wroght,

 ́   ́   ́ ‖ ́   ́   ́

Whan he of the apple ete and Eve it him betoght.[5]

It is extremely significant, however, that no examples of an accentual penta-
meter appear in English until well after the establishment of the accentual-
syllabic system and the dominance of literary iambic pentameter. There are, to
my knowledge, no examples from Old or Middle English, or from the lore of
the nursery. The five-beat line does not yield to the instinctive desire for accent-
ual symmetry.

Accentual pentameter does emerge, however, with other accentual meters
later in the nineteenth century, no doubt because of the dominance of iambic
pentameter. Here is a fine example by Robert Bridges; I have marked every syl-
lable, to show the easy freedom within the five-beat pattern:

˘   ́   ˘   ́ ˘ ́   ˘   ́   ˘   ́˘

When men were all asleep the snow came flying,

˘   ́   ˘   ˘   ́ ́   ˘   ́ ˘

In large white flakes falling on the city brown,

 ́   ˘˘ ˘   ˘ ́˘   ˘ ́ ˘   ˘   ́   ˘ ́˘

Stealthily and perpetually settling and loosely lying,

 ́   ˘   ˘   ́ ˘ ́ ˘   ˘   ˘   ́ ˘

Hushing the latest traffic of the drowsy town;

 ́   ˘ ˘   ˘ ́ ˘   ˘ ́ ˘   ́   ˘   ˘

Deadening, muffling, stifling its murmurs failing;

 ́ ˘˘ ˘   ˘ ́ ˘   ˘ ́ ˘   ́   ˘   ́

Lazily and incessantly floating down and down.

The Longer and Shorter Iambic Meters

While the power of four-beat accentual symmetry is crucial to the ballad qua-
train and all its variants, plus the various accentual meters, it also underlies the

---

[5]   Child, you are not a pilgrim but an alien guest:
Your days are numbered, your journeys planned.
Whichever way you go, north or east,
Death shall happen to you with bitter misery in your breast.
Lullay, lullay, little child, this suffering Adam made for you
When he ate the apple and Eve gave it to him.

effect of the different line lengths in accentual-syllabic meters. The success of iambic pentameter as the meter of literary poetry, as I have mentioned, is due directly to the fact that the five-foot line *prevents* the four-beat accentual symmetry of folk poetry from forming; verse in this meter thus tends to feel more reflective, more consciously calculated. Iambic tetrameter, on the other hand, clearly reflects its lilting folk origins, for reasons that should now be obvious, and iambic octameter, likewise, is a different way of printing much the same rhythm. The longer line perhaps gives the rhythm a sense of greater weight, or in the following example a comical insistence, the exclusion of both pauses and mid-line caesuras contributing to the breathlessness:

> I am the very model of a modern Major-General,
> I've information vegetable, animal and mineral,
> I know the kings of England and I quote the fights historical,
> From Marathon to Waterloo in order categorical ...[6]

Less obvious, however, is the fact that iambic heptameter lines (otherwise called *fourteeners*) are really just another way of printing the common meter ballad quatrain in two lines rather than four. Compare the following:

> As I in hoary winter's night stood shivering in the snow,
> Surprised I was with sudden heat which made my heart to glow;
> And lifting up a fearful eye to view what fire was near,
> A pretty babe all burning bright did in the air appear.

> As I in hoary winter's night
> Stood shivering in the snow,
> Surprised I was with sudden heat
> Which made my heart to glow;

Iambic heptameter virtually never appears without the caesura after the fourth foot that marks the ballad rhythm—just as in ballads, enjambment, while it rarely occurs after the fourth foot, almost never occurs after the seventh.

Another variant, enormously popular for a brief period in the sixteenth century, was called "Poulter's measure," after the practice of egg sellers ("poulters") selling eggs in lots of thirteen, or a dozen plus one. "Poulter's measure,"

---

[6] I am content with "iambic octameter" as a rough description of this meter, though more minute analysis reveals it as an example of *dipodic* verse, in which alternate feet, here odd-numbered feet, are more strongly accentuated than the even-numbered (the four primary accents falling on "am," "model," "modern," "general"). Dipodic phenomena occur in folk ballads and nursery rhymes, as well as technically astute versifiers like Gilbert.

an unequal couplet of a six-beat line plus a seven-beat line, is simply another way of printing the short meter form of ballad stanza:

> Laid in my quiet bed, | in study as I were,
> I saw within my troubled head | a heap of thoughts appear.
> And every thought did show | so lively in mine eyes,
> That now I sigh'd, and then I smil'd, | as cause of thought did rise
> I saw the little boy | in thought how oft that he
> Did wish of God to scape the rod, | a tall young man to be.

> Laid in my quiet bed,
> In study as I were,
> I saw within my troubled head
> A heap of thoughts appear.

Again, the regular caesuras identify the ballad quatrain roots of this meter.

The very short lines—iambic monometer, dimeter, trimeter—are also affected by the desire for accentual symmetry, though somewhat less noticeably. The same principle holds true for all the patterns—trochaic, anapestic, and dactylic, as well as iambic. Poems written in iambic monometer are understandably exceptional; Robert Herrick has given us the best known example, "Upon His Departure Hence":

> Thus I
> Pass by
> And die,
> As one
> Unknown,
> And gone:
> I'm made
> A shade,
> And laid
> I'th grave,
> There have
> My cave.
> Where tell
> I dwell,
> *Farewell.*

The effect of this, produced almost entirely by the peculiar meter, is complex: the air of virtuoso performance provides a feeling of ironic detachment from the poignant subject; the brevity of the lines suggests understatement; and the tendency to pause after each line imparts a delicate solemnity.

But a word of caution is needed here. Is this solemnity a product of the meter, one may ask, with its slight tendency to pause after each line? Or is it the product of the poem's subject, the author's own death? This is a nice philosophical question. If I were reading this poem to an audience, I would certainly read it slowly, observing the pauses; and those pauses are, I think, just as certainly inherent in the meter because of the tendency to accentual symmetry under discussion. But students often take such observations very crudely, very literally, almost as if there is a kind of magic power attributed to a particular formal structure: *there is no one-to-one relationship between any given abstract form and its expressive possibilities*. Iambic monometer also has an inherent need, obviously, for enjambment, and I can imagine a poem in this meter with a cheerful subject and quite a rollicking forward momentum, even though I know of no such poem. The movement of the poem—and this is the point—depends on a subtle interplay between the potential movement inherent in the abstract form, its handling by the poet, and the dramatic situation.

Iambic dimeter is not a common meter, but a somewhat more manageable one. Here, the lightness of the short line is reinforced by the weakness of pause:

> What should I say,
>   Since faith is dead,
> And truth away
>   From you is fled?
> Should I be led
>   With doubleness?
>   Nay nay, Mistress!

But again, the same meter has been, somewhat implausibly, used to combine a serious subject with end-stopped lines to produce a feeling of gravity:

> Hear me, O God!
> A broken heart
> Is my best part;
> Use still thy rod,
> That I may prove
> Therein my love.

Iambic trimeter is most often treated with end-stopping and an implied pause, like the trimeter lines in the ballad stanza. But without actual tetrameters present to establish the four-beat rhythm, the strength of the pause is much weakened. To my ear, continuous trimeter always creates an odd feeling of rhythmic ambiguity:

> Ah, my dear angry Lord,
> Since Thou dost love, yet strike;

Cast down, yet help afford;
Sure I will do the like.

I will complain, yet praise;
I will bewail, approve;
And all my sour-sweet days
I will lament and love.

The iambic hexameter line, or *alexandrine* (the only iambic line not yet discussed) tends to behave like a doubled trimeter: the oft-noted tendency of the alexandrine to break in the middle is partly a recollection of the pause after trimeter lines in the ballad stanza. This is not troublesome when a single alexandrine is used—as it so often is—as a kind of *stretched* iambic pentameter, a heightened or climactic line at the end of a stanza (the Spenserian stanza, for example) or an otherwise emphatic line in an iambic pentameter context (a common device in heroic couplet poetry). But in continuous iambic hexameter, the medial caesura is more problematic. It can sometimes attain the rude vigour of ballad meter:

Still let my tyrants know, I am not doomed to wear
Year after year in gloom, and desolate despair;
A messenger of Hope comes every night to me,
And offers for short life, eternal liberty.

He comes with western winds, with evening's wandering airs,
With that clear dusk of heaven that brings the thickest stars,
Winds take a pensive tone, and stars a tender fire,
And visions rise, and change, that kill me with desire.

But such robust treatment is exceptional. It is helped here by the forward momentum of the syntax carrying through the pauses, but the routine medial caesura easily becomes tedious. The meter has therefore not been popular. (Drayton's early-seventeenth-century *Polyolbion* is the only long poem of note that uses it.) It is sometimes successful if the poet treats it like iambic pentameter, disguising the medial break by moving the caesura:

The rain and wind, the rain and wind, raved endlessly.
On me the Summer storm, and fever, and melancholy
Wrought magic, so that if I feared the solitude,
Far more I feared all company: too sharp, too rude,
Had been the wisest or the dearest human voice.

This should be read aloud in a way that really disguises the hexameter line altogether.

The Trochaic Meters

Trochaic meters in English are found almost exclusively in lyric poetry. There are no notable long poems in the language written in a continuous trochaic meter, apart from Longfellow's *Hiawatha* (perhaps the exception that proves the rule[7]). For some reason, trochaic meters seem to lend themselves to subject matter removed in some way from the ordinary, subjects having to do with the supernatural, with incantations, spells, fairy lore, and the like:

> Double, double, toil and trouble,
> Fire burn and cauldron bubble.
> Cool it with a baboon's blood,
> Then the charm is firm and good.

Associations of this sort lend awe and mystery to Blake's "The Tyger":

> Tyger! Tyger! burning bright
> In the forests of the night,
> What immortal hand or eye
> Could frame thy fearful symmetry?

One might expect the accent falling always on the first syllable to restrict trochaic meters to ponderous effects, and these examples might bear this out; but in fact, trochaic meter can also achieve fairylike lightness:

> Queen and huntress, chaste and fair,
> Now the sun is laid to sleep,
> Seated in thy silver chair,
> State in wonted manner keep;
> Hesperus entreats thy light,
> Goddess excellently bright.

The meter is also quite at home in the nursery, as in the following incantation:

> Jack be nimble, Jack be quick,
> Jack jump over the candle stick.

For purposes of scansion, the same general principles hold true as those described for iambic meters. Metrical substitutions are possible—iambic, dactylic, or spondaic (rarely anapestic because of three consecutive unaccented

---

[7] Longfellow was imitating the meter of the Finnish *Kalevala*, a folk epic he apparently considered analogous to his version of Native American lore.

syllables: ´ ˘ | ˘ ˘ ´). But substitution occurs less frequently than in iambic meters, probably because the trochaic feeling seems more difficult to sustain. Scansion of trochaic meters uncovers, however, two peculiarities that the student should understand.

First: although the meter logically demands extra-syllable rhymes, poets still rely extensively on one-syllable rhyming, with the result that the final unaccented syllable is regularly omitted (or "truncated"[8]):

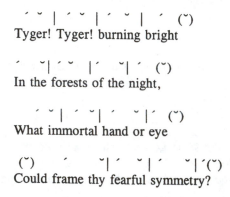

´ ˘ | ´ ˘ | ´ ˘ | ´ (˘)
Queen and huntress, chaste and fair,

´ ˘| ´ ˘| ´ ˘| ´ (˘)
Now the sun is laid to sleep,

´ ˘ |` ˘| ´ ˘ | ´ (˘)
Seated in thy silver chair,

´ ˘ | ´ ˘ | ´ ˘ | ´ (˘)
State in wonted manner keep.

Note that the name of this meter is still trochaic tetrameter, *not* trimeter. Students are often confused by the loss of the final syllable; but the four accented syllables still maintain the four-beat feeling, and the ear should be able to hear the four distinct beats. In lyric stanzas, poets often gain variety by systematically alternating extra-syllable with one-syllable endings.

A second and more troublesome peculiarity is that trochaic meters seem unstable, wanting to slip back into iambic patterns. The attentive reader may have noticed this in the Blake stanza above:

´ ˘ | ´ ˘ | ´ ˘ | ´ (˘)
Tyger! Tyger! burning bright

´ ˘| ´ ˘ | ´ ˘| ´ (˘)
In the forests of the night,

´ ˘ | ´ ˘| ´ ˘| ´ (˘)
What immortal hand or eye

(˘) ´ ˘| ´ ˘| ´ ˘|´(˘)
Could frame thy fearful symmetry?

---

[8] In trochaic and dactylic meters, some metrists use the ponderous terms "catalectic" for lines that omit the final slack syllables, and "acatalectic" for lines that preserve them.

In isolation, the last line could be understood as iambic; but the trochaic pattern is well established by the poem as a whole. The unaccented syllable on "could" in the fourth line is extra-metrical, like the extra-syllable ending in an iambic line: it does not enter into the formation of metrical feet. But it behaves quite differently from the extra-syllable ending. The iambic pentameter line, we remember, normally refuses (except in Chaucer, as noted above) to drop its first syllable; so when a trochaic line admits the initial unaccented syllable, the student may well ask, why does the line not immediately become iambic, thus:

$$\smile \quad \acute{} \mid \smile \quad \acute{} \mid \smile \quad \acute{} \mid \smile \quad \acute{}$$

Could frame thy fearful symmetry?

The question is not easy. There is no way to distinguish this line in isolation as "trochaic tetrameter" solely by ear: it is so labelled by its context in a largely trochaic poem. But in both cases, the *metrical frame of the poem determines how the line must both be pronounced and be rationalized by scansion.*

Yet another ambiguity can be observed in the second line. In isolation, this line could reasonably be heard as an iambic trimeter, thus:

$$\smile \quad \smile \quad \acute{} \mid \smile \quad \acute{} \mid \smile \quad \acute{}$$

In the forests of the night,

The only power that renders this scansion unacceptable is the context, the presence of the trochaic tick-tock established in the reader's ear (by the first line and by the whole context of the poem). Trochaic meters often promote an otherwise slack syllable in this way at the beginning of a line, and the reader must sometimes test alternatives to determine the best pronunciation.

There are many poems in which the extra-metrical unaccented syllable occurs so frequently that it is hard to say whether the basic meter is trochaic or iambic. In such cases, the label itself is arbitrary. But because iambic meters so rarely omit the first syllable, so rarely behave this way outside of Chaucer, the meter is usually called trochaic if a significant number of lines (not necessarily a majority) are clearly trochaic. The inventor of this type of verse is Milton, in his pair of early poems "L'Allegro" and "Il Penseroso":

$$(\smile) \; \acute{} \quad \smile \mid \acute{} \quad \smile \mid \acute{} \quad \smile \mid \acute{} \; (\smile)$$

But come thou goddess fair and free,

$$(\smile) \; \acute{} \quad \smile \mid \acute{} \quad \smile \mid \acute{} \; \smile \mid (\smile)$$

In Heav'n yclept Euphrosyne,

$$\acute{} \quad \smile \mid \acute{} \quad \smile \mid \acute{} \; \smile \mid \acute{} \; (\smile)$$

And by men heart-easing Mirth,

$$(\smile) \; \acute{} \quad \smile \mid \acute{} \; \smile \mid \acute{} \; \smile \mid \acute{} \; (\smile)$$

Whom lovely Venus at a birth

With two sister Graces more

To ivy-crownèd Bacchus bore ...

Haste thee nymph, and bring with thee

Jest and youthful Jollity,

Quips and Cranks and wanton Wiles,

Nods, and Becks, and wreathèd Smiles,

Such as hang on Hebe's cheek,

And love to live in dimple sleek;

Sport that wrinkled Care derides,

And Laughter, holding both his sides.

Come and trip it as ye go

On the light fantastic toe,

And in thy right hand lead with thee

The mountain nymph, sweet Liberty.

The suppleness and naturalness of the rhythms here, as they waver freely and unpredictably between trochaic and quasi-iambic patterns, strongly underline the relationship of this meter to the native English four-beat accentual line.[9]

The same array of line lengths is available in trochaic as in iambic meters, and the effects are somewhat parallel. If trochaic tetrameter is the most common version, however, trochaic pentameter has scarcely appeared at all, probably because of the difficulty maintaining it as distinct from the familiar rhythms of iambic pentameter. Robert Browning attempted it, with dubious success, in "One Word More," preserving the trochaic fall by insistent end-stopping and extra-syllable endings:

> I shall never, in the years remaining,
> Paint you pictures, no, nor carve you statues,
> Make you music that shall all-express me;
> So it seems: I stand on my attainment.
> This of verse alone, one life allows me:
> Verse and nothing else have I to give you.
> Other heights in other lives, God willing—
> All the gifts from all the heights, your own, Love!

The shorter lines generally parallel the effects of their iambic counterparts, and trochaic dimeter and trimeter have yielded curious effects. Pope, straying from his customary heroic couplet, uses trochaic dimeter comically in his "Lilliputian Ode":

> In amaze,
> Lost, I gaze.
> Can our eyes
> Reach thy size?
> May my lays
> Swell with praise
> Worthy thee?
> Worthy me?

Tennyson invests it with surprising brawn in "The Oak":

> All his leaves
> Fall'n at length,
> Look, he stands,
> Trunk and bough,
> Naked strength.

---

[9] This example from "L'Allegro" is highly trochaic; the rhythms of the more sombre "Il Penseroso" tend to be more iambic and spondaic.

Trochaic trimeter suggests a breathless movement, pushing through the half-implied pauses:

> Go not, happy day,
> From the shining fields,
> Go not, happy day,
> Till the maiden yields.
> Rosy is the West,
> Rosy is the South,
> Roses are her cheeks,
> And a rose her mouth.
>
> All mankind, I fancy,
> When anticipating
> Anything exciting
>   Like a rendezvous,
> Occupy the time in
> Purely random thinking,
> For when love is waiting,
>   Logic will not do.

The longer-lined trochaic meters, like all that extend beyond five or six beats, tend to seem like two shorter lines printed as one; poems printed in the longer line are few. Here is the scarce trochaic hexameter:

> Years have risen and fallen in darkness or in twilight,
> Ages waxed and waned that knew not thee nor thine,
> While the world sought light by night and sought not thy light,
> Since the sad last pilgrim left thy dark mid shrine.

Trochaic heptameter, like its iambic sibling, sounds like a ballad quatrain written out in long lines:

> Think'st thou to seduce me then with words that have no meaning?
> Parrots so can learn to prate, our speech by pieces gleaning;
> Nurses teach their children so, about the time of weaning.

Trochaic octameter, the long-lined equivalent to the popular trochaic tetrameter, is strongly associated with two well-known nineteenth-century poems that flaunt this unusual meter: in England Tennyson's "Locksley Hall," and in America Poe's "The Raven":

> In the spring a livelier iris changes on the burnished dove,
> In the spring a young man's fancy lightly turns to thoughts of love.

> Once upon a midnight dreary, while I pondered, weak and weary,
> Over many a quaint and curious volume of forgotten lore ...

The Triple Meters: Anapestic and Dactylic

The triple meters are characteristically associated with effects that are light, or quick, or lively, though in the Victorian period, their heyday, they easily became languorous. Anapestic meters behave in much the same way as the trochaic: the favoured version is anapestic tetrameter, and in practice in any given poem anapests and iambs freely intermingle so that it may seem arbitrary to decide which label should apply:

> ˘   ˊ|˘   ˊ|˘ ˘ ˊ | ˘   ˊ(ˇ)
> O swallow, sister, O fair swift swallow,

> ˊ ˘ | ˘   ˊ|˘ ˘   ˊ |˘ ˘ ˊ
> Why wilt thou fly after spring to the south,

> ˘ ˊ |˘   ˊ|˘ ˘ ˊ |˘ ˊ
> The soft south whither thine heart is set?

> ˘   ˊ| ˘ ˊ|˘   ˘ ˊ |˘   ˊ(ˇ)
> Shall not the grief of the old time follow?

I would probably call this anapestic tetrameter, because of the dominating triple rhythms (and their continuance in the rest of the poem), but I could not reject a description of iambic tetrameter with frequent anapests.

Anapestic pentameter, unlike the scarce trochaic pentameter, is used with about the same frequency as other anapestic lines. The triple meter seems sufficient to keep it distinct from iambic pentameter:

> And black in the oncoming darkness stood out in the trees
> And pink shone the ponds in the sunset ready to freeze
> And all was still and ominous waiting for dark
> And the keeper was ringing his closing bell in the park

Short anapestic lines, dimeter and trimeter, have effects roughly parallel to their iambic counterparts:

> O Rose, thou art sick!
> The invisible worm
> That flies in the night
> In the howling storm ...

> Ah, Sunflower! weary of time,
> Who countest the steps of the Sun,
> Seeking after that sweet golden clime
> Where the traveller's journey is done ...

The longer anapestic lines likewise reflect their folk ballad affiliations, with regular caesuras and occasional internal rhyming patterns:

> I would that we were, my beloved, white birds on the foam of the sea!
> We tire of the flame of the meteor, before it can fade and flee;
> And the flame of the blue star of twilight, hung low on the rim of the sky,
> Has awaked in our hearts, my beloved, a sadness that may not die.

> When you're lying awake with a dismal headache, and repose is taboo'd
>   by anxiety,
> I conceive you may use any language you choose to indulge in, without
>   impropriety;
> For your brain is on fire—the bedclothes conspire of the usual slumber
>   to plunder you:
> First your counterpane goes, and uncovers your toes, and your sheet slips
>   demurely from under you.

> Oh it isn't cheerful to see a man, the marvellous work of God,
> Crushed in the mutilation mill, crushed to a smeary clod,
> Oh it isn't cheerful to hear him moan; but it isn't that I mind,
> It isn't the anguish that goes with him, it's the anguish he leaves behind.

Dactylic meters are so rare that no one line can reasonably be called "commonest." The reason for their apparent unmanageability is their ambiguity. Dactylic meters, like anapestic, freely intermingle triple with duple rhythms; in addition, like trochaic meters, they have a tendency to accept the extra initial syllable. But even without these variations, the regular dactylic line is by itself ambiguous:

> ´ ˘ ˘ | ´ ˘ ˘ | ´ ˘ ˘ | ´ (˘ ˘)
> Why wilt thou fly after spring to the south,

> ´ ˘ | ˘ ´ | ˘ ˘ ´ | ˘ ˘ ´
> Why wilt thou fly after spring to the south,

As this example shows, a regular dactylic line can be understood equally well within an anapestic frame; this line itself, in fact, is taken not from a dactylic poem but from an anapestic example cited above. Dactylic meters thus easily lose their dactylic identity and slip into an anapestic feeling: to be maintained as recognizably "dactylic," they must be written with little metrical variation and thus quickly tire the ear.

Poets have nonetheless tried, at one time or another, most of the dactylic possibilities. Here are some examples, including a most exceptional dactylic monometer:

> Over the
>   seaworthy
> cavalry
>   arches a
> rocketry
>   wickerwork:
> involute
>   laceries
> lacerate
>   indigo
> altitudes
>   making a
> skywritten
>   filigree
> into which,
>   lazily,
> LCTs
>   sinuate ...

Eight o'clock, nine o'clock,
Coffee and oranges,
"Do you want eggs?" for the
Twenty-fifth time.
(*Orange* is singular.)
No, I want caviar,
Onions, black bread, and a
Vodka and lime.

Woman much missed, how you call to me, call to me,
Saying that now you are not as you were
When you had changed from the one who was all to me,
But as at first, when our day was fair.

The only dactylic meter that needs special comment is dactylic hexameter. When this meter occurs in English, it virtually always bears reference to its counterpart in Greek and Latin poetry, for this was the noble epic meter of Homer's *Iliad* and *Odyssey* and Virgil's *Aeneid*. Thus it brings dignity even to the rather sentimental tale Longfellow tells in his "Evangeline":

This is the forest primeval. The murmuring pines and the hemlocks
Bearded with moss, and in garments green, indistinct in the twilight,
Stand like Druids of eld, with voices sad and prophetic,
Stand like harpers hoar, with beards that rest on their bosoms.

This meter is usually handled, as here, with the line ending invariably on a dactyl plus a trochee (or spondee), as it does invariably in the classical languages.

Syllabic and Quantitative Systems

Syllabic thinking about meter has operated in English poetry in two different ways. During the earlier phase of the accentual-syllabic metrical tradition, iambic pentameter was often understood in terms of syllable count rather than feet, so that one finds syllable-counting terms like "numbers," the "decasyllabic line," "octosyllabics," and "fourteeners," while extra syllables were rationalized not as "anapestic substitutions" but as kinds of elision, collapsing two slack syllables to one. Such verse is easily analyzed through the accentual-syllabic foot system described here.

But a different kind of syllabic system was introduced early in the twentieth century by Robert Bridges in England and, more successfully, by Marianne Moore in America. In this system, lines are controlled solely by counting syllables, and accent is left to fall where it may. Bridges' experiments along these lines are, I think, failed poetry; Moore's, on the other hand, are widely admired. Even so, were this system confined to isolated experiments by these two poets, it would remain a curiosity, despite the exceptional artistry of Moore's achievement. But syllabic metric has been taken up by others—major figures like W.H. Auden, Dylan Thomas, Sylvia Plath, Thom Gunn, and Donald Davie—and it seems to offer unexplored potential for future development.

The principle is simple—so simple that scansion is unnecessary. One simply needs to say that the line maintains x number of syllables, or that the stanza has lines set out in a particular fixed syllable count.

Here is Thom Gunn's "Considering the Snail," a poem written in six-line stanzas with uniform lines of seven syllables each:

The snail pushes through a green
night, for the grass is heavy
with water and meets over
the bright path he makes, where rain
has darkened the earth's dark. He
moves in a wood of desire,

pale antlers barely stirring
as he hunts. I cannot tell

what power is at work, drenched there
with purpose, knowing nothing.
What is a snail's fury? All
I think is that if later

I parted the blades above
the tunnel and saw the thin
trail of broken white across
litter, I would never have
imagined the slow passion
to that deliberate progress.

Scansion in this instance is beside the point: all that is needed is confirmation that every line has (or—given the syllabic ambiguity of English—can reasonably be understood to have) the requisite number of syllables.

But further observations need to be made. First, the accents here fall completely by chance, without pattern: in fact, one of the most important functions of syllabic meter is to disrupt the habituated patterns of accentual-syllabic meter, its rhythms and the turns of phrase associated with them; consequently, lines with an odd number of syllables have a slight advantage because they are less likely to gather into the familiar two-syllable patterns of metrical feet. Syllabic verse, therefore, releases "prose rhythms" not found in traditional metrical poetry, but more closely allied with free verse. Secondly, because English is accent-timed, not syllable-timed, the syllable count itself can rarely be picked up by the ear alone; its function, then, is less aural than purely formal, a kind of discipline accepted by the poet as a self-imposed control or guide. Thirdly, since the lines are not organized by rhythmic groupings, they are most often marked for the ear by rhyme—here, an *abcabc* scheme; but the rhyming (possibly because of Marianne Moore's own practice) is generally light, unobvious. Finally, because the line endings do not coincide with rhythmic or phrasal groupings as they normally do in iambic meters, enjambment is customary, even with the light rhymes in place, and needs to be handled with great delicacy. Here, Gunn's line-end hesitations seem to me elegantly functional and expressive:

What is a snail's fury?   All

The word "all," separated from the question by caesura, seems at first the question's answer—before it rolls back over the line-end into the larger thrust of the poet's sentence.

Largely because of the avoidance of accentual patterns and the treatment of enjambment and line units, syllabic verse of this sort calls on many of the same formal perceptions as well-wrought free verse. The same is true in the elaborate stanzaic structures of Marianne Moore, with lines of different lengths, as here in the final stanzas of "The Fish":

All
external
    marks of abuse are present on this
    defiant edifice—
        all the physical features of

ac-
cident—lack
    of cornice, dynamite grooves, burns, and
    hatchet strokes, these things stand
        out on it; the chasm side is

dead.
Repeated
    evidence has proved that it can live
    on what cannot revive
        its youth. The sea grows old in it.

The stanza has five lines, with syllable counts of one, three, nine, six, and eight, and a rhyme scheme of *aabbx*. Moore's normal practice, apparent here, encompasses light rhyme and radical enjambment (as in the middle of a word, or over the end of a stanza). The stanza as a self-contained unit is not detectable by the ear alone, but is confirmed, aurally and visually, only on repetition.

Syllabic verse provides the contemporary poet with an attractive alternative to free verse, allowing a greater degree of discipline and control in the writing process, while projecting to the reader a higher sense of polish than free verse usually does.

Quantitative meters in English are wholly artificial: were it not for the prestige of Greek and Latin, they would certainly never have been attempted. "Quantity" refers to the time allotted to the pronunciation of vowel sounds, long or short. But in English, we simply do not attend to the length of time given to vowel sounds in our speech; long and short do not figure into the meaning, as they do in the classical languages. The patterning of vowel quantities was, however, the basis of meter in Greek and Latin. And because the education of the poets in the English tradition was, from the Middle Ages until recently, founded on the study of classical languages—including the obligatory composition of metrically correct verses in Latin and Greek—it seems inevitable that poets from time to time should have tried the same in English. Genuine appreciation of such writings depends as well, of course, on one's previous acquaintance with the classical models. The first great outburst of quantitative versifying took place in the Elizabethan period, with poets like Spenser and Thomas Campion. Since then, attempts to write English verse conforming to classical metrical patterns have been sporadic and generally unsatisfying—but frequent enough to merit mention.

These attempts have followed one of two different avenues: either the poet adopts the quantitative patterns and merely substitutes accents, more or less, for long quantities; or else the poet attempts to uncover actual quantities, normally ignored in the English words, and foreground them in a metrical pattern. In either case, rhyme is usually avoided, since rhyme never appears in classical Greek or Latin.

The first type is simpler and more common. Here again are the opening lines of Longfellow's "Evangeline," an accentual imitation of the classical dactylic hexameter (I have used the macron - to mark the "long," or accented, vowels, as is the custom):

<pre>
  ‾ ˘   ˘ | ‾ ˘   ˘ | ‾ ˘ || ˘ | ‾   ˘ ˘ | ‾   ˘   ˘ | ‾   ˘
This is the forest primeval. The murmuring pines and the hemlocks
  ‾ ˘   ˘ | ‾ ||˘ ˘ ˘ |‾ ‾ | ‾ ||˘ ˘|‾ ˘   ˘ | ‾ ˘ ˘
Bearded with moss, and in garments green, indistinct in the twilight,
  ‾   ‾ | ˘˘   ˘|‾ || ‾ | ‾ ‾|‾ ˘   ˘ | ‾ ˘ ˘
Stand like Druids of eld, with voices sad and prophetic,
  ‾   ‾ | ‾ ‾ |‾ || ‾ |‾   ‾ |‾ ˘   ˘ | ‾ ˘ ˘
Stand like harpers hoar, with beards that rest on their bosoms.
</pre>

In the classical line, the first four feet can be either dactyls or spondees, while the last two must be dactyl followed by spondee or trochee:

<pre>
  ‾ ˘ ˘ | ‾ ˘ ˘ | ‾ ˘ ˘ | ‾ ˘ ˘ | ‾ ˘ ˘ | ‾ ‾
  ‾ ‾ | ‾ ‾ | ‾ ‾ | ‾ ‾ | ‾ ˘
</pre>

Here, Longfellow establishes the triple sway of English dactylic meter in the first line, then allows "spondees" (really trochees for the most part) to intersperse at will. Such versification is not really quantitative at all, but an English accentual pattern that serves as a reminder of classical rhythms with which the reader is assumed to be familiar. The result is apt to seem stiff in English, though Longfellow's handling of it in "Evangeline" seems to me quite admirable technically.

Perhaps the commonest quantitative models in English are the lyric quatrains, the stanzas called "sapphic" and "alcaic." The sapphic quatrain consists of three lines like this, with the options indicated:

<pre>
  ‾ ˘ | ‾ ‾ | ‾ ˘ ˘ ˘ | ‾ ˘ | ‾ ‾
      | ‾ ˘ | | ‾ | ‾ ˘
</pre>

followed by a shorter one like this (called an adonic):

<pre>
  ‾ ˘ ˘ | ‾ ˘
</pre>

Here is a stanza of Isaac Watts' "The Day of Judgement," composed in an accentual replication of classical sapphics, which serve as an emotional control on the poet's fantasies of final destruction:

> Thoughts, like old vultures, prey upon their heart-strings,,
> And the smart twinges when the eye beholds the
> Lofty Judge frowning, and a flood of vengeance
>   Rolling afore him.

Here is the final stanza of Jay Macpherson's "A Lost Soul," for comparison:

> You were my soul: in arrogance I banned you.
> Now I recant—return, possess me, take my
> Hands, bind my eyes, infallibly restore my
>   Share in perdition.

In both examples, one notes the poet's free enjambment within the stanza, a feature found in the classical originals.

Efforts to compose genuinely quantitative verses in English are fewer. Campion's "Rose-cheeked Laura" and Milton's "Pyrrha" (a translation from Horace) are frequently anthologized. The following verses from Ezra Pound's "Apparuit" are a delicate attempt to reproduce the quantitative sapphic stanza in real English quantities:

$$\text{—} \; \breve{} \; | \; \text{—} \quad \breve{} \; | \; \text{—} \quad \breve{} \quad \breve{} \; | \; \text{—} \quad \breve{} \; | \; \text{—} \quad \text{—}$$

Golden rose the house, in the portal I saw

$$\text{—} \quad \breve{} \; | \; \text{—} \quad \breve{} \; | \; \text{—} \quad \breve{} \quad \breve{} \; | \; \text{—} \quad \breve{} \; | \; \text{—} \quad \breve{}$$

thee, a marvel, carven in subtle stuff, a

$$\text{—} \quad \breve{} \; | \; \text{—} \quad \text{—} \quad | \; \text{—} \quad \breve{} \quad \breve{} \; | \; \text{—} \quad \breve{} \quad | \; \text{—} \quad \breve{}$$

portent. Life died down in the lamp and flickered,

$$\text{—} \qquad \breve{} \quad \breve{} \; | \; \text{—} \quad \breve{}$$

        caught at the wonder.

$$\text{—} \qquad \breve{} \; | \; \text{—} \quad \breve{} \; | \; \text{—} \quad \breve{} \quad \breve{} \; | \; \text{—} \quad \breve{} \; | \; \text{—} \quad \text{—}$$

Green the ways, the breath of the fields is thine there,

$$\text{—} \quad \breve{} \; | \; \text{—} \quad \breve{} \; | \; \text{—} \quad \breve{} \quad \breve{} \; | \; \text{—} \quad \breve{} \; | \; \breve{} \breve{}$$

open lies the land, yet the steely going

$$- \ \smallsmile | - \ \ - | - \ \ \smallsmile \ \ \smallsmile | - \ \ - | - \ \smallsmile$$

darkly hast thou dared and the dreaded aether

$$- \ \smallsmile \ \ \smallsmile | - \ \ \smallsmile$$

parted before thee.

The reader should keep in mind that both the syllabic and the quantitative metrical systems described here are rare and largely a matter for the advanced student. It is helpful, however, to be aware from the beginning of the full range of metrical possibilities.

3

Stanza and Form

Students, lacking a technical vocabulary to deal with rhythm and sound, almost inevitably seize on one word: "flow." Whatever else may be happening within the prosody of a poem, the student is sure that it makes the poem "flow." As a teacher, exasperated, I have forbidden students to use the word "flow." But I will use it here. In some textbooks, the poetic stanza is presented as a fixed pattern, a static shape to be replicated x number of times in a poem—a mechanized facsimile. I prefer to think of it as a dynamic shape, a kind of river channel through which the syntax of the poem, with all its pent-up kinetic energy, all its forward momentum, must find a way, despite swerves and obstructions, to *flow*.

The Dynamics of Stanza and Form: Rhyme, Line and Closure

The obstructions that interfere with the forward thrust of the poetic sentence are formal and syntactic: formal obstructions are the line ends and the rhymes, and syntactic obstructions the amplifying phrases and clauses that delay completion of the sentence, often associated with caesura. W.B. Yeats records in his letters the discovery that he must seek, "not as Wordsworth thought, words in common use, but a powerful and passionate syntax and a complete coincidence of period and stanza."[1] He realized that the energy of a poem's movement is governed by the relationship between its syntactic current and the channel through which it must flow.

The stanza has its origins in lyric poetry written for music. In true lyric, each line of a stanza corresponds to a phrase of the tune. Poetry written for music tends strongly to end-stopping, with enjambment absent or weak, the rhyme word lingering in the ear to punctuate both the line-end pause and the end of the

---

[1] Letter to H.C. Grierson, 21 Feb. 1926, in *The Letters of W.B. Yeats,* ed. Alan Wade (London: Rupert Hart-Davis, 1954), p. 710. On the stanza in general, see Ernst Häublein, *The Stanza* (London: Methuen, 1978).

musical phrase. When stanzas are separated from their musical function and printed in books, enjambment enters far more freely, and far more supple effects of syntactic rhythm are possible. The literary lyric, intended not for singing but for reading, is fundamentally a kind of make-believe song in which the words themselves generate their own "music." Freed from musical performance, the literary lyric is capable of greater intricacy, not only of form but of intellectual substance.

Rhyme has a powerful capacity for structuring the dynamic movement of the stanza (see Chapter 1, pp. 30–31). The first rhyme word sets up an anticipation and thus forward momentum; the second creates satisfaction and thus the possibility of closure; any further rhymes create a sense of insistence, saturation, or excess. In consort with meter, this process is intimately linked to the dynamic movement within stanzas and forms.

The opening line of any stanza at once establishes a range of expectations and limitations. For example:

> There was a young lady from Venus ...

How many readers recognize the beginning of a limerick here? The opening line in this case establishes the expectation of a continued anapestic jingle, a particular rhyme scheme, and firm closure (one braces for the sting in the tail) not too many syllables away. The conventions are well known. In more sophisticated verse, conventional expectations are less determined, but they operate on the same principle:

> Shall I compare thee to a summer's day?
> Thou art more lovely, and more temperate ...

Many readers of these lines will know that they are confronting a sonnet. How? If not from foreknowledge of the author, or cues in the text, then perhaps from recognizing the familiar visual shape of a poem of a certain length on the page. Knowing or at least suspecting "sonnet," the reader again has expectations of metrical continuity, a certain length, and a structured formation of rhyme. Similar principles operate in the establishment of any stanzaic pattern.

A true song lyric by Thomas Campion (who wrote both words and music) provides a fairly simple example of rhyme's ability to regulate movement through a stanza:

> There is a garden in her face,
> Where roses and white lilies grow,
> A heavenly paradise is that place,
> Wherein all pleasant fruits do flow.
> These cherries grow, which none may buy
> Till "Cherry Ripe!" themselves do cry.

Here the reader recognizes the accentual symmetry of iambic tetrameter (the non-symmetrical pentameter is uncommon in song lyrics). The stanza unfolds in smooth, end-stopped lines, an exact fit between verbal phrase and musical phrase. The first two lines set up the expectation of rhyme, quickly satisfied by the next two, which introduce a new conceit but in parallel syntactic form. The last two lines create a rhymed couplet bringing the stanza to closure.

The pattern, with its simple *ababcc* rhyme scheme, is then repeated through two more stanzas, sung to identical music:

> Those cherries fairly do enclose
> Of orient pearl a double row,
> Which when her lovely laughter shows,
> They look like rosebuds filled with snow.
> Yet them nor peer nor prince can buy
> Till "Cherry Ripe!" themselves do cry.
>
> Her eyes like angels watch them still;
> Her brows like bended bows do stand,
> Threatening with piercing frowns to kill
> All that attempt with eye or hand
> Those sacred cherries to come nigh,
> Till "Cherry Ripe!" themselves do cry.

The second stanza makes us aware of one new formal element, a *refrain*—a final line repeated (with minor variation) from the first stanza and then repeated again, as expected, in the third. Otherwise, formal patterns are kept simple: continued end-stopping, minimal metrical variation (conforming to the musical phrase), syntax that scarcely diverges from normal word order and advances with little hesitation. The imagery likewise is conventional: the well-established conceit, presented most bluntly in the opening line, is developed with references to "cherries," "orient pearl," and "rosebuds," while the allusions to "heavenly paradise" and Eden are equally familiar.

Even such a conventional poem can have its subtleties, however, and Campion was a consummate artist. Formally, one can point to such elegant features as the internal rhyme on "grow" in the first stanza, the alliterative "nor peer nor prince" in the second, and the unexpected, somewhat suggestive, pressure of enjambment into the refrain couplet in the third. The shopworn imagery also yields fresh complexities: the high idealization of the garden and heaven images is undercut ironically by the refrain, which repeats the cries of fruit merchants heard on the streets of Campion's London. This irony is intensified by the pun on "angels"—the name of an English coin of the period—and by the music, which, repeating several times over, imitates the fruiterer's street call on the words "Cherry Ripe!" Something is for sale. Campion's love song is also a wily masculine joke. All this happens within the confines of a largely conventional song lyric.

W.B. Yeats's "No Second Troy," on the other hand, illustrates the interplay of rhyme scheme, end-stopping, enjambment, and closure, in a literary lyric not written for singing:

> Why should I blame her that she filled my days
> With misery, or that she would of late
> Have taught to ignorant men most violent ways,
> Or hurled the little streets upon the great,
> Had they but courage equal to desire?
> What could have made her peaceful, with a mind
> That nobleness made simple as a fire,
> With beauty like a tightened bow, a kind
> That is not natural in an age like this,
> Being high, and solitary, and most stern?
> Why, what could she have done, being what she is?
> Was there another Troy for her to burn?

This poem unfolds in a common *abab* scheme repeated three times, but printed without stanza breaks between quatrains. Its syntactic rhythm grows from a series of four questions. But the questions do not coincide with the quatrains; instead, the first question pushes through the first quatrain, coming to rest on the first *a* rhyme of the next, setting up anticipation for further unfolding. It is a dramatic enjambment of unseen stanzas. The second question also occupies five lines, again pushes through the quatrain structure, coming to rest on the first *b* rhyme of quatrain three, again demanding further completion, though the question closes on an emphatic spondee, "móst stérn." The rhymes are effective dynamically, yet they are themselves de-emphasized by the multiple enjambments. The third question occupies a line by itself, unexpectedly, completing the *a* rhyme but, for the first time in the poem, with imperfect rhyme. Closure is not complete. The final question occupies the last line by itself, bringing the poem to firm closure on a full, perfect *b* rhyme reaching back to the impassioned spondaic phrase. This formal analysis does not explain the great emotional force of Yeats's disillusioned love poem, but it does diagram the metrical and syntactic lines of force that imbue the questions with the fullest possible charge, and gives important guidance for any dramatic recitation.

Both Campion's and Yeats's lyrics operate within the confines of a single meter; but variation of the line lengths, too, participates in the regulation of stanzaic movement. Many stanzas mix line lengths (and sometimes even metrical feet) more or less freely. Lines shorter than the norm tend to light, lilting, rippling effects. The jingle of the iambic dimeter couplet in this context yields unmistakable irony:

> The glories of our blood and state
> Are shadows, not substantial things;

> There is no armour against fate,
> Death lays his icy hand on kings.
>   Sceptre and crown
>   Must tumble down
> And in the dust be equal made
> With the poor crooked scythe and spade.

Lines longer than the norm, like the alexandrine in the following example, generate a sense of stretch or expansiveness, usually (though not always) a slowing down:

> Hail to thee, blithe Spirit!
>   Bird thou never wert.
> That from Heaven, or near it,
>   Pourest thy full heart
> In profuse strains of unpremeditated art.

> Higher still and higher
>   From the earth thou springest
> Like a cloud of fire;
>   The blue deep thou wingest,
> And singing still dost soar, and soaring ever singest.

This complex and unusual stanza is built from lines of trochaic trimeter (trochaic, as so often, suggesting an otherworldly subject) with alternating extra-syllable and one-syllable rhymes, capped by an alexandrine—the trimeter doubled and transformed to iambic—which captures the soaring expansiveness of the bird. The rhyme scheme is *ababb*. A stanza like this, invented for a specific poem and not used again, is called a *nonce stanza*.

Nonce stanzas are infinite in their variety, but let us look at one more example to illustrate the principles under discussion. Here is the last stanza of Donne's "Valediction: Of Weeping":

>   O more than moon,
>   Draw not up seas to drown me in thy sphere;
>   Weep me not dead, in thine arms, but forbear
>   To teach the sea what it may do too soon.
>   Let not the wind
>   Example find
>   To do me more harm than it purposeth;
>   Since thou and I sigh one another's breath,
> Whoe'er sighs most is cruelest, and hastes the other's death.

This stanza of nine lines is divided in two parts by the rhymes, the first four and the next five lines being self-contained units, thus: *abbaccddd*. Most longer stanzas are such composites of smaller units. The short opening line isolates the poet's metaphorical address to his mistress, a command paralleled with another command in line 2. Enjambment prevents closure on the completion of the *b* rhyme, but the two parallel commands come to full stop on the completion of the *a* rhyme.

Closure might seem ensured, but a third command—fulfilling the climactic principle of threes—then begins with the jingly dimeter couplet, but enjambs into the pentameter line and comes to rest on "purposeth," yet unrhymed and thus pressing forward: when the *d* rhyme is realized, however, it enjambs yet again into the last line, which stretches out to a climactic heptameter and a satisfying third *d* rhyme.

This kind of analysis is an attempt to give specific meaning to the vague sense of "flow" that readers of poetry feel so instinctively. It arises in part, of course, from the metrical regularization of accents—but only in part. The interplay between syntax, rhyme scheme, line units, enjambment, and closure should be taken as a set of instructions for realizing the expressive syntactic momentum of any lyric stanza in oral, or silent, recitation. From a prosodic standpoint, the important thing is to incorporate the metrical, stanzaic, and rhyming structure into the dynamic movement of syntax, in order to realize poetry. The process appears complex under analysis, and it is; but a sensitive reader can quickly learn to be responsive to the signs.

Some Standard English Stanzas

Given the number of variables—the number of lines in a stanza, the length of each line, the possible rhyme schemes, the varieties of refrain—there is little hope of cataloguing all possible stanza forms. Yet a few have become well enough established to have names and histories of their own.

At one end of the scale, the line between stanzaic and continuous (or stichic) verse is blurred. Blank verse is continuous, organized into verse paragraphs (though on rare occasions it can be organized into blank verse stanzas of equal length, as in Tennyson's "Tears, Idle Tears," where the stanzaic closure is marked by an unrhymed refrain). On the other hand, stanzas of only two or three lines—couplets and tercets—are more frequently printed continuously and organized into verse paragraphs. Even quatrains (as in Yeats's "No Second Troy") can be so treated. Couplets, tercets, and quatrains are not properly called "stanzas" unless they are printed on the page with appropriate spacing.

The commonest forms of couplet poetry are iambic pentameter couplets of two kinds, either *heroic* (or *closed*) *couplets* or *open couplets* (see Chapter 1, pp. 26–27); iambic tetrameter couplets, or *octosyllabics;* and iambic heptameter couplets, or *fourteeners* (equivalent to ballad stanzas written as continuous couplets). Iambic pentameter couplets were introduced by Chaucer (if "iambic pentameter" is a term relevant to him at all), and the other types reach back even farther into literary history. All have prospered more or less through the centuries, though the heroic couplet, with its tendency to balance, parallelism, and pointed wit, has been unmistakably coloured by its dominance during the Augustan period, while octosyllabics and fourteeners carry overtones of light verse and folk poetry. Couplets of any type, with the immediate satisfaction of their closely juxtaposed rhymes, tend to antithesis, point, wit, aphorism, memorability.

> You see how far Man's wisdom here extends:
> Look next if human nature makes amends;
> Whose principles most generous are and just,
> And to those whose morals you would sooner trust.
> Be judge yourself, I'll bring it to the test,
> Which is the basest creature, Man or beast?
> Birds feed on birds, beasts on each other prey,
> But savage Man alone does Man betray.

> A thing of beauty is a joy forever:
> Its loveliness increases; it will never
> Pass into nothingness; but still will keep
> A bower quiet for us, and a sleep
> Full of sweet dreams, and health, and quiet breathing.
> Therefore, on every morrow, are we wreathing
> A flowery band to bind us to the earth,
> Spite of despondence, of the inhuman dearth
> Of noble natures, of the gloomy days,
> Of all the unhealthy and o'erdarkened ways
> Made for our searching ...

> Thou hast an house on high erect,
> Fram'd by that mighty Architect,
> With glory richly furnishèd,
> Stands permanent, though this be fled.
> It's purchasèd, and paid for too,
> By Him who hath enough to do.
> A price so vast as is unknown
> Yet by his gift is made thine own;
> There's wealth enough, I need no more,
> Farewell my pelf, farewell my store.
> The world no longer let me love,
> My hope and treasure lies above.

Tercets (or triplets) are normally printed as separate stanzas; the rhyme scheme *aaa* is commonest, though sometimes one line is left unrhymed. The most celebrated form of tercet, however, is the peculiar *terza rima,* invented by Dante for his great *Divine Comedy* and introduced to English early in the sixteenth century by Wyatt. This features a kind of chain-link rhyme that unfolds indefinitely: *aba bcb cdc ede fef* … The built-in forward momentum of the scheme is obvious, the engine of Dante's immense vision, or in English, of Shelley's fleet "Ode to the West Wind":

> Make me thy lyre, even as the forest is:
> What if my leaves are falling like its own!
> The tumult of thy mighty harmonies
>
> Will take from both a deep, autumnal tone,
> Sweet though in sadness. Be thou, Spirit fierce,
> My spirit! Be thou me, impetuous one!
>
> Drive my dead thoughts over the universe
> Like withered leaves to quicken a new birth!
> And, by the incantation of this verse,
>
> Scatter, as from an unextinguished hearth
> Ashes and sparks, my words among mankind!
> Be through my lips to unawakened earth
>
> The trumpet of a prophecy! O Wind,
> If Winter comes, can Spring be far behind?

Shelley's poem is distinctive in organizing the terza rima into "sonnets" of fourteen lines with couplets. Closure in terza rima, incidentally, can be achieved in two different ways: … *xyx yzy zz,* as here, or … *xyx yzyz.* Most instances of terza rima in English still carry hints of their Dantean origins.

Quatrains are by far the commonest stanzas in English, and they largely exist in relation to various manifestations of the ballad stanza, as discussed in Chapter 2. But one form of the iambic tetrameter (long meter) quatrain, with an envelope rhyme scheme *abba,* has been known as the *In Memoriam* stanza ever since Tennyson used it throughout his great elegy of that name:

> Behold, we know not anything;
> I can but trust that good shall fall
> At last—far off—at last, to all,
> And every winter change to spring.
>
> So run my dreams; but what am I?
> An infant crying in the night;

> An infant crying for the light,
> And with no language but a cry.

This rhyme scheme mutes the folk feeling of the *abab* arrangement of the quatrain, sustaining the momentum through the four lines without falling into two halves.

Two forms of iambic pentameter quatrain have been frequent, most notably the *elegiac quatrain*, rhymed *abab,* so called since its use in Thomas Gray's "Elegy Written in a Country Churchyard"[2]:

> The curfew tolls the knell of parting day,
> The lowing herd wind slowly o'er the lea,
> The ploughman homeward plods his weary way,
> And leaves the world to darkness, and to me.

To digress for a moment: Gray's stanza offers a fine illustration of the determining power of a poet's metrical choices. With minimal changes, this quatrain can be rewritten in two different ways. Try heroic couplets:

> The curfew tolls the knell of parting day,
> The ploughman homeward plods his weary way,
> The lowing herd wind slowly o'er the lea,
> And leave the world to darkness, and to me.

This revision destroys both the coherence and the sustained, leisurely expansiveness of the full quatrain. Try, then, substituting iambic tetrameter for pentameter:

> The curfew tolls the knell of day,
> The lowing herd wind o'er the lea,
> The ploughman homeward plods his way,
> And leaves the darkened world to me.

This revision loses the formal gravity of the iambic pentameter in favour of the lighter, folksier, and here much less appropriate form.[3]

The less common *Rubaiyat stanza,* rhymed *aaxa,* is named for Edward Fitzgerald's popular "Rubaiyat of Omar Khayyam":

---

[2] This form is sometimes called *heroic stanza,* after its use by John Dryden.

[3] This comparison is based on discussions by Lyle Glazier and Ian Jack printed in *Twentieth Century Interpretations of Gray's Elegy,* ed. H.W. Starr (Englewood Cliffs: Prentice-Hall, 1968).

> I sometimes think that never blows so red
> The Rose as where some buried Caesar bled;
> That every Hyacinth the Garden wears
> Dropt in her lap from some once lovely head.

Five-line and six-line stanzas are common enough, but few have attracted names. Versions in iambic tetrameter, or tetrameter plus trimeter, sound like extensions of the ballad quatrain:

> Why should you swear I am forsworn,
>   Since thine I vowed to be?
> Lady, it is already morn,
> And 'twas last night I swore to thee
> That fond impossibility.

> You who were darkness warmed my flesh
> where out of darkness rose the seed.
> Then all a world I made in me;
> all the world you hear and see
> hung upon my dreaming blood.

> "The time has come," the Walrus said,
>   "To talk of many things:
> Of shoes—and ships—and sealing wax—
>   Of cabbages—and kings—
> And why the sea is boiling hot—
>   And whether pigs have wings."

> She shall be sportive as the fawn
> That wild with glee across the lawn
>   Or up the mountain springs;
> And hers shall be the breathing balm,
> And hers the silence and the calm
>   Of mute, insensate things.

This last type—a ballad quatrain with doubled tetrameter lines—is sometimes known by the name *rime couée* (from Old French, "tailed rhyme").[4] The six-line *Burns stanza,* with its demanding fourfold rhyme *aaabab,* is another folk meter with a tetrameter base, found as far back as the fourteenth century, but now linked to the name of its most skilled writer:

---

[4] The terms "rime couée" and "tailed rhyme" sometimes include any stanza, like the Burns stanza, with final line or lines shorter than the base meter.

> But Mousie, thou art no thy lane,
> In proving foresight may be vain:
> The best laid schemes o' mice an' men
> > Gang aft a-gley.
> An' lea'e us nought but grief an' pain
> > For promised joy.

One seven-line iambic pentameter stanza, *rhyme royal,* rhymed *ababbcc,* appears most often in late medieval and early Renaissance poetry, though it has occasionally been revived. Having received its royal name from "The King's Quair," a poem apparently by King James I of Scotland, the form figures most prominently in Chaucer's *Troilus and Criseyde,* Wyatt's celebrated "They Flee from Me," Sir John Davies' "Orchestra," and Shakespeare's "The Rape of Lucrece," much later emerging in Wordsworth's "Resolution and Independence," where it is further elevated with a final alexandrine. This example is from Davies:

> This is true Love, by that true Cupid got,
> Which danceth galliards in your amorous eyes,
> But to your frozen heart approacheth not;
> Only your heart he dares not enterprise;
> And yet through every other part he flies,
> And everywhere he nimbly danceth now,
> That in yourself, yourself perceive not how.

Ottava rima, the most famous iambic pentameter eight-line stanza, rhymed *abababcc,* has a curious history. Like the sonnet and terza rima, it was introduced from Italian in the sixteenth century first by Wyatt and then by Sir John Harington's monumental translation of Ariosto's *Orlando Furioso,* where the couplet is often given ironic point. Revived in the Romantic era, most notably by Byron, its threefold rhyme followed by a pointed couplet provides the great comic instrument of his *Don Juan:*

> Sagest of women, even of widows, she
> Resolv'd that Júan should be quite a paragon,
> And worthy of the noblest pedigree,
> (His sire was from Castille, his dam from Aragon):
> Then for accomplishments of chivalry,
> In case our Lord the King should go to war again,
> He learned the arts of riding, fencing, gunnery,
> And how to scale a fortress—or a nunnery.

But early in this century, W.B. Yeats turned to the form and found in it, unexpectedly, the depths of some of his most passionate and profound meditations:

> Labour is blossoming or dancing where
> Body is not bruised to pleasure soul,
> Nor beauty born out of its own despair,
> Nor blear-eyed wisdom out of midnight oil.
> O chestnut tree, great-rooted blossomer,
> Are you the leaf, the blossom, or the bole?
> O body swayed to music, O brightening glance,
> How can we know the dancer from the dance?

No better illustration can be found, I think, of the dangers of associating a particular effect or feeling too closely with any particular abstract form.

The nine-line *Spenserian stanza* is the longest, most elaborate named stanza in our poetry. It is in iambic pentameter rhymed *ababbcbcc,* always with a final alexandrine. Like ottava rima and many other unnamed longer stanzas, it opens with a quatrain and closes with a couplet. Spenser, in his epic romance *The Faerie Queene,* taught Milton and subsequent poets the climactic and closural possibilities of the final alexandrine. His stanza was revived in homage, first during the eighteenth century by James Thomson in "The Castle of Indolence," then more vigorously by later Romantics, notably Keats in "The Eve of Saint Agnes" and Shelley in "Adonaïs." In this century, it has again fallen into disuse. This is Keats:

> Awakening up, he took her hollow lute—
> Tumultuous—and, in chords that tenderest be,
> He played an ancient ditty, long since mute,
> In Provence called "La Belle Dame sans Merci":
> Close to her ear, touching the melody;
> Wherewith disturbed, she uttered a soft moan:
> He ceased—she panted quick—and suddenly
> Her blue affrayèd eyes wide open shone:
> Upon his knees he sank, pale as smooth-sculptured stone.

Though often used in narrative, this is a leisurely, ornamental stanza, ill suited to rapid movement. The principal difficulties, apart from the fourfold *b* and threefold *c* rhymes, are preventing a too obvious break after the fourth line, and sustaining, building the matter to a suitably impressive alexandrine.

Stanzas longer than nine rhymes have appeared as nonce forms; but the longer the stanza, the more difficult it is to sustain momentum and preserve internal coherence.

Beyond the Single Stanza

Besides the formal structure of the individual stanza, lyric poems sometimes feature devices that link one stanza to another. A refrain, like that in Campion's

"Cherry Ripe," above, is a simple device that most powerfully reminds us of the relation between lyric poetry and music, even when it appears in a printed text. It can be almost any length in keeping with the proportions of the poem, from a single monosyllable or a nonsense phrase like the "fa-la-la" of madrigals, to a single line, a couplet, or a full-blown separate stanza, repeated as a chorus between the other verses. In general, it reinforces a sense of parallelism and connection from stanza to stanza. It usually reinforces the general mood of the poem, but can also question or contradict it (see Yeats's "The Apparitions").

Refrains can also be varied to reflect progress from one stanza to the next. In Sir Walter Ralegh's "The Lie," the refrain appears "And give the world the lie," "Then give them both the lie," "Give potentates the lie," and so on. Sometimes the last appearance of a refrain is altered, creating a sense of closure: Herbert's "Virtue" turns "For thou must die," repeated three times, into "Then chiefly lives."

Although refrains usually appear between stanzas, they can also punctuate stanzas internally. The song that ends Shakespeare's *Twelfth Night* rotates two refrain lines:

> When that I was and a little tiny boy,
> *With hey, ho, the wind and the rain,*
> A foolish thing was but a toy,
> *For the rain it raineth every day.*
>
> But when I came to man's estate,
> *With hey, ho, the wind and the rain,*
> 'Gainst knaves and thieves men shut their gate,
> *For the rain it raineth every day.*

Other linking devices between stanzas include patterned repetitions of words or phrases, and the interlocking of rhymes. All of these devices are featured in the so-called "French forms" (see below), and in fact English poetry has been rather negligent of them in comparison with some other languages. But they do appear. Frost's well-known "Stopping by Woods on a Snowy Evening" uses rhyme-linked quatrains, *aaba bbcb ccdc,* in the manner of terza rima.

A lyric from Eliot's "Dry Salvages" borrows a device from the troubadours of Provence, rhyming from one stanza to the next, but not within the stanza itself (sustaining some very challenging rhymes through six stanzas):

> Where is there an end of it, the soundless wailing,
> The silent withering of autumn flowers
> Dropping their petals and remaining motionless;
> Where is there an end to the drifting wreckage,
> The prayer of the bone on the beach, the unprayable
> Prayer at the calamitous annunciation?

There is no end, but addition; the trailing
Consequence of further days and hours,
While emotion takes to itself the emotionless
Years of living among the breakage
Of what was believed in as most reliable—
And therefore the fittest for renunciation.

One can find in Sylvia Plath's "Black Rook in Rainy Weather" an extraordinary adaptation of this device. Elizabeth Barrett Browning's "A Musical Instrument" sustains a complex pattern through seven stanzas. "The great god Pan" is a refrain phrase, the word "river" concludes the second and last line of each stanza, and the rhyme scheme *ABaccB* stays constant:

What was he doing, the great god Pan?
    Down in the reeds by the river?
Spreading ruin and scattering ban,
Splashing and paddling with hoofs of a goat,
And breaking the golden lilies afloat
    With the dragonfly on the river.

He tore out a reed, the great god Pan,
    From the deep cool bed of the river;
The limpid water turbidly ran,
And the broken lilies a-dying lay,
And the dragonfly had fled away
    Ere he brought it out of the river.

With internal refrains and multiple refrains, linked rhyme schemes, and refrain words or phrases, innumerable formal combinations become possible, limited only by the inventiveness of the poet (or musician).

Some Virtuoso Pieces

One should not pass by the topic of rhyme and stanza without recognizing the brilliance and inventiveness some poets have displayed. Rhyme especially—being the showiest feature of poetic form—has given poets many opportunities for virtuoso feats. The fields of light and popular verse have produced some of the most impressive of these. Theater rhymesters from W.S. Gilbert to Cole Porter to Stephen Sondheim have startled and delighted audiences with their verbal dexterity. This is not surprising, since rhyme is one of the elements of verse technique most associated with play. On the other hand, poets at their most serious have hardly restricted themselves to plain blank verse, as the writings of Herbert and Hopkins and Dylan Thomas testify. What follows is a small collection of inventive (and one or two profound) explorations of rhyme and stanza.

Four means of rhyming for display are rhyming on unusual or seemingly impossible words (the troubadours called this "scarce rhyme"); rhyming insistently on the same sound; rhyming in close proximity; and rhyming in intricate or concealed patterns. These types do not exhaust the possibilities, but cover many examples.

Rhyming on unusual or almost impossible words is usually a comic effect (though the Eliot example above shows a more serious tone):

> But—Oh! ye lords of ladies intellectual,
> Inform us truly, have they not hen-peck'd you all?

> Beside this thoroughfare
> The sale of half-hose has
> Long since superseded the cultivation
> Of Pierian roses.

Included in this group are those who twist words into rhyme:

> Farewell, farewell, you old rhinoceros,
> I'll stare at something less prepoceros.

Also included would be *macaronic* rhymes—rhymes between two languages:

> Unaffected by "the march of events,"
> He passed from men's memory in *l'an trentiesme*
> *De son eage*; the case presents
> No adjunct to the Muses' diadem.

In Gilbert and Sullivan's *Pirates of Penzance,* one character sings a patter song in which he teases the audience by pretending to have difficulty finding the rhyme:

> I am the very model of a modern Major-General,
> I've information vegetable, animal and mineral,
> I know the kings of England and I quote the fights historical,
> From Marathon to Waterloo in order categorical;
> I'm very well acquainted too with matters mathematical,
> I understand equations, both the simple and quadratical,
> About binomial theorem I'm teeming with a lot o' news—
> > [*Lot o' news? Lot o' news? Ah!*]
> With many cheerful facts about the square of the hypotenuse.

Rhyming relentlessly on the same sound has comic effect, but can also underscore a serious inevitability. My favourite example is Thomas Hardy's meditation on "scientific" approaches to the Bible, "The Respectable Burgher on 'The Higher Criticism'":

> Since Reverend Doctors now declare
> That clerks and people must prepare
> To doubt if Adam ever were;
> To hold the flood a local scare;
> To argue, though the stolid stare,
> That everything had happened ere
> The prophets to its happening sware;
> That David was no giant-slayer ...

The poem continues for a full thirty-six lines, leaving the reader breathless (and possibly agnostic).

Rhyming in close proximity encompasses a surprising number of poems that use the "echo" convention:

> Fair rocks, goodly rivers, sweet woods, when shall I see peace? *Peace.*
> Peace! what bars me my tongue? who is it that comes me so nigh? *I.*
> Oh, I do know what guest I have met, it is Echo. *'Tis Echo.*
> Well met, Echo, approach; then tell me thy will too. *I will too.*

Also there is Thomas Hood's amazing one-of-a-kind triple play:

> Even is come; and from the dark park, hark,
> The signal of the setting sun—one gun!
> And six is sounding from the chime, prime time
> To go and see the Drury Lane Dane slain,
> Or hear Othello's jealous doubt spout out ...

The poem sustains this procedure for thirty-four lines.

Hood's poem is an outrageous stunt, in the same class with a number of un-classifiable rhyming tricks. George Herbert's very seriously clever "Paradise" uses *aaa* tercets, subtracting from the rhyme one letter each line:

> I bless thee, Lord, because I GROW
> Among thy trees, which in a ROW
> To thee both fruit and order OW.
>
> What open force, or hidden CHARM
> Can blast my fruit, or bring me HARM,
> While the inclosure is thine ARM?

The rhyming that I personally find most fascinating, however, occurs in intricate patterns. This has a long history going back to the origins of rhyme itself in European literatures, and is not confined to the comic. Here is the opening of a fifteenth-century Scottish hymn to the Virgin Mary:

> Haile! sterne superne. Haile in eterne,
> In Godis sicht to shine.
> Lucerne in derne for to discerne
> Be glory and grace divine.
> Hodiern, modern, sempitern,
> Angelicall regine,
> Our tern inferne for to disperne,
> Helpe! rialest rosine.[5]

Internal rhymes have not seemed to interest English poets to any great degree, but there was a spate of activity in the 1930s, with impressive results. A superb lyric by C. Day Lewis begins:

> Do not expect again a phoenix hour,
> The triple towered sun, the sky complaining;
> Sudden the rain of gold, and heart's first ease,
> Tranced under trees by the eldritch light of sundown.

This is not blank verse, as first appears, but subtle internal rhyme that continues for three more stanzas.[6] A well-known poem by W.H. Auden takes such devices to great lengths, integrating patterns of end rhyme, internal rhyme, and alliteration, in a single, intricate quatrain four times repeated. I have italicized the patterns:

> "*O where are you going?*" said *reader to rider,*
> "That *valley* is *fatal* where *fur*naces *burn,*
> Yonder's the *midden* whose odours will *madden,*
> That *gap* is the *grave* where the *tall* re*turn.*"

---

[5] Hail star on high! Hail in eternity,
In God's sight to shine.
Lamp in darkness, to perceive
By glory and grace divine.
Of today, now existing and everlasting,
Angelic queen,
Our doom below to drive away,
Help, most royal rose!

[6] If you cannot hear it, the pattern begins *hour/towered,* and continues for four stanzas.

"*O do you imagine?*" said *fearer to farer*,
"That *d*usk will *d*elay on your *p*ath to the *pass*,
Your diligent *looking* discover the *lacking*
Your *f*ootsteps *f*eel from *g*ranite to *grass?*"

These are just a few examples that illustrate but do not exhaust the possibilities of rhyme and stanza. English is often said to be poor in rhyme, and so it is compared with some other languages. But the inventiveness of poets is inexhaustible, and the desire to make patterns out of language is essential to human creative genius. For convenience, I have tabulated various kinds of rhyming and rhyme terms in Appendix 1.

Some Standard Verse Forms: Fixed and Not So Fixed

The Sonnet

Besides its recognized stanza forms, English poetry also features a number of "fixed forms"—that is, forms that govern the design of entire poems—all of which have been imported from other languages. By far the commonest and best known of these is the sonnet. Having arisen in Italian poetry, it was taken up by Dante and later Petrarch, and then passed along to poets of the French Renaissance. Since its introduction from the Italian early in the sixteenth century by Wyatt (who translated from Petrarch and wrote original sonnets) and Surrey (who established the English form), and since the phenomenal craze at the end of that century for sonnet cycles (by Sidney, Spenser, Shakespeare, Daniel, and many others), the sonnet has maintained a presence almost continuously in our poetry to the present day, with only the Augustan decades seeming to lack enthusiasm for the form.[7]

Unlike some of the less common "fixed" forms described below, the sonnet has shown a high degree of flexibility. Textbook descriptions have not always followed suit. Students are shown the two major sonnet types, the original *Italian* (or *Petrarchan*) and the native *English* (or *Shakespearean*), but are given

---

[7] Among many studies of the sonnet, see John Fuller's brief introduction *The Sonnet* (London: Methuen, 1972) or Paul Oppenheimer's more recent *The Birth of the Modern Mind: Self, Consciousness and the Invention of the Sonnet* (New York: Oxford Univ. Press, 1989), which speculates that the sonnet, the oldest poetic form still widely used, is "the first lyric form since the fall of the Roman Empire intended not for music or performance but for silent reading" (p. 3), and is therefore bound up with the emerging modern sense of self.

little indication of the many variants that can be found in the wild, in the continental traditions as well as in English. Both types are normally iambic pentameter poems of fourteen lines. The Italian sonnet is divided into two major parts of eight and six lines each, known as the *octave* and the *sestet,* rhyming *abbaabba cdecde.* The English sonnet is divided into four major parts, three quatrains plus a couplet, rhyming *abab cdcd efef gg.* Ideally then, we are frequently told, the Italian sonnet lends itself to bipartite treatment of a subject—a description, say, followed by reflections on the scene, or a statement followed by counterstatement. The move at line 9 from octave to sestet is then called the *turn.* Such is the case often enough:

> I must not think of thee; and, tired yet strong,
> I shun the thought that lurks in all delight—
> The thought of thee—and in the blue Heaven's height,
> And in the dearest passage of a song.
> Oh, just beyond the fairest thoughts that throng
> This breast, the thought of thee waits, hidden yet bright;
> But it must never, never come in sight;
> I must stop short of thee the whole day long.
> But when sleep comes to close each difficult day,
> When night gives pause to the long watch I keep,
> And all my bonds I needs must loose apart,
> Must doff my will as raiment laid away,—
> With the first dream that comes with the first sleep
> I run, I run, I am gathered to thy heart.

The English sonnet, on the other hand, ideally exhibits tripartite treatment of its subject, followed by snappy closure in the couplet, like this:

> That time of year thou mayest in me behold
> When yellow leaves, or none, or few, do hang
> Upon those boughs which shake against the cold,
> Bare, ruined choirs where late the sweet birds sang.
> In me thou see'st the twilight of such day
> As after sunset fadeth in the west;
> Which by and by black night doth take away,
> Death's second self, that seals up all the rest.
> In me thou see'st the glowing of such fire
> That on the ashes of his youth doth lie,
> As the deathbed whereon it must expire,
> Consumed with that which it was nourished by;
> This thou perceiv'st, which makes thy love more strong,
> To love that well which thou must leave ere long.

So say the textbooks. But the English sonnet, perhaps influenced by its Italian sibling, frequently features a clear turn after line 8, producing a bipartite effect:

> They that have power to hurt and will do none,
> That do not do the thing they most do show,
> Who, moving others, are themselves as stone,
> Unmovèd, cold, and to temptation slow;
> They rightly do inherit heaven's graces
> And husband nature's riches from expense;
> They are the lords and owners of their faces,
> Others but stewards of their excellence.
> The summer's flower is to the summer sweet,
> Though to itself it only live and die,
> But if that flower with base infection meet,
> The basest weed outbraves its dignity:
> For sweetest things turn sourest by their deeds;
> Lilies that fester smell far worse than weeds.

Here, the octave introduces the subject and the sestet the principal metaphor, and Shakespeare seems to underline the turn with the rhyme of "power" (line 1) and "flower" (line 9).

Such disposition of subject matter neatly within the confines of the rhyme scheme is the rule to be expected. But the account given in dogmatic textbooks overlooks several things. One is the play of the poet's rhetoric *against* form, using enjambment in the manner of Yeats's "No Second Troy" (above), itself almost a sonnet. The textbook use of the form tends to symmetry, neatness, a sense of logic, stability—the same qualities projected by the Augustan heroic couplet; the other tends to the energy of enjambment and, possibly, formal instability. As always, the fit between content and form is a matter not of textbook rule but expressiveness. Milton, whose command of enjambment in *Paradise Lost* is exemplary, shows the same power in his sonnets, where he frequently drives his syntax straight through the expected turn. Here, angered by a recent political massacre, he employs the sonnet form for an unexpected subject:

> Avenge, O Lord, thy slaughtered saints, whose bones
> Lie scattered on the Alpine mountains cold,
> Even them who kept thy truth so pure of old
> When all our fathers worshipped stocks and stones,
> Forget not: in thy book record their groans
> Who were thy sheep and in their ancient fold
> Slain by the bloody Piedmontese that rolled
> Mother with infant down the rocks. Their moans
> The vales redoubled to the hills, and they
> To Heaven. Their martyred blood and ashes sow

> O'er all th'Italian fields where still doth sway
> The triple tyrant; that from these may grow
> A hundredfold, who having learnt thy way
> Early may fly the Babylonian woe.

Another variable is the rhyme scheme itself. Milton's sonnet, one may notice, uses not the prescribed *cdecde* scheme for the sestet, but *cdcdcd*. There are many possible rearrangements for the sestet rhymes—*cdeced, cdcede,* and so on—and poets use them interchangeably. As well, a more relaxed octave can introduce a third rhyme, *abbaacca*. Students are often surprised and confused by these freedoms, but then, poets are generally less pedantic than students.

One common variant of the sestet, *cdcdee,* produces a hybrid sonnet that begins Italian and ends English (a form much favoured by John Donne): *abbaabba cdcdee.* Or the procedure can be reversed, as it is in one of the most vivid short poems in the language, Yeats's "Leda and the Swan," which begins English and ends Italian: *ababcdcd efgefg.* A surprising effect is achieved by moving the couplet forward, as in the magical still point of Dante Gabriel Rossetti's "Silent Noon":

> Your hands lie open in the long fresh grass—
> The finger-points look through like rosy blooms:
> Your eyes smile peace. The pasture gleams and glooms
> 'Neath billowing skies that scatter and amass.
> All round our nest, far as the eye can pass,
> Are golden kingcup-fields with silver edge
> Where the cow-parsley skirts the hawthorn-hedge.
> 'Tis visible silence, still as the hour-glass.
>
> Deep in the sun-searched growths the dragonfly
> Hangs like a blue thread loosened from the sky:
> So this wing'd hour is dropt to us from above.
> Oh! clasp we to our hearts, for deathless dower,
> This close-companioned inarticulate hour
> When twofold silence was the song of love.

Because of the popularity and prestige of sonnet form, poets have tried many variations.[8] Spenser's sonnets feature an interlocked rhyme scheme recalling his own Spenserian stanza, *ababbcbccdcdee*—a demanding form that has had few imitators. One of Shakespeare's sonnets is written in iambic tetrameter, several of Sidney's in hexameter. Hopkins uses accentual meters, Elizabeth

---

[8] One should also note that the word "sonnet" during the Renaissance period was often applied indiscriminately to any short lyric poem.

Daryush syllabic. Milton's "On the New Forcers of Conscience" is a "tailed" sonnet—an Italian sonnet with several lines appended. Keats, for a joke, wrote a sonnet "On the Sonnet" with a nonsensical rhyme scheme *abcabdcabcdede*. Countee Cullen's "Yet Do I Marvel" begins with two quatrains and finishes with three couplets. Rupert Brooke wrote a "Sonnet Reversed," with the couplet at the beginning: *aababacdcdefef*. Poe's "Sonnet—Silence" has fifteen lines; George Meredith's sequence "Modern Love" is made up of sixteen-line sonnet-like poems. Edna St. Vincent Millay's *Sonnets from an Ungrafted Tree* all conclude with a line of heptameter. Robert Lowell at the end of his career produced a large number of fourteen-line blank verse poems that look and act like sonnets in every way except rhyme. The possibilities are endless, and the student should expect to find poets experimenting, stretching the limits of the textbook recipes.

The French Forms

English poetry has borrowed a few complex forms from continental models, primarily French, that do (normally) adhere to textbook prescriptions. Poets who attempt them consciously rise to the technical challenge. These forms all feature types of stanzaic linkage—refrains, double refrains, and the like—and their demands are so severe that poets treat them as virtuoso challenges, tests of skill and ingenuity. Interest in these forms surfaced first on the continent in the later medieval and early Renaissance periods, arising primarily out of the Provençal troubadours, whose dazzling range of experimentation in stanza and rhyme were emulated by poets in other vernacular languages. English poets from Chaucer through Sidney and Spenser in the sixteenth century imitated several of these forms, which then disappeared. They were revived in the later nineteenth century, spurred by the renewed interest in medievalism, and have attracted many formally minded twentieth-century poets as well. In many cases, the form was first treated as a *tour de force* of light verse until, in the hands of a strong poet, it was invested with seriousness and depth.

　　The shortest and rarest of these is the *triolet*, a shorter version of the *rondel* (see below) which has, in the space of only eight lines, two refrain lines, *ABaAabAB*.[9] The meter is usually iambic trimeter or tetrameter:

> Rose kissed me today.
> Will she kiss me tomorrow?
> Let it be as it may,
> Rose kissed me today
> But the pleasure gives way
> To a savour of sorrow;

---

[9] There is no widely recognized shorthand for these complex forms; I offer only what seems sensible.

Rose kissed me today—
Will she kiss me tomorrow?

This unprepossessing example shows how confining the form is, with five of the eight lines determined by the two refrains.

One might think it impossible to dance in such a straightjacket; but see what Thomas Hardy does with it in his exceptional double triolet "The Coquette, and After":

For long the cruel wish I knew
That your free heart could ache for me
While mine should bear no ache for you;
For long—the cruel wish!—I knew
How men can feel, and craved to view
My triumph—fated not to be
For long! ... The cruel wish I knew
That your free heart could ache for me!

At last one pays the penalty—
The woman—women always do.
My farce, I found, was tragedy
At last! One pays the penalty
With interest when one, fancy free,
Learns love, learns shame ... Of sinners two
At last *one* pays the penalty—
The woman—women always do!

This poem offers a valuable study in extracting multiple meanings and contrastive inflections from the simple refrain lines. The result is a poignant short dramatic monologue, powerful in dramatic reading.

The *villanelle,* more frequently met with, also features a double refrain, this time on the same rhyme: *A'bA" abA' abA" abA' abA" abA'A".*[10] The meter can be iambic trimeter, tetrameter, or pentameter (or, I suppose, any meter a poet can sustain). Like the triolet, this form, which was associated with pastoral in French Renaissance poetry, was also imported for light verse by minor figures like Austin Dobson. When James Joyce in his novel *Portrait of the Artist as a Young Man* wanted to demonstrate his hero's "arrival" as an artist, he had him produce a villanelle:

---

[10] The A' and A" signs mark the rhyming dual refrains. On villanelle, see Ronald E. McFarland, *The Villanelle: The Evolution of a Poetic Form* (Moscow: Univ. of Idaho Press, 1987).

> Are you not weary of ardent ways,
> Lure of the fallen seraphim?
> Tell no more of enchanted days.
>
> Your eyes have set man's heart ablaze
> And you have had your will of him.
> Are you not weary of ardent ways?
>
> Above the flame the smoke of praise
> Goes up from ocean rim to rim.
> Tell no more of enchanted days.
>
> Our broken cries and mournful lays
> Rise in one eucharistic hymn.
> Are you not weary of ardent ways?
>
> While sacrificing hands upraise
> The chalice flowing to the brim,
> Tell no more of enchanted days.
>
> And still you hold your longing gaze
> With languorous look and lavish limb!
> Are you not weary of ardent ways?
> Tell no more of enchanted days.

Critics still debate whether Joyce intended this poem as a serious sign of his hero's skill, or as a parody of late romantic excesses.

There is no question of parody, however, in the many fine examples of villanelle in the twentieth century—Robinson's "House on the Hill," Auden's "Miranda's Song" from *The Sea and the Mirror,* William Empson's "Missing Dates," Theodore Roethke's "The Waking," Elizabeth Bishop's "One Art," or Dylan Thomas' celebrated elegy for his father, with its moving refrain lines

> Do not go gentle into that good night,
> Rage, rage against the dying of the light.

In all of these examples, and many others besides, the poets successfully meet the test of motivating the repetitiveness of the form. In Thomas, the refrains dramatize the obsessiveness of grief, in Roethke the riddles of existence. A more recent example, Molly Peacock's "Little Miracle," finds formal latitude by contrasting three-beat refrain lines against metrically variable free lines, and by other licences with the paradigm:

> No use getting hysterical.
> The important part is: we're here.
> Our lives are a little miracle.

My hummingbird-hearted schedule
beats its shiny frenzy, day into year.
No use getting hysterical—

it's always like that. The oracle
a human voice could be is shrunk by fear.
Our lives are a little miracle

—we must remind ourselves—whimsical,
and lyrical, large and slow and clear.
(No use getting hysterical!)

All words other than *I love you* are clerical,
dispensable, and replaceable, my dear,
Our inner lives are a miracle.

They beat their essence in the coracle
our ribs provide, the watertight boat we steer
through others' acid, hysterical
demands. Ours is the miracle: *we're here*.

Two related forms, the *rondel* and the *rondeau,* also occur. Both, like the villanelle, employ refrains and only two rhymes (though neither form is observed by poets with quite the same rigidity as the villanelle usually is). In its most usual manifestation, the rondel is a poem of fourteen lines in which the first two reappear as a refrain: *ABbaabAB abbaAB.* Here is a charming example from the fifteenth-century:

My ghostly father, I me confess,
   First to God, and then to you,
   That at a window (wot ye how)
I stole a kiss of great sweetness,
Which done was out of advisedness,
   But it is done, not undone, now,
My ghostly father, I me confess,
   First to God, and then to you.

But I restore it shall doubtless
   Again, if so be that I mow,
   And that, God, I make a vow,
Or else I ask forgiveness—
My ghostly father, I me confess,
   First to God, and then to you.

In the fifteen-line rondeau, the opening word or phrase of the first line reappears twice as a refrain, *aabba aabR aabbaR*. A famous example was written by a Canadian soldier who died during the First World War, John McCrae:

> In Flanders fields the poppies blow
> Between the crosses, row on row,
>   That mark our place; and in the sky
>   The larks, still bravely singing, fly
> Scarce heard amid the guns below.
>
> We are the Dead. Short days ago
> We lived, felt dawn, saw sunset glow,
>   Loved and were loved, and now we lie
>   In Flanders fields.
>
> Take up our quarrel with the foe:
> To you from failing hands we throw
>   The torch; be yours to hold it high.
>   If ye break faith with us who die
> We shall not sleep, though poppies grow
>   In Flanders fields.

The most elaborate, prolonged, challenging—in fact astonishing—of all these forms, however, is also the most frequently attempted: the *sestina*. As its name suggests, the sestina uses a six-line stanza; but unlike the other forms described here, it uses not refrain lines but refrain words, end words repeated in each stanza. The words are not repeated in their original order, but according to a strictly prescribed set of mathematical permutations that has to be seen to be believed. The abstract structure looks like this, but I will leave it to the reader to discover the internal logic:

> 1: a b c d e f
> 2: f a e b d c
> 3: c f d a b e
> 4: e c b f a d
> 5: d e a c f b
> 6: b d f e c a

At the end, there is a three-line *envoi* in which all six refrain words must be repeated, usually fb/ad/ec. The sestina, writes Ezra Pound, is "like a thin sheet of flame folding and infolding upon itself."[11] This bizarre form was invented

---

[11] In English practice, the order often varies in the envoi, sometimes with repetitions of only three of the refrain words at line ends. Pound's comment appears in *The Spirit of*

in the twelfth century by Arnaut Daniel, one of the troubadours of Provence who collectively initiated the European tradition of lyric poetry in vernacular languages. (Any curious reader interested in forms whose complexity far exceeds anything in English should look into the Provençal troubadours.[12]) Arnaut Daniel's form was imitated by Dante in one of his most celebrated lyrics ("Al poco giorno"), and then passed into the modern European languages, all of which are sprinkled with sestinas.

The technical difficulty of simply meeting these demands is obvious. The difficulties of writing a *good* sestina include motivating the vast amount of repetition: the subject of the poem must be sufficiently haunting or obsessive. The poet should also find suitable refrain words—words that will determine the tone of the entire poem. Finally, the poet must sustain the subject in a logical development through six stanzas plus envoi. Even so, poets have sometimes increased the difficulties for themselves. Sidney's celebrated "Ye Goatherd Gods," for example, is a *double* sestina, in which two speakers in dialogue run through the entire set of permutations twice. Auden's "Kairos and Logos" is a sequence of four sestinas. The prize for the most unmanageable refrain words probably goes to Canadian poet Earle Birney, whose "Sestina for the Ladies of Tehuantepec" triumphantly manoeuvres the words "hotsprings," "earthquakes," "iguanas," "Diaz," "isthmus," and "women." Other fine examples have been written by Swinburne, Pound, Muriel Rukeyser, Elizabeth Bishop, Anthony Hecht, John Ashbery, and (in free verse) Diane Wakoski. But my personal favourite, despite its rather drab refrain words, remains Rudyard Kipling's "Sestina of the Tramp-Royal," a dramatic monologue that, within the confines of the form, magically creates the dialect voice of a free-spirited folk philosopher. The poem builds to a deeply moving extended simile in the sixth stanza:

> Speakin' in general, I 'ave tried 'em all—
> The 'appy roads that take you o'er the world.
> Speakin' in general, I 'ave found 'em good
> For such as cannot use one bed too long,
> But must get 'ence, the same as I 'ave done,
> An' go observin' matters till they die.

Romance (1968; New York: New Directions, 1920), p. 27. On sestina, see Marianne Shapiro, *Hieroglyph of Time: The Petrarchan Sestina* (Minneapolis: Univ. of Minnesota Press, 1980).

[12] Useful anthologies are Frederick Goldin, *Lyrics of the Troubadours and Trouvères* (New York: Doubleday Anchor, 1973), Anthony Bonner, *Songs of the Troubadours* (New York: Schocken, 1972), and Meg Bogin, *The Women Troubadours* (New York: Norton, 1980). A scholarly survey of troubadour forms is Istvan Frank, *Répertoire métrique de la poésie des troubadours* (Paris: Champion, 1966).

What do it matter where or 'ow we die,
So long as we've our 'ealth to watch it all—
The different ways that different things are done,
An' men an' women lovin' in this world;
Takin' our chances as they come along,
An' when they ain't, pretendin' they are good?

In cash or credit—no, it aren't no good;
You 'ave to 'ave the 'abit or you'd die,
Unless you lived your life but one day long,
Nor didn't prophecy nor fret at all,
But drew your tucker somehow from the world,
An' never bothered what you might ha' done.

But Gawd, what things are they I 'aven't done?
I've turned my 'and to most, and turned it good,
In various situations round the world—
For 'im that doth not work must surely die;
But that's no reason man should labour all
'Is life on one same shift—life's none so long.

Therefore, from job to job I've moved along.
Pay couldn't 'old me when my time was done,
For something in my 'ead upset it all,
Till I 'ad dropped whatever 'twas for good,
An', out at sea, be'eld the dock-lights die,
An' met my mate—the wind that tramps the world!

It's like a book, I think, this bloomin' world,
Which you can read and care for just so long,
But presently you feel that you will die
Unless you get the page you're readin' done,
An' turn another—likely not so good;
But what you're after is to turn 'em all.

Gawd bless this world! Whatever she 'ath done—
Excep' when awful long—I've found it good.
So write, before I die, "'E liked it all!"

All of these "fixed forms" are of Western European origin, deriving from Provençal, Italian, or French. In the past century, however, poets have become aware of poetic traditions from a more global viewpoint. None of these forms is as thoroughly Englished as the sonnet, or even the sestina, and all retain specific traces of their cultural origins; but they are practised with increasing frequency. Ezra Pound (despite all his well-earned disrepute for anti-semitism) paradoxically merits credit as the first non-Eurocentric major author in our language for his efforts to raise consciousness of the poetry and culture of China and Japan. He was not the first to attempt the Japanese *haiku* (sometimes spelled *hokku*), but he was the most influential. This brief syllabic form—a three-line unrhymed poem with syllable structure of 5, 7, 5—is now well known in English, though translators usually discard the syllabic structure, and most poets imitate not its formal pattern (or its other elaborate Japanese conventions) but its paradoxes and logical dislocations, the Zen spirit that underlies the tradition and that seems compatible with Western theories like imagism. Here are two examples, translations from the first great master of the form, Basho, and a later master, Issa:

> On the wide seashore
> a stray blossom and the shells
> make one drifting sand.

> White, sifted mountain
> reverberates in the eyes
> of a dragonfly.

The form often creates an implied metaphor by juxtaposing elements, like the tiny ephemeral dragonfly and the huge and unchanging mountain in the second example.[13] The haiku's cousin, the *tanka*—with a syllable structure of 5, 7, 5, 7, 7—appears even more rarely in English with its form intact, but here is an example by Amy Lowell:

> Roses and larkspur
> And slender serried lilies;
> I wonder whether
> These are worth your attention.
> Consider it, and if not—

From a different source, the Afro-American *blues* has become another recognizable form often imitated or incorporated into larger structures, but typically retaining the cry of distress common to the folk originals. Unlike Afro-American religious spirituals, which have no regular verse form, blues always assume a three-part pattern, having two repetitions (with variation) of the original statement, plus a conclusion (a variant of the classic German *AAB Barform*, familiar from hymns and chorales). Langston Hughes' "Widow Woman" is a literary version of blues that remains close to the original spirit and form, with the radically enjambed lineation pointing the jazz emphasis of the presumed singer:

---

[13] These examples are from William Howard Cohen, *To Walk in Seasons: An Introduction to Haiku* (Rutland: Charles E. Tuttle, 1972), pp. 25 and 39.

Oh that last long ride is a
Ride everybody must take.
Yes, that last long ride's a
Ride everybody must take.
And that final stop is a
Stop everybody must take.

When they put you in the ground and
They throw dirt in your face,
I say put you in the ground and
Throw dirt in your face,
That's one time, pretty papa,
You'll sure stay put in your place.

Many other forms have been imported, and there is no room to include
them all. Complex Welsh forms, for example, have often lured English poets,
but never (in my experience) to the point of sustained successful imitation. The
ghazals of several Middle Eastern traditions are couplet poems rhyming on the
same rhyme, always signed at the end with the poet's name. The term occurs
in English even in the early nineteenth century, with Thomas Moore's "Gazel,"
but Adrienne Rich has appropriated it loosely for a number of free verse poems
in unrhymed couplets (see, for example, "Ghazals: Homage to Ghalib"), and her
example has been followed. The *pantoum,* of Malayan origins, is a quatrain ver-
sion of terza rima, in which the second and fourth lines of each stanza rhyme
with the first and third of the next. It has not, to my knowledge, been frequently
attempted in the past (Louis MacNeice's "Leaving Barra" is perhaps the best-
known adaptation), but younger poets have begun to pick it up. Here is a recent
version by David Trinidad using not rhymes but alternating refrain lines, on the
villanelle principle:

It is almost time to grow up
I eat my TV dinner and watch
Nancy Sinatra in 1966
All boots and thick blonde hair

I eat my TV dinner and watch
The daughter of Frank Sinatra
All boots and thick blonde hair
She appears on "The Ed Sullivan Show"

The daughter of Frank Sinatra
She sings "These Boots Are Made For Walkin'"
She appears on "The Ed Sullivan Show"
The song becomes a number one hit ...

All such forms remain "exotic" until poets collectively have familiarized them to the point that their conventions—the expectations they presuppose—are widely known. But this should not discourage writers from imitating whatever forms and genres they may discover in world literatures. English poetry has shown in its history a remarkable ability to absorb every kind of formal principle from other languages, and there is no indication that the process has slowed down.

The Ode

The term "ode" is loosely given to any stanzaic lyric that addresses a serious subject with a certain degree of elaborateness, elevation, or ceremony. As such, it includes many of the most notable and familiar poems in our language. But a full understanding of this multifarious term, with its often contradictory applications, requires a long view of literary history.[14] The contradictions extend straight back to origins in Greek and Latin poetry, where the ode appeared in three distinct types.

The simplest odes—those of Anacreon and his followers—were short lyrics in simple stanzas on frivolous subjects, like drinking. The Anacreontic ode explains why the word in English, especially during the Renaissance, sometimes appears in connection with such short, light poems. (The word "sonnet" is used similarly during the same period.) The odes of Horace, however, often rose above the level of the Anacreontic, treating serious subjects in common lyric stanzas: Andrew Marvell's "Horatian Ode upon Cromwell's Return from Ireland" is a self-conscious English imitation.

The type that most concerns us here in relation to English poetic forms, however, is the Pindaric ode. This elaborate form, by far the earliest to appear, originated with the poems of Pindar in the fifth century B.C., written to celebrate the victors of the original Olympic games, and reappeared in the choric odes of the Greek tragedy. This is a form in which there are units of three stanzas, known as strophe, antistrophe, and epode (or turn, counterturn, and stand). As these terms suggest, the Greek ode, performed at formal occasions, was not only sung but danced. The stanzas of the strophe and antistrophe are typically elaborate, long and with a variety of line combinations; the antistrophe repeats the strophe exactly, but the epode finds a different structure. This entire threefold pattern can then be repeated any number of times.

The true Pindaric ode is exceedingly rare in English literature.[15] The sole

---

[14] See Carol Maddison, *Apollo and the Nine: A History of the Ode* (London: Routledge Kegan Paul, 1960), or more briefly, John D. Jump, *The Ode* (London: Methuen, 1974) or John Heath-Stubbs, *Ode* (New York: Oxford Univ. Press, 1969).

[15] It was attempted a few times in the eighteenth century by such poets as Congreve, Collins, Gray, and Rogers, and is all but unknown in American poetry (Bayard Taylor

undisputable masterpiece in the form is also the earliest, Ben Jonson's "To the Immortal Memory and Friendship of That Noble Pair, Sir Lucius Cary and Sir Henry Morrison," written to console Cary for the untimely death of his friend. Here, to illustrate the pattern, is the third of four repetitions of the three-stanza sequence, with the labels as Jonson himself printed them:

The Turn

It is not growing like a tree
In bulk doth make man better be;
Or standing long an oak, three hundred year,
To fall a log at last, dry, bald, and sere:
A lily of a day
Is fairer far in May;
Although it fall and die that night,
It was the plant and flower of light.
In small proportions we just beauties see,
And in short measures life may perfect be.

The Counterturn

Call, noble Lucius, then for wine,
And let thy looks with gladness shine;
Accept this garland, plant it on thy head,
And think, nay know, thy Morisson's not dead.
He leap'd the present age,
Possess'd with holy rage
To see that bright eternal day;
Of which we priests and poets say
Such truths as we expect for happy men,
And there he lives with memory, and Ben

The Stand

Jonson! who sung this of him, ere he went
Himself to rest,
Or taste a part of that full joy he meant
To have expressed
In this bright asterism;
Where it were friendship's schism
(Were not his Lucius long with us to tarry)

---

being the most notable exception).

> To separate these twi-
> lights, the Dióscuri,
> And keep the one half from his Harry.
> But fate doth so altérnate the design,
> Whilst that in heaven, this light on earth must shine.

Despite the magnificence of Jonson's poem, I would not take time with its form if it did not have wider consequences. Though true Pindaric is most rare, its formal influence extends in two directions. One is the so-called pseudo-Pindaric, or "irregular ode"—a form introduced in the seventeenth century by Abraham Cowley and widely imitated for two centuries thereafter. Cowley was most impressed by the wildness and licence of Pindar's language (reflected in the Jonson passage by the radical enjambments), so he wrote poems that mixed line lengths and rhyme schemes with total abandon, no two stanzas the same. The principle may be seen in the free, irregular, non-repeated stanzas of Dryden's two St. Cecilia odes, in Coleridge's "Dejection," and, most notably, in Wordsworth's "Ode on the Intimations of Immortality." Before the advent of free verse, the pseudo-Pindaric ode offered poets the greatest degree of freedom from formal constraint.

The irregularity of the Pindaric ode is likewise a precedent for elaborate and irregular—but repeated—stanzas like those in the odes of Keats:

> My heart aches, and a drowsy numbness pains
>   My sense, as though of hemlock I had drunk,
> Or emptied some dull opiate to the drains
>   One minute past, and Lethe-wards had sunk:
> 'Tis not through envy of thy happy lot,
>   But being too happy in thine happiness—
>   That thou, light-wingèd Dryad of the trees,
>   In some melodious plot
> Of beechen green, and shadows numberless,
>   Singest of summer in full-throated ease.

This nonce stanza, repeated eight times in the poem, seems descended from the irregularity of the pseudo-Pindaric tradition. Odes written in complex nonce stanzas like this are quite frequent.

4

Figures of Speech

Rhetoric, as every modern writer on the subject points out, has a bad name. We speak of "mere rhetoric"—style without substance, insincerity, artificiality: "It's *just* a figure of speech." Aristotle, on the other hand, identified mastery of one particular figure, metaphor, as the defining power of the poet. And the study of rhetoric, for all the centuries from Aristotle through the Middle Ages and Renaissance and into the nineteenth century, has formed the heart of all education. Even in the twentieth century, despite the decline of classical rhetoric, rhetorical criticism has remained a thriving industry. The subject of "rhetoric" is thus an immense one, far larger than this book can hope to encompass. Historically, rhetoric, the "art of persuasion," was the study of oratory: the art of speaking in an effective way to sway audiences. Its first concern was prose, and it treated questions like the various types of speeches to be made (judicial, deliberative, epideictic), the component parts of a speech (introduction, narration, division, confirmation, confutation, conclusion), the levels of diction (high, middle, low), the character of the orator, and so on. All of these matters have clear relevance to the study of poetry, and indeed, the speeches in the epic poems of Homer have served as examples throughout the entire tradition. But I must leave them for more advanced study.[1] One part of rhetoric, however, has immediate relevance to the patterning of poetic language: the figures of speech.

Rhetoric and Figure

All modern introductions to poetry include some discussion of figurative language. But most are child's play compared with the exhaustive analyses found

---

[1] The serious student can do no better than Edward P.J. Corbett, *Classical Rhetoric for the Modern Student* (New York: Oxford Univ. Press, 2d ed., 1971). See also Brian Vickers, *Classical Rhetoric in English Poetry* (1970; Carbondale: Southern Illinois Univ. Press, 1989), and Richard Lanham, *A Handlist of Rhetorical Terms* (Berkeley: Univ. of California Press, 1969), and Sr. Miriam Joseph, *Shakespeare's Use of the Arts of Language* (New York: Columbia Univ. Press, 1949).

in the rhetorical tradition, with its hundreds of figures defined and illustrated. There are many reasons why a modern reader of poetry should pay attention to this neglected subject.

First, the poets studied it themselves. Ever since the first rhetoric textbook written in England (by the Venerable Bede, circa A.D 700), schoolboys were drilled in long catalogues of figures. Brian Vickers has described the process: "What pupils actually did when confronted with these compilations may be expressed in a quite bald way: 'first learn the figures, secondly identify them in whatever you read, thirdly use them yourself.'" It was simply the accepted routine, he notes, "and given the crushing degree of memorization, one can assume that anyone who had been at school in sixteenth-century England (or Europe) would know a goodly portion of Susenbrotus' 132 figures and tropes."[2] Such was the training that produced Spenser, Sidney, and Shakespeare, and throughout the two centuries after them the tradition remained alive.

Only with the Romantic revolution in the nineteenth century did classical rhetoric fall into disrepute ("the age of Rhetoric, like that of Chivalry, has passed amongst forgotten things," lamented Thomas De Quincey in 1828[3]). But even then, classically educated poets like Tennyson were schooled in their figures, and later poets have repeatedly rediscovered them. "I use everything and anything to make my poems work," declared Dylan Thomas: "old tricks, new tricks, puns, portmanteau words, paradox, allusion, paronomasia, paragrams, catachresis, slang, assonantal rhymes, vowel rhymes, sprung rhythm. Every device there is in language is there to be used if you will."[4] Poets have always delighted in the beauty and expressive power of the figures, which enable them to treat language as a malleable, plastic substance for making new shapes.

Secondly, study of the figures is important because it is only through conscious awareness of them that they exist. This is one of the paradoxes of poetry. *The figure comes into existence experientially only when it is recognized as a figure.* We read "Achilles was a lion on the battlefield," and understand at once that he was fearless and ferocious. But the process of understanding is complex: we must first recognize that Achilles was *not* a lion—literally—and take steps to decode a suitable meaning. We do this intuitively, of course, without putting the name "metaphor" to the process. But this intuition for language is precisely what the reading of poetry can heighten. Living in an all-prose world, we are apt to become helplessly literal minded. But by learning to decode the figurative language of poetry, and understanding how the process works, we expand our power over language immeasurably. Acquaintance with the names of the figures

---

[2] Vickers, pp. 48–49.

[3] Quoted in Vickers, p. 49.

[4] Quoted in William T. Moynihan, *The Craft and Art of Dylan Thomas* (Ithaca: Cornell Univ. Press, 1966), p. 62.

teaches us to become sensitive to these linguistic moments. Although the naive reader will feel the effects of figuration—just as she will sense poetic rhythms—without consciously understanding the causes, the full experience of poetry requires awareness of the figurative processes in language.

The language of prose, typically, is practical and transparent, but the language of poetry is more self-conscious; one way poetic language calls attention to itself is by departing from the norms of prose. Take Pope's description of an English tea:

> From silver spouts the grateful liquors glide,
> While China's earth receives the smoking tide.

For a moment, the reader imagines that some cataclysmic natural disaster has occurred in a distant region of the globe: "China's earth receives the smoking tide." But recognizing that this meaning is unsuitable to the context of an English parlour, the mind quickly performs an operation of decoding, and supplies a meaning more fitting: a teacup is filled with tea. In so doing, the reader, smiling, notes a discrepancy between the inflated metaphors (technically "periphrases") and their mundane signification.

This complex decoding procedure is one of the principal pleasures of poetry. The reader must first notice something "wrong" with the text, and then take steps to correct it. Figures of speech, writes Jonathan Culler, "are instructions about how to naturalize the text by passing from one meaning to another—from the 'deviant' to the 'integrated.'" The figure itself "is nothing other than an awareness of the figure, and its existence depends wholly on the reader being conscious of the ambiguity of the discourse before him."[5] This process, as I have said, happens at one level intuitively; but one's mental agility will, without question, improve with practice. Thus the reader who passes too quickly to the so-called meaning—who writes down in his notes that Poem *X* has Meaning *Y*— misses all the fun.

The terminology, alas, is difficult and Greek. But it repays study nevertheless. The serious student of literature will find it invaluable. The less serious will learn—even after forgetting some of the terms themselves—that *the concept of language patterned consciously, language used as a plastic, shapable substance, remains*.

For the schemes and tropes (and this is my third point) are ways of imposing pattern on language, and in this sense they are closely related to the poetic functions of meter, stanza, and form, even though they are not usually so treated in books on poetic form. But as well as "imposing" pattern on language, the

---

[5] *Structuralist Poetics* (Ithaca: Cornell Univ. Press, 1975), pp. 179-80. See also Gérard Genette, *Figures of Literary Discourse* (New York: Columbia Univ. Press, 1982).

rhetorical figures—particulary the neglected schemes—are devices *for revealing and heightening the patterns that naturally exist in language.* If you have ever called someone a "turkey," or an "Einstein," or exclaimed "Holy Cow!" you have used a rhetorical figure. Far from being artificial distortions of language, the figures have developed from patterns that naturally appear when language is used with great emotion or energy. As such, they provide one means of identifying patterns that emerge in free verse and help give it formal organization (we shall return to this approach in the next chapter).

What follows, then, is a catalogue of some of the more common, familiar schemes and tropes, with illustrations and commentary. My list is descended from a distinguished heritage. Throughout I have preferred the most frequently used terms in the working critical vocabulary. In the long history of rhetoric, different classifications of the figures have been used. One essential distinction is between *schemes* and *tropes,* that is, between "figures of speech" and "figures of thought." In Brian Vickers' words, a trope "involves a change or transference of meaning and works on the conceptual level," while a scheme "essentially works on the physical level of the shape or structure of language... A trope affects the meaning of words; a [scheme] only affects their placing or repetition."[6] Tropes have received abundant attention. The study of metaphor alone has reached staggering proportions. The lowlier schemes, however—more closely related to patterning of the physical language like meter, rhyme, and stanza—have been slighted.

Beginning with the schemes, I use the following classification:

1.   Figures of balance and parallelism
2.   Figures of repetition
3.   Figures of amplification or omission
4.   Figures of address (apostrophe)
5.   Figures of syntactic deviation (inversion)
6.   Figures of verbal play (puns and coinages)

The Schemes

Figures of Balance and Parallelism

Parallelism, whether in poetry or prose, is not ornamental: it is basic to good sense. It is where syntactic arrangement most deeply engages with reason. According to one of the most cherished guidebooks to good writing, equivalent things *must* be set out in co-ordinate grammatical structures: "Nouns must be yoked with nouns, prepositional phrases with prepositional phrases, adverb

---

[6] P. 86.

clauses with adverb clauses. When this principle is ignored, not only is the grammar of co-ordination violated, but the rhetoric of coherence is wrenched ... Violations of parallelism are serious not only because they impair communication but because they reflect disorderly thinking."[7] In other words, there are two choices: *either ideas are parallel, or they are not parallel*. So with syntax. The principle of parallel structure is thus fundamental to the logical structure of language, and it is common to both prose and poetry. Student writers, however, fearing to sound repetitious, avoid it and thus create needless and misleading muddles. In figures of balance, words, phrases, or clauses are placed in positions of equivalence, either alike or opposite. The parallel syntax itself conveys the meaning: "these two (or more) thoughts are equal in importance."

Simple *parallelism* sets corresponding ideas in similar syntactic forms:

> One speaks the glory of the British Queen,
> And one describes a charming Indian screen;
> A third interprets motions, looks, and eyes;
> At every word a reputation dies.

> To see the world in a grain of sand
> And heaven in a wild flower
> Hold Infinity in the palm of your hand
> And Eternity in an hour

Such lines have logical point, clarity, memorability. The formal structure of the couplet, the heroic couplet especially, lends itself to all figures of balance and parallelism.

Parallelism can be elaborated into highly complex structures. Milton extracts lyrical beauty from his blank verse in this extraordinary description of dawn in the Garden of Eden:

> Sweet is the breath of morn, her rising sweet,
> With charm of earliest birds; pleasant the sun
> When first on this delightful land he spreads
> His orient beams, on herb, tree, fruit, and flower,
> Glistering with dew; fragrant the fertile earth
> After soft showers; and sweet the coming on
> Of grateful evening mild, then silent night
> With this her solemn bird, and this fair moon
> And these the gems of heaven, her starry train:
> But neither breath of morn, when she ascends
> With charm of earliest birds, nor rising sun
> On this delightful land, nor herb, fruit, flower,

---

[7] Corbett, pp. 463-64.

Glistering with dew, nor fragrance after showers,
Nor grateful evening mild, nor silent night
With this her solemn bird, nor walk by moon
Or glittering starlight, without thee is sweet.

An equally stunning passage at the end of Wordsworth's "Tintern Abbey" illustrates the use of parallelism to sustain a sonorous poetic voice and sort out a complex series of logical connections that would otherwise be incomprehensible. The passage is in blank verse, but I print it to point up the multiple use of parallelism. Here, one can see how the interlocking parallel structures bind the complex logic of the passage into a coherent, comprehensible whole:

Oh! yet a little while may I behold in thee what I was once, my dear,
                                        dear Sister! and this prayer I make,
Knowing that Nature never did betray the heart that loved her;
'Tis her privilege through all the years of this our life to lead from
                                                    joy to joy:
For she can ‖ so inform the mind that is within us,
             ‖ so impress with quietness and beauty,
     and ‖ so feed with lofty thoughts,
   That neither ‖ evil tongues,
             ‖ rash judgments,
             ‖ nor the sneers of selfish men,
             ‖ nor greetings where no kindness is,
             ‖ nor all the dreary intercourse of daily life
   Shall e'er ‖ prevail against us
       or ‖ disturb our cheerful faith that all that we
                                behold is full of blessings.
Therefore ‖ let the moon shine on thee in thy solitary walk;
     and ‖ let the misty mountain winds be free to blow against
                                                        thee:
And in after years,   ‖ when these wild ecstasies shall be matured
                                        into a sober pleasure,
             ‖ when thy mind shall be a mansion for all
                                        lovely forms,
             ‖ thy memory be as a dwelling place for all
                                    sweet sounds and harmonies:
Oh! then if ‖ solitude,
           ‖ or fear,
           ‖ or pain,
           ‖ or grief, should be thy portion,
With what healing thoughts of tender joy wilt thou
           ‖ remember me,
           ‖ and these my exhortations!

Wordsworth's principal signposts here are logical and temporal: For she (Nature) can so inform, impress, and feed … Therefore let the moon and winds have influence … and consequently in after years, despite the trials of aging, this healing influence will endure. But the powers of parallelism enable Wordsworth to enrich his blessing with the kind of specificity that acknowledges the negatives, the sneers and fears, while holding them in subordinate position within the grand structure of his rhetorical design.

In *antithesis,* where the equivalence is one not of similarity but of opposition, grammatical parallelism is still obligatory. Again, the effect is of point, condensation, clarity, memorability:

>Wandering between two worlds, one dead,
>The other powerless to be born.

>The best lack all conviction, while the worst
>Are full of passionate intensity.

>So subtly is the fume of life designed,
>To clarify the pulse, and cloud the mind,

Even more than parallelism, antithesis is a manifestation of logic. While parallelism asserts similarity, antithesis asserts both similarity and difference. Both parallelism and antithesis are so closely tied to rational expression, however, that they may become inappropriate dramatically. When Neil Armstrong stepped out on the moon, for example ("One small step for man, one giant leap for mankind"), his antithesis, however "memorable," was out of place, too obviously programmed. His script-writers should have known that he needed an expression of excitement, not cool reason.

Chiasmus, which means "criss-cross," is an elegant variation of parallelism or antithesis that repeats the terms in inverse order, *A* is to *B* as *B* is to *A,* thus:

>Featur'd like him, like him with friends possess'd

>My eyes are full of tears, my heart of love,
>My heart is breaking, and my eyes are dim.

>Odour of blood when Christ was slain
>Made all Platonic tolerance vain,
>And vain all Doric discipline.

Chiasmus is capable of complex effects. In "To the Girls of My Graduating Class," Irving Layton addresses

>Golda, Fruma, Dinnie, Elinor,
>My saintly wantons, passionate nuns.

The two phrases are parallel in syntax (adjective plus noun), but form a semantic chiasmus, "saintly" belonging more logically with "nuns," "wantons" with "passionate." Wallace Stevens ends a well-known poem with a similar pattern:

> In ghostlier demarcations, keener sounds.

Here, the two phrases are again parallel in syntax, antithetical in meaning; "demarcations" seems semantically to belong with "keener," and "sounds" with "ghostlier"—a chiasmus of meaning (that incidentally produces examples of "transferred epithet" and oxymoron—see below). The mysterious, haunting effect of both lines surely owes much to their intricate, yet compact, figurative patterning.

Chiasmus has a specialized form, *antimetabole* ("turn about"), in which *identical* words or phrases appear in reversed order. The effect is always conspicuous and self-conscious. When President Kennedy, in a famous speech, declared, "Ask not what your country can do for you, ask what you can do for your country," he seems to have known that he was putting into currency a ready-made quotation; and his rhetoric was indeed remarkably effective for a time in mobilizing public sentiment.[8] In poetry, as in prose, antimetabole often appears with witty effect:

> Yet graceful ease, and sweetness void of pride,
> Might hide her faults, if Belles had faults to hide.

But the same figure informs the solemn culmination of Coleridge's "Frost at Midnight":

> so shalt thou see and hear
> The lovely shapes and sounds intelligible
> Of that eternal language which thy God
> Utters, who from eternity doth teach
> Himself in all, and all things in himself.

Parallel syntax is often arranged in ascending sequences, a figure known as *climax* (technically "*auxesis*" or "*gradatio*"). This figure often has an oratorical ring, as in John of Gaunt's patriotic deathbed speech in Shakespeare's *Richard II:*

> This blessed plot, this earth, this realm, this England.

---

[8] Corbett rephrases: "Do not ask what America can do for you. You would do better to ask whether your country stands in need of *your* services." It would be a profitable exercise, he says, to take several examples of antimetabole, and convert them to ordinary prose. "Such an exercise would undoubtedly reveal what the schemes add to the expression of thought" (p. 477).

But it can also suggest relentlessness or inevitability, as it does in the following poem by Emily Dickinson:

> The Heart asks Pleasure—first—
> And then—Excuse from Pain—
> And then—those little Anodynes
> That deaden suffering—
>
> And then—to go to sleep—
> And then—if it should be
> The will of its Inquisitor,
> The privilege to die—

Figures of Repetition

Simple repetition of a word or phrase is one of the most basic forms of emotional emphasis:

> The woods decay, the woods decay and fall

The device (technically called "iteratio") is easy, yet it beautifully underscores the elegiac feeling of reluctant acceptance at the beginning of Tennyson's poem. Compare the following:

> For Lycidas is dead, dead ere his prime
>
> In the bleak mid-winter
>   Frosty wind made moan,
> Earth stood hard as iron,
>   Water like a stone;
> Snow had fallen, snow on snow,
>   Snow on snow,
> In the bleak mid-winter
>   Long ago.

More energetic multiple repetition ("epizeuxis," or "fastening on") can express extreme agitation, as in King Lear's famous outburst:

> Never, never, never, never, never!

Multiple repetitions seem to require extreme situations. Milton's Samson laments his blindness:

> O dark, dark, dark, amid the blaze of noon,
> Irrecoverably dark, total eclipse
> Without all hope of day!

Archibald MacLeish imagines the end of the world:

> There is the sudden blackness, the black pall
> Of nothing, nothing, nothing—nothing at all.

Verbal repetitions enter into a number of sustained formations where the repetition assumes a patterning function. Repetition of a word or phrase in an initial position, the commonest form, is called *anaphora* ("carrying back"):

> The time of the seasons and the constellations
> The time of milking and the time of harvest
> The time of the coupling of man and woman
> And that of beasts.

This device is essential to the long catalogues of Walt Whitman:

> To think the thought of death merged in the thought of materials,
> To think of all these wonders of city and country, and others taking
>   great interest in them, and we taking no interest in them,
> To think how eager we are in building our houses,
> To think others shall be just as eager, and we quite indifferent.
> (I see one building a house that serves him a few years, or seventy
>   or eighty years at most,
> I see one building the house that serves him longer than that.)

The opposite form is *epistrophe* ("a turning away"), somewhat more subtle and less common, where the repetition appears in a final position. Here it energizes Ezra Pound's denunciation of carnage in the First World War:

> Daring as never before, wastage as never before.
> Young blood and high blood,
> fair cheeks and fine bodies;
>
> fortitude as never before
>
> frankness as never before,
> disillusions as never told in the old days

Compare a prose speech by Malcolm X: "As long as the white man sent you to Korea, you bled. He sent you to Germany, you bled. He sent you to the South Pacific to fight the Japanese, you bled." Like anaphora, epistrophe has the power to evoke inevitable consequences.

A combination of anaphora and epistrophe—double repetition at *both* beginning and end—is called *symploce* ("intertwining"); it is understandably rare, but striking in its insistence:

> We are the hollow men
> We are the stuffed men

Repetition of the same word or phrase at both the beginning and end of a single line or phrase, *epanalepsis* ("resumption"), though rare in prose, is surprisingly frequent in poetry:

> All day, the same our postures were,
> And we said nothing all the day

> Roll on, thou deep and dark blue Ocean, roll!

> The splendid silence clings
> Around him, and around
> The saddest of all kings,
> Crowned, and again discrowned.

> We keep the wall between us as we go.
> To each the boulders that have fallen to each.

Perhaps the feeling of stasis inherent in this figure makes it appropriate to the seemingly timeless experience of lyric poetry.

Repetition of the last word of one phrase at the beginning of the next, in a chain-link fashion, is called *anadiplosis* ("doubling back"). This "heel-treading verse" was very popular with some Renaissance poets:

> For I have lovéd long, I crave reward,
> Reward me not unkindly: think on kindness,
> Kindness becometh those of high regard—
> Regard with clemency a poor man's blindness.

If not overdone, it can also have a conversational effect:

> At six o'clock we were waiting for coffee,
> Waiting for coffee and the charitable crumb

Repetition of the same root word with different grammatical inflections is called *polyptoton:*

> Love is not Love
> Which alters when it alteration finds,
> Or bends with the remover to remove

> Remember me when I am gone away,
> Gone far away into the silent land;
> When you can no more hold me by the hand,
> Nor I half turn to go yet turning stay.

In this second example, Christina Rossetti's placement of the key word "turning" beautifully captures the departing lover's hesitation. Shelley addresses his ecstatic skylark in an eloquent double polyptoton arranged in chiasmus:

> The blue deep thou wingest
> And singing still doth soar, and soaring ever singest.

All of these patterned forms of repetition can not only operate on a small scale, but also sustain longer passages. They appear frequently through the long period of rhetorical dominance, but also, as the Whitman examples suggest, remain available as organizing devices in free verse. One other, *ploce* ("plaiting"), is a general term used to cover all cases of insistent repetition that fall into no set patterns. Occurrences are very frequent, yet the term itself (probably because it is so general) is not often used by critics except those with a specific inclination to rhetoric. Rhetorically self-conscious poets, however, work the figure vigorously:

> Tell me no more of minds embracing minds,
>   And hearts exchang'd for hearts;
> That spirits spirits meet, as winds do winds,
>   And mix their subtlest parts.

Sir Philip Sidney goes to outrageous lengths, with multiple puns that demand a reader's close attention:

> I hear a cry of spirits faint and blind,
> That, parting thus, my chiefest part I part,
> Part of my life, the loathed part to me,
> Lives to impart my weary clay some breath;
> But that good part, wherein all comforts be,
> Now dead, doth show departure is a death—
> Yea, worse than death; death parts woe and joy.
> From joy I part, still living in annoy.

Again, ploce is used as a means to suggest formal organization in lines of free verse; the multiple repetitions in D.H. Lawrence's beautiful "Bavarian Gentians" are worth study from this angle:

> Bavarian gentians, big and dark, only dark,
>   darkening the day-time, torch-like with smoking blueness of Pluto's
>   gloom,

> ribbed and torch-like, with their blaze of darkness spread blue
>   down
> flattening into points, flattened under the sweep of white day
> torch-flower of the blue-smoking darkness, Pluto's dark blue daze,
> black lamps from the hall of Dis, burning dark blue,
> giving off darkness, blue darkness, as Demeter's pale lamp gives off
>   light,
> lead me then, lead the way.
>
> Reach me a gentian, give me a torch!
> let me guide myself with the blue, forked touch of this flower
> down the darker and darker stairs, where blue is darkened on
>   blueness

Figures of Amplification and Omission

Going beyond figures of repetition, figures of amplification extend the meanings of otherwise plain statement, building a sense of magnitude, and sometimes generating further levels of figuration. Figures of omission, on the other hand, tend not to diminish their subjects, but instead to condense, concentrate, refine them to a point. Both deviations from normal prose syntax serve to emphasize, to heighten.

The simplest poetic amplification is the *epithet*, an adjective notably vivid or just:

> You spotted snakes with double tongue,
> Thorny hedgehogs, be not seen.

> the curious phenomenon of your occipital horn

In Marianne Moore's "To a Snail," why, one may ask, is her phrase "occipital horn" for the snail's shell so arresting? Learning to answer such questions is one of the rewards of studying poetry.

The *fixed epithet,* a special variety found in epic poetry, is the repeated use of an adjective or phrase for the same subject: thus in Homer's *Odyssey*, the wife Penelope is always "prudent," the son Telemachus is always "sound minded," and Odysseus himself is "many minded." This feature, natural to oral poetry like Homer's, has been imitated in literary epics like Virgil's *Aeneid*, where Aeneas is always "dutiful" and his friend Achates "faithful."

The figure of *parenthesis* ("put beside") has exactly the same meaning it does in ordinary usage: a word, phrase, or clause inserted as an aside into a sentence complete in itself:

> They fought with God's cold—
> And they could not and fell to the deck

> (Crushed them) or water (and drowned them) or rolled
>   With the sea-romp over the wreck.

Note that it can be punctuated not only with parentheses, but also dashes or commas. Parenthesis is a device for complicating a simple statement in a concise way. It has the effect sometimes of a second voice intruding for a moment over the primary voice—expanding, commenting, explaining.

The figure of *epanorthosis* (*correctio,* "setting straight") is an immediate correction of a word or phrase just used. It often has the effect of making the speaker appear singularly honest or precise:

> These hedgerows, hardly hedgerows, little lines
> Of sportive wood run wild

> O stay, three lives in one flea spare,
> Where we almost, yea, more than married are.

Sometimes the correction is introduced for comic effect:

> He learned the arts of riding, fencing, gunnery,
> And how to scale a fortress—or a nunnery.

> Whose prose is grand verse, while his verse, the Lord knows,
> Is some of it pr——No, 'tis not even prose,

With the figure of *periphrasis* (circumlocution), the scheme of amplification moves strongly in the direction of trope, a true figure of thought. Periphrasis, a word or phrase describing a thing without naming it, is often metaphorical. The device has acquired a bad name, because in mundane prose we are supposed to write directly, *without* redundant circumlocution, and pragmatic or literal-minded students sometimes reject the figure with hostility. Even euphemisms, the refuge of polite society, are nowadays frowned upon in favour of unadorned, candid expression. Poets, however, have long enjoyed the riddling, figurative indirectness of periphrasis. The anonymous poets of Old English developed a repertoire of periphrastic phrases known as "kennings," with vivid metaphorical content: the "whale's road" for "sea," the "bone-house" for the "body."

Periphrasis remains one of the commonest and most important of the schemes. It is capable of complex effects:

> What passion cannot music raise and quell?
>   When Jubal struck the chorded shell

Dryden alludes here to the ancient origins of the lyre, cords of animal hide stretched across a tortoise's shell, but in the process also creates a pun on musical "chords." Purists of diction in the eighteenth century used periphrasis to avoid low, vulgar wording:

> What idle progeny succeed
> To chase the rolling circle's speed,
> Or urge the flying ball?

Thus Thomas Gray recalls boyhood games without having to use the low vernacular "hoop." Wordsworth, for all his railing against the poetic diction of his predecessors, shyly mentions

> A game too humble to be named in verse,

and thus avoids having to name tic-tac-toe. Gerard Manley Hopkins employs multiple periphrasis to project the grandeur of his windhover:

> I caught this morning morning's minion, king-
> dom of daylight's dauphin, dapple-dawn-drawn Falcon, in his riding
> Of the rolling level underneath him steady air

In a darker mood, the graveyard thoughts of William Cullen Bryant become more vivid rather than less when death and the coffin, or rather, when

> The breathless darkness, and the narrow house
> Make thee to shudder.

The power of periphrasis is not to be scorned.

Pleonasm ("excess"), or redundancy, has likewise a bad name, perhaps for better reason, since it is easily abused. Yet it can also project a feeling of exuberance:

> At the round earth's imagined corners, blow
> Your trumpets, angels, and arise, arise,
> From death, you numberless infinities
> Of souls.

The pleonasm, of course, is "numberless infinities," but who would wish it away from John Donne's extravagant evocation of the Last Judgement?

An extreme form of amplification is *congeries* ("heap"), a word heap, or accumulation of words and phrases. The same Donne sonnet offers another example:

> All whom war, death, age, agues, tyrannies,
> Despair, law, chance, hath slain.

George Herbert's moving sonnet "Prayer" is nothing but a congeries of periphrastic phrases describing its subject:

Prayer, the Church's banquet, Angel's age,
God's breath in man returning to his birth,
The soul in paraphrase, heart in pilgrimage,
The Christian plummet sounding Heav'n and earth;
Engine against th'Almighty, sinner's tower,
Reverséd thunder, Christ-side-splitting spear,
The six-day's world transposing in an hour,
A kind of tune, which all things hear and fear;
Softness, and peace, and joy, and love, and bliss,
Exalted Manna, gladness of the best,
Heaven in ordinary, man well dresst,
The milky way, the bird of Paradise,
Church bells beyond the stars heard, the soul's blood,
The land of spices; something understood.

This figure is obviously closely related to (and not clearly distinguished from) the *catalogue*—an extended list of anything. Catalogues are prominent in the poetry of Whitman, who, attempting to embrace the entire cosmos in language, built a career of them. But ever since Homer, *epic catalogues* have been one of the conventions of that genre. *The Iliad* features a long catalogue of ships, which builds up our conviction that an enormous, even cosmic confrontation is taking place. The catalogue appears in more modest forms as well, like this from Spenser's "Epithalamion":

Hark how the cheerfull birds do chaunt theyr laies
And carroll of loves praise.
The merry Larke hir mattins sings aloft.
The thrush replyes, the Mavis descant playes.
The Ouzell shrills, the Ruddock warbles soft,
So goodly all agree with sweet consent,
To this dayes merriment.

I have left one of the commonest figures of amplification for the last, so that it can be paired with its corresponding figure of omission. In *polysyndeton* ("many connections"), the poet repeats the connective between each term in a series:

Poor Cornus sees his frantic wife elope,
And curses wit, and poetry, and Pope.

Whose dwelling is the light of setting suns,
And the round ocean and the living air,
And the blue sky, and in the mind of man.

What lips my lips have kiss'd, and where, and why

> Pull down thy vanity, it is not man
> Made courage, or made order, or made grace

The effect has a deliberateness, attesting that each item has been weighed with care, each equally important.

Its opposite is *asyndeton* ("without connections"), the omission of connectives:

> I may, I must, I can, I will, I do,

affirms Sidney's determined lover, Astrophel.

> I pant, I sink, I tremble, I expire!

exclaims the depleted speaker of Shelley's "Epipsychidion." The figure suggests hurry, excitability. But asyndeton can reach more subtle levels of feeling. Here, Christina Rossetti's asyndeton in the last line (together with subtle metrical hesitation) magically captures a gesture of passion spent:

> I loved my love from green of spring
>   Until sere autumn's fall;
> But now that leaves are withering,
>   How should one love at all?
>   One heart's too small
> For hunger, cold, love, everything.

Curiously, both polysyndeton and asyndeton have an effect of poetic emphasis by dislocating the normal syntactic treatment of series, though they dislocate in opposite directions. Gerard Manley Hopkins, at the climactic moment of "The Windhover," combines both figures with stirring effect in the same line:

> Brute beauty and valour and act, oh, air, pride, plume, here
> Buckle!

The most general term for a figure of omission is *ellipsis*, leaving out any word or phrase that is understood:

> Good nature and good sense must ever join;
> To err is human, to forgive divine.

In Pope's famous maxim, the word "is" is not present but understood, in the second phrase; in the following, the phrase understood is "seemed to be":

> This land's sharp features seemed to be
>   The century's corpse outleant;

> His crypt the cloudy canopy,
>   The wind his death lament.

Ellipsis is clearly a device that increases condensation and point. It is used more frequently in poetry than prose, because poetry is expected to be more condensed than prose, and much twentieth-century poetry is elliptical in the extreme. But it occurs in ordinary speech far more than one might expect: "the people [whom] I like best," "let the dog [go] out." When Claudius, fearing Hamlet, tells his courtiers to prepare for a voyage,

> And he to England shall along with you,

Shakespeare's ellipsis is not so much a poetic effect as a dramatist's simulation of rapid speech. Compare the radical, excited ellipses of Blake's "The Tyger":

> And what shoulder, and what art
> Could twist the sinews of thy heart?
> And when thy heart began to beat,
> What dread hand? And what dread feet?
>
> What the hammer? What the chain?
> In what furnace was thy brain?
> What the anvil? What dread grasp
> Dare its daily terrors clasp?

One special form of ellipsis is called *zeugma* ("yoking"), in which a single verb governs more than one object, each in a different way. The result is a kind of pun, and the effect is most often one of pointed wit:

> Since saucy jacks so happy are in this,
> Give them thy fingers, me thy lips, to kiss.

Not surprisingly, then, the master of zeugma is Pope at his wittiest:

> Here thou, great Anna! whom three realms obey,
> Dost sometimes counsel take, and sometimes tea.
>
> Atoms or systems into ruin hurl'd,
> And now a bubble burst, and now a world.
>
> Whether the nymph shall break Diana's law,
> Or some frail China jar receive a flaw;
> Or stain her honour, or her new brocade ...

Great Anna, queen of the realm, takes "counsel" and "tea" without distinguishing them too carefully; bubbles and worlds burst with equal inconsequence; and the nymph's moral honour is no more important than her gown.

Figures of Address

Figures of address occur when the poetic speaker addresses someone or thing. Often using a verb form other than the indicative, it encompasses forms of direct address, rhetorical questions, exclamations, commands, and hortatory subjunctives (blessings and curses). In the classical languages, these grammatical situations all have their own distinct verb forms, which they do not always have in English. Yet the situations are quite clear.

The most general term is *apostrophe* ("turning away").[9] Loosely used, it covers all forms of address. Most precisely, it applies only to moments in the midst of a text when the speaker breaks off suddenly to address directly some person or thing present, or even absent. In this precise usage, as the root sense "turning away" suggests, apostrophe remains close to the origins of rhetoric in public oratory. Yet in poetry, the same effect can be dramatic and highly moving. Wallace Stevens, after about forty lines of philosophical puzzling in "The Idea of Order at Key West," suddenly uses apostrophe to bring his point beautifully home:

> Ramon Fernandez, tell me, if you know,
> Why, when the singing ended and we turned
> Toward the town, tell why the glassy lights,
> The lights in the fishing boats at anchor there,
> As the night descended, tilting in the air,
> Mastered the night and portioned out the sea.

T.S. Eliot, imitating the device from Baudelaire (whom he quotes), suddenly turns upon his reader, savagely:

> You! hypocrite lecteur!—mon semblable,—mon frère!

And Dylan Thomas ends his elegy for his dying father with this direct apostrophe:

> And you, my father, there on the sad height,
> Curse, bless, me now with your fierce tears, I pray,

---

[9] Do not confuse this term with the punctuation mark for possessives and contractions, also called an apostrophe.

Do not go gentle into that good night,
Rage, rage against the dying of the light.

Apostrophe at the beginning of a poem obviously cannot be a "turning away"; yet, as Jonathan Culler has shown in a celebrated analysis, this device is essential to the workings of many familiar poems, particularly many of the great Romantic odes.[10] Using this figure, the poet seems to summon up his subject from nowhere, creating it by naming it, addressing it:

Thou still unravished bride of quietness,
Thou foster child of silence and slow time

Hail to thee, blithe spirit!
Bird thou never wert

But the device is hardly restricted to the Romantics, or to the elevated style of the ode. Chaucer writes an ironic lament for his own poverty by apostrophizing his empty purse:

To you, my purs, and to noon other wight
Complaine I, for ye be my lady dere.

And modern poets continue the practice—a public-spirited Carl Sandburg apostrophizes the city of Chicago:

Hog Butcher for the World,
Tool Maker, Stacker of Wheat,
Player with Railroads and the Nation's Freight Handler;
Stormy, husky, brawling,
City of the Big Shoulders

And an ironic William Carlos Williams first apostrophizes his own nose, then asks it a rhetorical question:

O strong-ridged and deeply hollowed
nose of mine! what will you not be smelling?

The possibilities are clearly various.

---

[10] "Apostrophe," in Jonathan Culler, *In Pursuit of Signs* (Ithaca: Cornell University Press, 1981), pp. 135–54. See also J. Douglas Kneale, "Romantic Aversions: Apostrophe Reconsidered," *E.L.H.*, 58 (1991), pp. 141–65.

One specialized form of apostrophe is the *invocation,* another of the figures that belongs to the conventions of epic poetry. The invocation, the plea to the Muses for aid in telling the story, was originally an oral formula for getting started, not unlike "once upon a time." The invocation of Homer's *Odyssey* is almost casual:

> Tell me, Muse, about the man of many turns, who many
> Ways wandered when he had sacked Troy's holy citadel ...
> Begin the tale somewhere for us also, goddess, daughter of Zeus

But writers of literary epic elevated the formula, which passed through Virgil's hands into the European traditions. The sonorous invocation to Milton's *Paradise Lost* is analysed in Appendix 2. But here is a twentieth-century variant, from the opening of Hart Crane's modernist epic, *The Bridge:*

> O Sleepless as the river under thee,
> Vaulting the sea, the prairies dreaming sod,
> Unto us lowliest sometime sweep, descend
> And of the curveship lend a myth to God.

Like all elevated formulas, however, the invocation invites parody, and Byron does not miss this point in his comic adventure *Don Juan:*

> Hail Muse! *et cetera*—We left Don Juan sleeping

The *rhetorical question ("erotesis"* or *"interrogatio"*)—a question to which no answer is needed or expected—is another form of address, and it likewise has the dramatic effect of confronting the reader directly, sometimes offguard. In apostrophe, question, and command, the poetic speaker can adopt virtually an aggressive stance towards the reader. By its demands, it can powerfully affect the response of the audience. Shelley ends his "Ode to the West Wind" triumphantly:

> O Wind,
> If Winter comes, can Spring be far behind?

Dylan Thomas demands to know:

> What is the meter of the Dictionary?
> The size of genesis? the short spark's gender?

And Harlem Renaissance poet Langston Hughes wonders, provocatively:

> What happens to a dream deferred?

Like apostrophe, the rhetorical question figures in epic conventions; as part of the invocation, the *epic question* is posed to the Muses by the poet in apparent disbelief. Here is the second verse paragraph of Virgil's *Aeneid*, as translated by Dryden:

> O muse! the causes and the crimes relate;
> What goddess was provoked, and whence her hate;
> For what offence the queen of heaven began
> To persecute so brave, so just a man ...
> Can heavenly minds such high resentment show,
> Or exercise their spite in human woe?

Pope, with his customary wit, gives this a mock-epic turn in "The Rape of the Lock":

> Say what strange motives, Goddess, could compel
> A well-bred Lord t'assault a gentle Belle?
> Or say what stranger cause, yet unexplored,
> Could make a gentle Belle reject a Lord?

The simple *exclamation* (technically *exclamatio,* "shouting out") means exactly what it does in ordinary usage: a cry of emotion, often grammatically incomplete. Chaucer's hypocritical Pardoner uses it with false indignation:

> O glotonye, ful of cursednesse!
> O cause first of oure confusioun!
> O original of oure dampnacioun,
> Til Christ hadde bought us with his blood again!

Tennyson exclaims more gently in his poetic acceptance of dying:

> Sunset and evening star,
>   And one clear call for me!
> And may there be no moaning of the bar
>   When I put out to sea.

This example from Tennyson begins with exclamation and ends with a version of the final figure of address, the *command*. There are two basic types of this figure. One is the expression of blessings or curses, stated wishes for the future, often taking the form "may it" or "let it." In Latin, this situation calls grammatically for the hortatory subjunctive verb form, and in English it sometimes produces the common but poorly understood subjunctive form as well (the "be" in the first example that follows):

> Honor, riches, marriage blessing,
> Long continuance and increasing,
> Hourly joys be still upon you,
> Juno sings her blessings on you.
>
> My lizard, my lively writher,
> May your limbs never wither,
> May the eyes in your face
> Survive the green ice
> Of envy's mean gaze
>
> Earth, receive an honoured guest;
> William Yeats is laid to rest:
> Let the Irish vessel lie
> Emptied of its poetry.

The command as a direct order, a vigorous call to action, is technically termed *"proclees."*

> Burn off my rusts and my deformity;
> Restore thine image so much, by thy grace,
> That Thou may'st know me, and I'll turn my face.
>
> Make me thy lyre, even as the forest is:
> What if my leaves are falling like its own!
> The tumult of thy mighty harmonies
> Will take from both a deep, autumnal tone,
> Sweet though in sadness. Be thou, Spirit fierce,
> My spirit! Be thou me, impetuous one!

Figures of Syntactic Deviation

The general term for deviation from normal word order is *inversion* (also called *"hyperbaton"* or *"anastrophe"*). The effect is usually to throw emphasis on the inverted word or phrase placed conspicuously at the beginning or end:

> Numb were the beadsman's fingers, while he told
> His rosary

The device is one of the easiest ways poetry has to differentiate itself from the prosaic. But modern taste, with its liking for unaffected, conversational language, tends to frown on poetical inversions. Modern poets have used them effectively nonetheless:

> What kept him from remembering what it was
> That brought him to that creaking room was age.

On the other hand, inversions can be carried to tasteless extremes, as in this ghastly beginning of a sonnet:

> Who prop, thou ask'st, in these bad days, my mind?
> He much, the old man, who clearest-souled of men

One common structure of syntactic inversion is the straddled adjective, an elegance favoured by Milton and passed by him to generations of later writers:

> Such are those thick and gloomy shadows damp
> Oft seen in charnel vaults

> Full many a gem of purest ray serene

> He, the young man carbuncular, arrives

Eliot, in this last example, self-consciously uses the Miltonic locution for ironic effect.

In *anacoluthon* ("inconsistent") the syntax is not merely inverted but deliberately ungrammatical, often changing grammatical structure mid-sentence:

> To my quick ear the leaves—conferred—
> The bushes—they were Bells—

This grammatical deflection is common in ordinary speech, but suggests a degree of excitation. Sometimes the effect of anacoluthon is rather as if the voice, overcome by deep feeling, has run ahead of the brain. Yeats captures this beautifully in thoughts about a dead friend:

> And that enquiring man John Synge comes next,
> That dying chose the living world for text
> And never could have rested in the tomb
> But that, long travelling, he had come
> Towards nightfall upon certain set apart
> In a most desolate and stony place,
> Towards nightfall upon a race
> Passionate and simple like his heart.

And Robert Frost activates what might have been an ordinary meditation on the changing seasons with a dramatic anacoluthon, stern in its warning, followed by polysyndeton and dazzling antimetabole:

> The trees that have it in their pent-up buds
> To darken nature and be summer woods—
> Let them think twice before they use their powers
> To blot out and drink up and sweep away
> These flowery waters and these watery flowers
> From snow that melted only yesterday.

Another syntactic shock effect is to leave a sentence unfinished—break it off. This is called *aposiopesis* ("becoming silent"); a famous example occurs in the opening scene of Virgil's *Aeneid*, where an angry Neptune scolds the rebellious winds:

> Is it for you to ravage seas and land,
> Unauthorized by my supreme command?
> To raise such mountains on the troubled main?
> Whom I—but first 'tis fit the billows to restrain.

The dramatic effect can be highly charged. Here Shakespeare uses it to capture the blustering impotence of the aging Lear:

> I will have such revenges on you both,
> That all the world shall—I will do such things—

Here Byron uses it comically to underscore a seduction scene in *Don Juan*:

> Or else 'twere easy to withdraw her waist;
> But then, the situation had its charm,
> And then—God knows what next—I can't go on ...

Grammatical expectations can also be jolted if the poet substitutes a "wrong" part of speech—a figure called *anthimeria* ("one part for another"):

> Where did you come from, baby dear?
> Out of the everywhere into here.

"Everywhere," normally an adverb, becomes (by adding a definite article "the") a noun. In common speech, the figure is colourful. Shakespeare loves it: I will "knee [as a verb] the way into his mercy," say a character in *Coriolanus*; "His complexion is perfect gallows," says a character in *The Tempest*. But some writers of the twentieth century, Cummings for example, have made anthimeria the virtual cornerstone of their technique:

> Women and men (both dong and ding)
> summer autumn winter spring

> reaped their sowing and went their came
> sun moon stars rain

The device commonly called *transferred epithet* ("*hypallage*") is an adjective
that applies logically to something other than its grammatical object:

> Come away, come away, death,
> And in sad cypress let me be laid.

The cypress itself, of course, is not "sad"—but it is poetic to think so. One
graveyard poet contemplates

> The flat, smooth stones that bear a name,
> The chisel's slender help to fame.

"Slender" seems to belong to "chisel," but the phrase "slender help" has an
added poignancy. Transferred epithets are frequent in poetry, though rare in
prose, and they easily slip by without being noticed:

> The space between is but an hour,
> The frail duration of a flower.

> And silent was the flock in woolly fold

> The grasshoppers spin into my ear
> A small innumerable sound

> The woman keeps the kitchen, makes tea,
> Sneezes at evening, poking the peevish gutter.

The effect of this figure is enigmatic: I would suggest that the adjective, in being
dissociated from its logical object, suffuses the entire scene: the flock, not the
fold, is "woolly," but woolliness then becomes the dominant quality the speaker
perceives; the woman, not the gutter, is "peevish," but peevishness then domi-
nates the entire household.

Two other scarce but startling figures of deviation are *hendiadys* and *dia-
cope*. In hendiadys ("one by means of two") an adjectival meaning is expressed
with two words joined by "and":

> What seest thou else
> In the dark backward and abysm of time?

> When all my five and country senses see

> If I had what hypocritical poetasters crocodilely call lucre and filthy

The effect of this is hard to describe: perhaps it is just the general defamiliariza-
tion. In diacope (or "*tmesis*"—"cleft, gash") there is a radical separation of the
elements of a grammatical unit:

> My heart in hiding
> Stirred for a bird—the achieve of, the mastery of the thing!

Here anthimeria ("achieve" for "achievement") and diacope (break after "of")
combine to suggest the speaker's breathlessness.

Figures of Verbal Play

Various kinds of wordplay are assembled under this heading, principally *puns*
and *coinages*. Puns are a familiar form of everyday wit, and, like rhyme or ono-
matopoeia, create moments of comedy, discovery, and sometimes serious insight
out of the arbitrary accidents of the physical language. Many attempts have been
made to classify various kinds of puns—by the classical rhetoricians and by
others since—but none has been truly successful. Puns depend too much on the
unpredictabilities of language. But three terms have gained sufficient currency
in rhetorical analysis to be mentioned here. *Syllepsis* ("taking together") is a pun
that involves a *double entendre* on a single word:

> And the heaviest nuns walk in a pure floating
> Of dark habits.

Antanaclasis ("bending back") is a pun on a word repeated with a second mean-
ing, as in Walter Savage Landor's complaint against old age:

> Ah! he strikes all things, all alike,
> But bargains, those he will not strike.

Paronomasia is a pun that plays on similarity of sound:

> O Eve, in evil hour thou didst give ear
> To that false Worm.

Coinages—*neologisms*—are creative acts of diction, the minting of new
words, and poets have left a legacy of such creations, often quite memorable:

> And hearken to the birds' lovelearnèd song,

> I sound my barbaric yawp over the roofs of the world

> The moment in the draughty church at smokefall

A special kind of neologism is the so-called *portmanteau word*—a term invented and explained by Lewis Carroll in *Through the Looking Glass*, where his wonderful nonsense poem "Jabberwocky" is made up of such inventions:

> 'Twas brillig, and the slithy toves
> Did gyre and gimble in the wabe.

As Humpty Dumpty explains, "Well, *slithy* means 'lithe and slimy' ... You see it's like a portmanteau—there are two meanings packed up into one word." At least three of Carroll's invented portmanteau words from this one poem—"burbled," "galumphing," and "chortled"—have passed into common usage. The concept also provided a model for James Joyce's monumental *Finnegans Wake*. Portmanteau words are not common in poetry, but they can occur with striking effect:

> Come, thou mortal wretch,
> With thy sharp teeth this knot intrinsicate
> Of life at once untie.

Cleopatra's play on "intrinsic" and "intricate" powerfully blends those meanings.

One other special type of wordplay is known as *malapropism,* named for a character in Sheridan's play *The Rivals*, Mrs. Malaprop, who repeatedly confuses the meanings of words: "He is the very pineapple of politeness!" she exclaims (meaning "pinnacle"). The device is not unknown to the classical rhetoricians (who called it "*acrylogia*" or "*cacosyntheton*"), but it is rare. Poets themselves occasionally fall victim to Mrs. Malaprop's errors—as when Elizabeth Barrett Browning contemplates

> Our Euripides, the human,
> With his droppings of warm tears,

or Walt Whitman blurts:

> O culpable! I acknowledge! I exposé!

Even the masters of language are fallible human beings after all.

The Tropes

The tropes, or figures of thought, take us from the patterning, the schematizing of poetic language, deeper into the substance. These figures are semantically far more complex than the schemes, but (the reader will be relieved to know) there are fewer of them. Metaphor in particular has been the focus of impressive scholarly industry, not all of it poetical or abstruse. In *Metaphors We Live By*, George Lakoff and Mark Turner demonstrate how deeply embedded are common metaphors in our everyday thinking and behaviour—life is a journey, life is a play, life is a burden and death a deliverance.[11] We construct our very experience of existence through metaphor.

The present discussion, however, can attempt to do little more than identify the major tropes and provide examples. For purposes of discussion, I sort them into four groups; but these groups, I warn the reader ahead of time, have an internal logic not immediately obvious:

1. Metaphor and simile
2. Metonymy and synecdoche
3. Personification
4. Irony (hyperbole, understatement) and paradox

Metaphor and Simile

Metaphor (*translatio*, "transference") is often used loosely as a general term for any figure of speech (as are the words "figure" and even "trope"). But in the more precise sense here, metaphor refers specifically to an assertion that two things in some way similar are identical:

> The moon was a ghostly galleon, tossed upon cloudy seas

> The fruit-bat swings on its branch, a tongueless bell

The poet does not declare that the moon was *like* a galleon, but that it *was* a galleon: the silent fruit-bat, by way of grammatical apposition, *is* a bell. There is an air of mystery about the identity of the two, the literal and the figurative—a mystery some literal-minded students find hard to accept. The word "metaphor" derives from Greek words meaning "to ferry over," and the process is a voyage from one plane of existence to another:

> But soft! What light through yonder window breaks?
> It is the East, and Juliet is the sun!
> Arise, fair sun, and kill the envious moon,
> Who is already sick and pale with grief,
> That thou, her maid, art far more fair than she.

---

[11] *Metaphors We Live By* (Chicago: Univ. of Chicago Press, 1980). See also their *More Than Cool Reason: A Field Guide to Poetic Metaphor* (Chicago: Univ. of Chicago Press, 1989).

Juliet *is* the sun, and her presence causes a change in Romeo's cosmos like the sun's rising. Ordinary people do not have such an effect on us, but chosen individuals do. The metaphor opens the lover's mind to the audience.

Simile differs from metaphor in that the similarity is made explicit—there is no pretence of absolute identity. Textbooks usually define it as a comparison using "like" or "as," but other markers ("thus," "so") sometimes appear. Because the explicit similarity also recognizes the differences between the compared items, simile has a more rational feel than metaphor. Like metaphor, simile is sometimes incidental, decorative, as when Marianne Moore describes her cat:

> the mouse's limp tale hanging like a shoelace from its mouth.

But simile often acquires the full force of the metaphorical identity. Here the poet, grief-stricken, mourns the death of his wife:

> But hark, my pulse, like a soft drum
> Beats my approach, tells thee I come.

The simile not only likens the pulse to the drumbeat, but it evokes the presence of the funeral cortege approaching its inevitable destination. (The prosody of these exquisite lines also repays study.)

Simile has its special place in epic as the *epic simile*. Like all such conventions, the epic simile is a feature of Homer's oral style that has been consciously imitated by epic poets ever since. In Homer, warlike characters are likened unto lions falling on helpless sheep, sometimes in a fairly perfunctory way. But the epic simile, as opposed to normal similes, is often greatly elaborated, and introduced with certain formulas. Odysseus, sleepless on the night before his decisive struggle, is described memorably:

> But he himself turned this way and that,
> As when a man shifts an intestine full of fat and blood
> On a great blazing fire quickly this way and that
> And longs for it to be roasted very rapidly;
> So this way and that did he toss about, pondering
> How he might lay his hands upon the shameless suitors,
> Being one man against many.

The formula "As when ... So ..." is the sign of epic simile.

Because metaphor is so central to poetic language, and has been recognized as central for so many centuries, many conditions of metaphor have been specially labelled. *Conceit* is a particularly slippery word, even for a literary term. It derives from Italian *concetto,* or "concept," giving us the common usage: conceited people are too full of their own ideas. As a literary term, it derives from Italian usage as a general synonym for metaphor or simile, a point of like-ness, and in English criticism sometimes means no more. Dryden, however, by uniting it with an adjective borrowed from philosophy, coined the phrase *meta-physical conceit,* which has come to define the chief characteristic of a number of seventeenth-century poets. In metaphysical conceit, according to Samuel Johnson's famous account, "the most heterogeneous ideas are yoked by violence together." And though Johnson's admiration for the metaphysicals is severely qualified, he does conclude that "to write on their plan, it was at least necessary to read and think."[12] When John Donne compares two lovers to "stiff twin compasses"—to cite the standard example—one senses the intellectual strain and ingenuity required to justify the comparison:

> If they be two, they are two so
> As stiff twin compasses are two,
> Thy soul, the fix'd foot, makes no show
> To move, but doth, if t'other do.
>
> And though it in the center sit,
> Yet when the other far doth roam,
> It leans, and harkens after it,
> And grows erect, as it comes home.

As a consequence, "conceit" is often used to designate a particularly far-fetched metaphor (like catachresis, below), or a more fully extended metaphor, like these:

> A process in the weather of the heart
> Turns damp to dry; the golden shot
> Storms in the freezing tomb.
> A weather in the quarter of the veins
> Turns night to day; blood in their suns
> Lights up the living worm.
>
> A startled stag, the blue-grey Night,
>   Leaps down beyond black pines.
> Behind—a length of yellow light—
>   The hunter's arrow shines:
> His mocassins are stained with red,
>   He bends upon his knee,
> From covering peaks his shafts are sped,
> The blue mists plume his mighty head—
>   Well may the swift Night flee!

---

[12] Johnson, "Life of Cowley."

Catachresis ("misapplication") is an extravagant, far-fetched metaphor. This is Donne, exulting over his mistress in bed:

> Oh my America, my new found land,
> My kingdom, safeliest when with one man manned.

E.E. Cummings enlivens some simple patriotic thoughts with this disarming proposition:

> as freedom is a breakfastfood

Not all metaphors take the explicit form "A *is* B." Many, if not most, in fact, are *submerged metaphors* in which the semantic identity is sunk into the grammatical forms of the language; the items to be compared must be deduced from context:

> The heart has need of some deceit
> To make its pistons rise and fall;
> For less than this it would not beat,
> Nor flush the sluggish veins at all.

Ascribing "pistons" to the heart turns the physical organ into an engine. The comparison is not original, but in this poem it refocuses the conventional association of "heart" with "feeling" (itself a figure of metonymy; see below) and startles us into recognizing the hard physical basis of existence. In the following lines, "heart" becomes a tree afire:

> Whatever flames upon the night
> Man's own resinous heart has fed.

All writers—not just poets—are obliged to attend to the effects of their metaphors on the literal level. When the politician proclaims that "the population explosion has paved the way towards new economic growth," we are more likely to laugh than be persuaded, if we are paying attention. Because of the essentially metaphoric nature of language, however, it is impossible *not* to mix metaphors to some extent. The important thing for the writer is to keep the lines from tangling, to avoid unintended absurdities. When poets lose sight of their own metaphors, the results can embarrass:

> Fir'd with that name,
> I bridle in my struggling Muse with pain,
> That longs to launch into a nobler strain.

These lines by Joseph Addison are cited by Samuel Johnson, who proceeds to annihilate them: "To 'bridle' a goddess is no very delicate idea," he notices.

"But why must she be 'bridled'? because she longs to 'launch'—an act which was never hindered by a bridle: and whither will she 'launch'? into 'a nobler strain.' She is in the first line a horse, in the second a boat: and the care of the poet is to keep his horse or his boat from singing."[13]

Addison's difficulties arose because his metaphorical language was half-conscious. He doubtless "bridled" his Muse because he pictured her as the mythical Pegasus, a conventional embodiment of poetic power. But he clearly did not picture her vividly enough. The metaphors are worn-out clichés, or *dead* metaphors: "heart of the matter," "foot of the page," "eye of the storm," "dead end." One of the roles of poetry is to keep its language's metaphors alive; but when a poet is inattentive, the clichés will swarm:

> A wanderer is man from his birth.
>   He was born on a ship
> On the breast of the river Time;
> Brimming with wonder and joy
> He spreads out his arms to the light,
> Rivets his gaze on the banks of the stream.

This dreadful example from a respected poet begins with two master metaphors, "life as a journey" and "time as a river," both capable of seemingly infinite variation; but it then sets a ship afloat upon a "breast," and endows something that "brims" with spreading arms and a gaze that "rivets." Poor Matthew Arnold failed to see that the figures sleeping in his weary language might awaken and strangle each other. On the other hand, poets can bring dead metaphors miraculously back to life:

> While scholars speak authority
> And wear their ulcers on their sleeves ...

Metonymy and Synecdoche

A second group of major tropes includes *metonymy* and *synecdoche*. Metonymy ("change of name"), the broader term, means using one object (or concept) to stand for another to which it is closely or customarily related; the relationship is not one of similarity, as in metaphor, but of common association. The figure permeates everyday speech: "blood" for self-sacrifice, "sweat" for hard work, "heart" for strong feeling, "cold shoulder" for indifference. "All hands on

---

[13] Samuel Johnson, "Life of Addison."

deck"—"Give us this day our daily bread." In poetry, the figure is even more
colourful:

> When flowing cups run swiftly round,
>   With no allaying Thames

Thus Richard Lovelace cheers that there is no water in his wine ("Thames" is
metonymy for "water"). At a more recent party, attended by John Berryman,

> Two daiquiris
> withdrew into a corner of the gorgeous room
> and one told the other a lie.

On a darker note, Robert Lowell laments a dying cousin:

> This Easter, Arthur Winslow, less than dead
> Your people set you up in Phillips' House
> To settle off your wrestling with the crab—
> The claws drop flesh upon your yachting blouse.

The "crab" in question here is the disease cancer, an association that requires
acquaintance with either Latin or astronomy.

Synecdoche ("understanding one by another") is a form of metonymic asso-
ciation that involves substitution of the part for the whole, genus for species, or
vice versa. When T.S. Eliot's Prufrock, in a famous moment of fantasy,
reflects:

> I should have been a pair of ragged claws
> Scuttling across the floors of silent seas,

presumably he wishes to be the entire creature, not just its claws; when he
claims (somewhat unconvincingly):

> And I have known the arms already, known them all,

presumably he has known the persons in question in an undismembered state.
Tennyson uses the figure beautifully in one of his best-known lyrics:

> Now sleeps the crimson petal, now the white;
> Nor waves the cypress in the palace walk;
> Nor winks the gold fin in the porphyry font.

The substitution of "petal" for "flower" is synecdoche; but if "crimson" and
"white" are associated with the conventional "red and white" colours of love

poetry, the figure is metonymic. The use of "fin" in the third line is mysteriously splendid synecdoche, considering that Tennyson might have written:

> Nor winks the gold fish in the porphyry font.

Feeling the difference here is, I suggest, one test of an appreciation for poetry.

One special form of metonymy called *antonomasia* ("to name instead") involves the substitution of a proper name for a particular quality associated with it. We call a traitor a "Judas," a petty tyrant a "Napoleon," and we read "Emily Brontë" (meaning her writings). This figure is quite common. Hart Crane recalls meeting with an old sailor:

> Murmurs of Leviathan he spoke,
> and rum was Plato in our heads

Rum "was Plato" because, being very drunk, the two imagined they were being profoundly philosophical.

Metonymy and synecdoche are in practice often difficult to distinguish:

> Perhaps in this neglected spot is laid
> Some heart once pregnant with celestial fire;
> Hands that the rod of empire might have swayed,
> Or waked to ecstasy the living lyre.

"Heart," in this resplendently troped quatrain, is conventional metonymy for "spirit" or "being;" but Thomas Gray is contemplating a real graveyard that presumably houses real hearts, not to mention hands, so the figure is synecdoche as well. "Rod of empire" for political power and "living lyre" for music or poetry provide further examples of metonymy. Many rhetoricians, understandably, do not press the distinction between metonymy and synecdoche; but both terms appear regularly in critical discourse.

The relation between metonymy and metaphor is an even more complex matter. Both figures seem to be intimately related to the essential processes by which language produces meaning, but in opposite ways. It is thus possible to distinguish between poetic styles intensely metaphoric (like the condensed language of Gerard Manley Hopkins or Dylan Thomas) and those intensely metonymic, working through association and juxtaposition (like the collage assemblages of Ezra Pound). In reading a poem by Thomas, one experiences things that seem to merge into one another, unsuspected congruities being revealed, no verbal identity being distinct. In reading Pound, one finds things presented literally, concretely, but which seem to branch off in surprising chains of association.

The linguist Roman Jakobson has backed up this observation through medical studies of patients whose language skills have been injured by stroke: in some the ability to form similarities by metaphor is damaged, in others the ability to relate words by metonymic association.[14] The two faculties thus seem to stand in a complementary relationship, and the full use of language requires both working together.

The relationship between my third and fourth categories of trope is similarly enigmatic, but I think instructive.

Personification

Personification and irony are not usually linked in any way. But I see them too, like metaphor and metonymy, as paired opposites. *Personification* (or *prosopopoeia*) is one of the best known and widely recognized of the figures:

> My Love is of a birth as rare
> As 'tis for object strange and high;
> It was begotten by Despair
> Upon Impossibility.

Here, three abstractions are personified: that is, they assume human qualities and behave in human ways. Personification is frequently combined with apostrophe, the thing addressed being treated as human:

> Care-charmer Sleep, son of the sable night

> Thou still unravished bride of quietness

Like metaphor, personification can also be submerged:

> The candle starts and flickers,
> Interrogates the shadows, leaves them still more secret.

Prosaic candles "flicker," but they never "interrogate"—that activity is decidedly human.

Personification is closely associated with *allegory,* which may be defined (very loosely) as personification extended through a passage of description or narration. The passage may be book length. Major allegories, like *The Romance of the Rose* or *Pilgrim's Progress*, spin long tales about walking abstractions. The great allegorical poems of Dante and Spenser, of course, extend their resources far beyond simple personifications. But allegory can occur on a much

---

[14] Roman Jakobson, "Two Aspects of Language and Two Types of Aphasic Disturbances," *Language in Literature* (Cambridge: Harvard Univ. Press, 1987).

smaller scale. In just over a hundred lines, Anne Bradstreet's "The Flesh and the Spirit" represents her two opposed principles as an argument between two sisters "close by the banks of lacrim flood" (tears, figured as a river). Here is an even more familiar example:

> Because I could not stop for Death—
> He kindly stopped for me—
> The Carriage held but just Ourselves—
> And Immortality.

Emily Dickinson's little tale of a chaperoned social outing with her gentleman caller, Death, lasts six short stanzas.

According to some theorists, personification is closely related to the mythic imagination. A world populated by personified abstractions, by things or concepts behaving in human ways, is not far removed from a world populated by gods and goddesses, fairies and sprites. Personification is thus a rationalization of a primitive, animistic vision. In William Collins' tiny elegy for fallen soldiers, "How sleep the brave," personified Honour and Freedom coexist naturally with other "forms unseen":

> By fairy hands their knell is rung,
> By forms unseen their dirge is sung;
> There Honour comes, a pilgrim gray,
> To bless the turf that wraps their clay,
> And Freedom shall awhile repair
> To dwell a weeping hermit there.

Personification is thus a trope that elevates the natural world by seeing analogues to human life in it.

Irony and Paradox

Irony ("dissimulation"), on the other hand, is in its broadest sense a trope of debasement, of dehumanizing. This is not true of irony in all its forms, perhaps; but irony is fundamental to satire, to expressions of ridicule and rejection.

Defined simply, irony is the use of expressions meaning the opposite, or nearly the opposite, of what is literally said. All forms of irony involve the consciousness of a discrepancy. As a literary term, irony has wide applications, and one hears of "dramatic irony," "romantic irony," "cosmic irony." These broad uses of the term have to do with large-scale situations, attitudes, points of view. As a figure of speech, however, irony operates in a more local way. Simple irony of a word or phrase, commonly called sarcasm, is technically called "*antiphrasis*" ("speaking opposite"). When Brutus in Shakespeare's *Julius*

Caesar repeatedly declares of Caesar's assassins, "So are they all, honourable men," the Roman mob quickly understand otherwise.

Two other, more specific forms of irony are *hyperbole* ("exaggeration") and *meiosis* ("lessening"), or, more simply, overstatement and understatement. In either case, the reader recognizes the discrepancy and makes appropriate corrections:

> Inebriate of Air—am I—
> And Debauchee of Dew.

Thus avows Emily Dickinson, and even without knowing the personal character of this writer, we recognize that the substances in question are hardly conducive to inebriation and debauchery: we recognize hyperbole. Likewise, John Donne sings:

> She's all states, and all princes I,
> Nothing else is.

We recognize the hyperbolic (and unbelievable) claims of the conventional lover. Despite its overt claims, then, hyperbole is ironic in its tacit recognition of human limitations.

On the other hand, John Crowe Ransom suggests a measured, restrained grief through meiosis, or understatement:

> The little cousin is dead, by foul subtraction,
> A green bough from Virginia's aged tree,
> And none of the country kin like the transaction,
> Nor some of the world of outer dark, like me.

The figure called *litotes* is often equated with meiosis, sometimes even treated as a synonym; it is more useful, however, as a term for the special meiosis involving a double negative that ironically, even tentatively, affirms the positive:

> Hear, then, a noble Muse thy praise rehearse
> In no ignoble verse.

There is another closely related pair of terms that for some reason rarely appear in critical discourse, though the devices are commonplace: *cacozelia* ("bad imitation") and *tapinosis* (or *bdelygmia,* "humiliation") refer to diction that is on one hand more elevated than necessary, or on the other more debasing. Cacozelia is the ironic use of elevated language; thus Ezra Pound has a jealous lover warn:

> But in one bed, in one bed alone, my dear Lyncaeus,
> I deprecate your attendance.

And Eliot in "The Waste Land" celebrates the clerk-typist's underwear with cacozelia and a grandiloquent alexandrine:

> Out of the window perilously spread
> Her drying combinations touched by the sun's last rays

Tapinosis, on the other hand, is a descent to vulgar diction:

> Lord, confound this surly sister,
> Blight her brow with blotch and blister,
> Cramp her larynx, lung and liver,
> In her guts a galling give her.

Tapinosis can be more subtle than this; when Robert Frost foresees the apocalypse, he cautions:

> There would be more than ocean water-broken
> Before God's last *Put out the Light* is spoken.

The quoted phrase sounds less like a righteous God fulfilling providence than like an exasperated parent. A related term—far more frequently encountered than "cacozelia" or "tapinosis"—is *bathos,* sudden sinking of tone, usually comical (whether or not it is intentional):

> Do I dare
> Disturb the universe?

inquires Eliot's Prufrock, and the question makes him appear absurd. And Edwin Arlington Robinson characterizes a pathetically high-flown daydreamer thus:

> Miniver loved the Medici,
>   Albeit he had never seen one;
> He would have sinned incessantly,
>   Could he have been one.

Still another pair of terms names unusual ironic devices capable of great dramatic subtlety. *Apophasis* ("denial") is an act of pretending to deny what is really affirmed. When the politician tells us that she will *not* mention her opponent's repeated adulteries and traffic violations, she is able to place herself in a high moral light with the audience, while at the same time reminding them forcefully of the opponent's peccadilloes. Poets use the same ironic obliquity:

> Let me not to the marriage of true minds
> Admit impediments.

Thus begins Shakespeare's deflation of ideal marriage. *Aporia* ("difficulty") is a speaker's feigned or true ignorance about circumstances, or the ability to express them, a display of modesty that is likely to win the reader's sympathy:

> But words came halting forth, wanting Invention's stay,
> Invention, Nature's child, fled stepdame Study's blows;
> And others' feet still seemed but strangers in my way.

Thus begins Sidney's Astrophel (though his aporia does not prevent him from producing more than a hundred sonnets.) When Shelley declares of the dead John Keats,

> He wakes or sleeps with the enduring dead,

aporia allows him to take an agnostic position of uncertainty about the state of afterlife.

Figures that openly violate common sense are governed by the major trope of *paradox*—a seemingly contradictory or impossible statement:

> Stone walls do not a prison make,
> Nor iron bars a cage.

Paradox, like irony, demands that the reader convert the explicit and inconsistent assertion into a comprehensible form. Reading these lines, recognizing a challenge to one's ordinary experience, one is forced to rationalize a meaning: "If freedom is a state of mind," let us say, "then stone walls and iron bars are powerless." This process of decoding paradox is so fundamental to the reading of poetry that some critics—notably the "New Critics" of the mid-twentieth century—proclaimed that "the language of poetry is the language of paradox."[15] Few would make such a hyperbolic claim today, but the figure is indeed one of the most frequent. Irony and paradox together now rival metaphor as the fundamental tropes of poetry. There is in paradox, writes Edward Corbett, "as in most metaphorical language, what Aristotle considered a special mark of genius: the ability to see similarities."[16]

Paradox is a form of irony because it reminds us of the irrational nature of the world we live in; yet since it can be resolved into meaning, it also suggests an over-riding, less apparent kind of order. Because it lies on the boundary between the rational and the irrational, paradox is a favourite device of religious thought, and religious poetry:

---

[15] Cleanth Brooks, *The Well Wrought Urn* (New York: Harcourt Brace, 1947), p. 3.

[16] P. 491.

> I saw Eternity the other night
> Like a great ring of pure and endless light

Vaughan's chatty and absurd "the other night" somehow validates the cosmic sweep of his vision, convinces us of its reality. Donne pleads paradoxically for God's violent intervention:

> Divorce me, or untie that knot again,
> Take me to you, imprison me, for I,
> Except you enthral me, never shall be free,
> Nor ever chaste, except you ravish me.

And Wordsworth condenses a Platonic doctrine in paradox:

> Our birth is but a sleep and a forgetting

Twentieth-century poetry and criticism, concentrating on the irrationalities of everyday language and experience, have turned to paradox as a matter of course. One of the most oft-quoted poetic definitions of poetry itself is a series of paradoxes:

> A poem should be palpable and mute
> As a globed fruit,
>
> Dumb
> As old medallions to the thumb,
>
> Silent as the sleeve-worn stone
> Of casement ledges where the moss has grown—
>
> A poem should be wordless
> As the flight of birds.

And paradox remains a stock-in-trade of love poetry. James Reaney paradoxically undercuts the idea of "Platonic love":

> Come sit on my knee, green emptiness
> Here's a kiss for you, puff-of-air

Edna St. Vincent Millay echoes the conventional paradoxes of the masculine Renaissance love sonnet from a feminist point of view:

> So wanton, light and false, my love, are you,
> I am most faithless when I most am true.

Paradox is the most general term, but there are several other expressions that suggest logical incongruity. A highly condensed paradox—in two or three words—is an *oxymoron* ("pointedly foolish"). Witty observers like to spot the oxymorons that penetrate common speech: a soldier is assigned to "Military Intelligence," a voter casts her ballot for the "Progressive Conservatives," a diner orders "jumbo shrimp." In literature, Milton's account of Hell at the beginning of *Paradise Lost* is riddled with celebrated oxymorons: the fallen angels find themselves amid "darkness visible," with "ever-burning sulphur unconsumed," valuing their "precious bane." T.S. Eliot uses the same shock effect for his account of aging:

> First, the cold friction of expiring sense
> Without enchantment, offering no promise
> But bitter tastelessness of shadow fruit
> When body and soul begin to fall asunder.

Yet William Cullen Bryant assures that, after death:

> Thou shalt lie down
> With patriarchs of the infant world.

Non sequitur ("it doesn't follow") is another violation of logic, a statement that does not follow logically from the preceding. The term is found in ordinary educated usage, as well as in criticism. It is related to bathos, in that it involves an unexpected continuation, but it does not require a sudden tumble. A dramatic example is the turn of Yeats's great sonnet "Leda and the Swan":

> A shudder in the loins engenders there
> The broken wall, the burning roof and tower,
> And Agamemnon dead.

The apparent *non sequitur,* the relatively minor sexual event that issues in the death of kings and the fall of civilizations, brings into focus the evil consequences of isolated acts of violence and the plight of individuals helplessly caught in the larger processes of history. This is an isolated example: some highly metonymic poems that depend on constant juxtaposition, like Pound's *Cantos*, could be said to elevate *non sequitur* into a method.

Hysteron proteron ("the latter the former") involves a startlingly illogical or unidiomatic reversal of sequence:

> Th'Antoniad, the Egyptian Admiral,
> With all their sixty, fly and turn the rudder

Here the agitation of the moment has grammatical consequences, the ships seeming to fly *before* they turn. The figure is rare, but the term is found occasionally; it is related to the *non sequitur,* but also to other deviations that suggest excitability, like anacoluthon and diacope.

Synaesthesia may also be considered a form of paradox, or oxymoron, in that it involves a deliberate confusion of the senses, though it might also be classed as a peculiar kind of metaphor. In the past two centuries it has become a dominant figure. Not many poets, however, have gone farther in a single line than Keats:

> And taste the music of that vision pale

It is a figure not often found before the Romantics put it into currency and their symbolist successors erected it into a stylistic preference; but Milton ventured synaesthesia in "Comus":

> At last a soft and solemn breathing sound
> Rose like a steam of rich, distill'd perfumes

Emily Dickinson describes a hummingbird as "a resonance of emerald" ("A Route of Evanescence"), and imagines a common housefly with "Blue—uncertain stumbling Buzz" ("I heard a fly buzz"). Synaesthesia is most prized, however, by post-Romantic poets of a decadent tendency:

> I am engulphed, and drown deliciously.
> Soft music like a perfume, and sweet light
> Golden with audible odours exquisite,
> Swathe me in cerements for eternity.

This completes a survey of recognized figures of speech, most of which are in common use in current critical discourse. The list is far from complete. But any student or aspiring writer who studies these devices, used so very consciously by so many generations of poets, who grasps how they work, who learns to recognize them in the wild on first encounter with an unfamiliar poem, will find that poetic language speaks with far greater force than before. As for using them in one's own writing, no one pretends that mastery of the figures is a shortcut to excellence. Practice and experiment, and above all sensitivity, are essential. But the figures do identify what Brian Vickers has called "pockets of energy" in language. To release this potential energy, as with meter, the aspiring writer must first do consciously what she hopes eventually to do with ease.

5

Form in Free Verse

Free verse is writing presented as "verse" that does not employ traditional metrical systems. Beyond this bare statement no further generalization can be made. There are no rules; the kinds of free verse writing are limited only by the capacity of human inventiveness in language.

Perceiving form in non-metrical verse, talking about it intelligently—making generalizations—is therefore difficult, and criticism has made few advances to help the student or the general reader.[1] Perceiving form at all depends first on the inherited convention that writing presented as verse has form, and that formal patterns are meaningful; in other words, it depends on the reader's expectation of form. It depends therefore on one's ability to discover formal patterns, often by translating the "rules" of metrical poetry into more abstract principles that operate in free writing. This process is *ad hoc*—that is, it depends on the peculiar properties of the specific poem in question—and it is heuristic, a matter of continuous discovery. What I can offer here, then, are not rules, but instead a few suggestions about ways to discover and talk about free verse form.

Twentieth-century poets have loudly insisted that free verse has formal significance. "No verse is *libre* for the man who wants to do a good job," proclaimed T.S. Eliot, and he has been echoed ever since, but rarely with any notion of how to tell a "good job" from a bad one.[2] I will risk advancing a view—heretical for a prosodist—that some poetry remains interesting despite unremarkable formal skill, interesting for reasons other than form. Just as much metrical verse is metrically routine, much free verse shows little interest in verse technique of any kind. Yet even in such writing, an expectation of basic formal

---

[1] Among the best writings on this subject are Charles O. Hartman, *Free Verse: An Essay on Prosody* (Princeton: Princeton Univ. Press, 1980); passages in Veronica Forrest-Thomson, *Poetic Artifice: A Theory of Twentieth-Century Poetry* (Manchester: Manchester Univ. Press, 1978); and Stephen Cushman, *William Carlos Williams and the Meanings of Measure* (New Haven: Yale Univ. Press, 1985).

[2] Eliot, "The Music of Poetry," in *On Poetry and Poets* (London: Faber, 1957), p. 37.

competence, and the conventions relating sound to sense, remain.

Free verse, then, is verse without meter, but also verse that observes other formal conventions besides meter. The verse line, lacking an audible organization of accented and unaccented syllables, remains a visible unit on the page. It has a beginning, an ending, and a syllable count, all of which participate in the sense of verse form. It is frequently, though not always, justified to the left margin. Rhythm remains, though not rhythmic regularity or predictability. As in metrical verse, the lines may form stanzas, and they may use rhyme. To a much greater extent than metrical verse, free verse depends on the typographic conventions of poetry, the visual layout on the page. Because it dispenses with metrical regularity, it also dispenses with the predictability of metrical verse, and therefore with the sense of tension between verse rhythm and the metrical frame. But it gains a sense of freedom, and with it a potential for exploring new or more subtle rhythms than metrical verse, or at least rhythms organized in ways that are neither symmetrical nor predictable.

Before the free verse revolution was started by Walt Whitman's 1855 edition of *Leaves of Grass*, the greatest freedom ventured by poets was in the irregular ode, where poets mixed lines of different and unpredictable lengths and rhyme schemes, as in Dryden's St. Cecilia odes or Wordsworth's "Immortality Ode." Milton, in the choruses of *Samson Agonistes* modelled after the choric odes of Greek tragedy, daringly abandoned rhyme to mark the irregular line ends, and thus is sometimes said to have written free verse:

> This, this is he; softly a while;
> Let us not break in upon him.
> O change beyond report, thought, or belief!
> See how he lies at random, carelessly diffus'd,
> With languish'd head unpropt,
> As one with hope abandon'd,
> And by himself given over.
> In slavish habit, ill-fitted weeds
> O'erworn and soiled.
> Or do my eyes misrepresent? Can this be he?
> That heroic, that renowned,
> Irresistable Samson whom, unarmed,
> No strength of man or fiercest wild beast could withstand.

Such a passage is in fact metrical and can be scanned within the accentual-syllabic system. But the effect of unpredictability remains, particularly in the absence of rhyme to mark the lines. Furthermore, in the absence of a metrical paradigm, choices between alternative scansions are impossible to resolve. Thus, line 2 can be scanned as an anomalous trochaic line (or even iambic tetrameter lacking the first syllable):

˘ ˘ | ´ ˘ ˘ | ´ ˘ | ´ ˘   ˘

Let us not break in upon him.

Or as an iambic trimeter:

˘ ˘   ´ | ˘   ´ | ˘   ´   (˘)

Let us not break in upon him.

This kind of scannable but variable verse continues to appear even to the present, with Matthew Arnold's irregularly rhymed "Dover Beach" a justly admired example. For the analyst, this means that any given poem, even though it appears to be "free" verse, must first be tested by the other available systems before it can safely be called "free verse."

Apart from the irregular ode, however, earlier poetry can show only a few oddities: Swift's comical "Mrs. Francis Harris's Petition," in which the lower-class speaker is given unmetrical but rhyming doggerel; the "prose poems" of Ossian, which pretend to be translations of ancient Scottish poetry; the psalm-like madhouse verses of Smart's "Jubilate Agno"; and the long lines of Blake's later prophetic books, which are founded on the ballad fourteener but depart from it radically.

The success of Whitman's great experiment established the possibility of a significant, fully developed poetic corpus in non-metrical forms. For Whitman, the matter of his visionary message far outweighed his formal interests. Drawing from the anti-formalist bias of his mentor Emerson (who had proclaimed, "it is not meters, but a meter-making argument that makes a poem"[3]) and from the anti-formalist bias of the American culture that he celebrated, Whitman discarded meter altogether. Still, formal interest survives in Whitman, as we shall see below: his long lines, partly modelled on the form and rhetoric of the Old Testament psalms, establish him within the tradition of the cultural visionary and prophet.

At first, imitators were few and tentative. Stephen Crane tried short-lined free verse in his brief poetic parables, but with little influence. It was only after the turn of the century that a group of poets—mainly Americans though living in London, and well aware of parallel developments in French poetry, where free verse was also establishing itself—initiated the "Imagist Movement": free verse again impressed itself on the consciousness of readers.[4] The controversies

---

[3] Emerson, "The Poet" (1844). Even before Whitman, American poets were straining against conventional forms, as evidenced in much of Emerson's own verse as well as the irregular stanzas of Poe.

[4] Early imagist poems and poetics are conveniently gathered in Peter Jones, ed., *Imagist Poetry* (Harmondsworth: Penguin, 1972). Subsequent quotations are from "Imagisme" (*Poetry*, March 1913), variously attributed to Pound and F.S. Flint; Amy Lowell,

that surrounded this movement encapsulate the longer debate that has persisted ever since. "As for meter," Ezra Pound declared, we compose "in the sequence of the musical phrase, not in the sequence of the metronome." Amy Lowell seized on this principle in the name of American democracy: "We do not insist upon 'free-verse' as the only method of writing poetry. We fight for it as for a principle of liberty." And in a real sense, political overtones are inescapable: free verse is disruptive of order, a sign of liberty, a rejection of traditional authorities. Pound, however, while espousing free verse, recognized the necessity of verse conventions: "Rhythm MUST have meaning," he wrote in a letter; "It can't be merely a careless dash off, with no grip and no real hold to the words and sense." To Pound, the point of free verse is not so much liberation from form, as a freedom that makes new formal discoveries possible. Both Pound and Amy Lowell affirmed that the invention of new rhythms made possible the expression of emotions that escape metered verse. But the revolutionary political rhetoric of Lowell is characteristically American, and this possibly explains why free verse has generally found a more comfortable home in the New World than in England.

What follows is discussion of some of the ways critics have found to talk about form in free verse. There have been many attempts to categorize the many forms free verse assumes, without satisfactory results. I have assumed that the phrase "free verse" encompasses a large and diverse range of formal procedures, but I have made no attempt to categorize them. Instead, I offer three basic analytic approaches: through the poetic line, through metrical presences, and through syntax. All of these are available for any free verse poem, regardless of its general type. But in any one poem, one kind of analysis may clearly return greater rewards than others.

Lines: The Master Convention of Free Verse

When meter is removed from verse, what is left? Lines. As many writers have noted, the principal difference between poetry and prose is the obvious one: poetry is written in lines, while prose runs to the right-hand margin.[5] (I will consider the peculiarities of the so-called prose poem below.) This means that,

---

Preface to *Some Imagist Poets* (1915); and Ezra Pound, letter to Harriet Monroe, January 1915. Timothy Steele, *Missing Measures: Modern Poetry and the Revolt against Meter* (Fayetteville: Univ. of Arkansas Press, 1990), is a searching analysis of this movement, but tendentious and covertly hostile.

[5] Credit for this observation is due to philosopher Jeremy Bentham: "Prose is where all the lines but the last go on to the margin—poetry is where some of them fall short of it." See Bentham's 1808 letter to Lord Holland (*Works*, Edinburgh 1838–43, X, p. 442).

by general agreement, when prose is *re*printed, the lineation is arbitrary and can be adjusted at will; but when poetry is reprinted, the integrity of the line must be preserved. This convention is carried over from metrical verse to free verse, even though the lines themselves have no internal metrical structure. In reciting free verse aloud, as well, the convention of marking the line endings with some kind of pause or hesitation (as is usual in metrical verse) is usually observed.

There is an important corollary to be remembered here, however. In metrical verse, the lines have an audible structure based on distribution of syllables and stresses; in free verse, they do not. Confronted with a passage from, say, Wordsworth's *Prelude* printed as prose, an experienced reader can reconstruct the lineation; confronted with any free verse poem, she can not. Thus in metrical verse, the auditory structure generates the printed structure; in free verse, the printed structure generates the auditory. Various kinds of free verse, then, are dependent, to greater or lesser degrees, on the specifics of the print medium.

What happens, then, when a piece of non-metrical writing is set up in lines? English critic Veronica Forrest-Thomson has given a most ingenious example.[6] Take the following passage of prose, a particularly humdrum editorial from the *London Times*:

> The Government have taken their time in appointing the new chairman of the BBC, which is a measure both of the importance now attached to the office and of the difficulty in persuading somebody of the necessary quality to take it on a part-time basis at £6,000 a year.

But set up the identical words as lines of "free verse" and observe what happens:

> The Government have taken their time
> in appointing the new chairman of the
> BBC
> which is a measure both
> of the importance now attached to the office
> and of the difficulty in persuading somebody
> of the necessary quality
> to take it
> on a part-time basis
> at £6,000 a year

A reader alert to the line breaks begins to notice potential intonations that continuous prose smoothed over: "The Government have taken their time" (well, isn't that typical of governments?)—"in appointing the new chairman of the→/ BBC" (such an important institution, to fill up a whole line by itself!)—

---

6 Pp. 22–25.

"which is a measure both" (sense of anticipation ...)—"of the importance now attached to the office" (ah yes, they haven't just forgotten about it)—"and of the difficulty in persuading *somebody*" (just anybody?)—"of the necessary quality" (ahem)—"to take it" (please, anybody, *just take it!*)—"on a part-time basis" (so it's not that important after all?)—"at £6,000 a year" (well, you can't expect the government to be extravagant ...).

The sensitive reader of poetry has learned to probe words and phrases for their fullest implications. In free verse, the line breaks, cunningly placed, open up slight hesitations that focus attention on implications just under the surface. In this case, the stuffiest newspaper prose proves compact with unintended satirical innuendoes about governments, bureaucrats, and cultural institutions. One of the functions of free verse, it seems, with its disruptive fragmentations, is to expose the various undertones in language that continuous prose glosses over. The line break, carried over from the conventions of end-stopping and enjambment in metrical verse, is one of its most powerful devices.

Treatment of the line unit and the line end is thus a defining feature for many different kinds of free verse. Line length is not determined metrically; but in a very general way, the length of the line interacts with human physical capacities. Very long lines, like those favoured by Whitman, stretch the limits of the human breath:

> Ah, what can ever be more stately and admirable to me than mast-
>   hemmed Manhattan?
> River and sunset and scallop-edg'd waves of flood-tide?
> The sea-gulls, oscillating their bodies, the hay-boat in the
>   twilight, and the belated lighter?
> What gods can exceed these that clasp me by the hand, and with
>   voices I love call me promptly and loudly by my nighest name as
>   I approach?
> What is more subtle than this which ties me to the woman or man
>   that looks in my face?
> Which fuses me into you now, and pours my meaning into you?

The simple fact of excessive line length contributes to the sense of a superhuman, larger-than-life vatic persona that Whitman creates. This persona of prophet-bard is continued, along with the long verse line, in such successors of Whitman as D.H. Lawrence, Robinson Jeffers, and Allen Ginsberg. On the other hand, very short lines, like those in the Forrest-Thomson example, tend to isolate words and phrases with a kind of nervous, intellectual scrutiny, not vatic and expansive, but cryptic and sibylline:

> Still the walls do not fall,
> I do not know why;

there is zrr-hiss,
lightning in a not-known,

unregistered dimension;
we are powerless,

dust and powder fill our lungs
our bodies blunder

through doors twisted on hinges,
and the lintels slant

crosswise

Here the short lines, fragmenting and disrupting the syntactic flow, call attention to connotations and aural effects, like the poise of "still" against "fall" in line 1; the semantically suggestive chiming of "lightning" and "not-known," or "powder" and "blunder;" the assonance of "twisted," "hinges" and "lintels;" the dramatic isolation of "crosswise" which releases overtones of crucifixion from an adverb that is otherwise merely descriptive.

The artificial line boundary thus interacts with other natural boundaries in language. We organize language into syntactic groups. Words in any passage organize themselves in a descending hierarchy which speakers of a language recognize instinctively: (1) sentences are made of (2) clauses and (3) phrases, which are in turn made of (4) individual words, which are in turn made of (5) syllables, which are in turn made of (6) indivisible letters or phonemes. Enjambment, as in metered verse, feels more forceful as one descends this scale. As linguist Roger Fowler observes, "it seems that the smaller the grammatical unit concerned, the greater its resistance to being stretched over a metrical boundary."[7]

In Whitman's long lines, enjambment is all but non-existent: line ends coincide with sentences or phrases, and the long lines seem both majestic and stable. Vast quantities of free verse early in this century, influenced by imagist demands for precision and concentration, favour a shorter line than Whitman's but at the same time avoid strong enjambment, adhering to the phrase boundary. Here are two examples, the first by Amy Lowell:

The snow whispers about me,
And my wooden clogs
Leave holes behind me in the snow.
But no one will pass this way
Seeking my footsteps,

---

[7] Quoted in Cushman, p. 32.

And when the temple bell rings again
They will be covered and gone.

And another by Carl Sandburg:

One arch of the sky
Took on a spray of jewels.

The crystals gleamed on the windows
Weaving their wintrish alphabets
Of spears and ovals fixed in frost
Fastened to a glass design
With a word: This must be.

Here, the greatest pressure at the line ends is felt in the need to continue and complete the sentences. Proponents of free verse at this innovative time wrote a great deal about "cadence," and the falling intonation that marks phrase boundaries to the ear are emphasized by the lineation to produce this kind of "cadenced," or what I call "phrasal," free verse.

This, technically the simplest kind of free verse, continues to have successful practitioners; witness Audre Lorde's "A Small Slaughter":

Day breaks without thanks or caution
past a night without satisfaction or pain.
My words are blind children I have armed
against the casual insolence of morning
without you
I am scarred and marketed
like a streetcorner in Harlem
a woman
whose face in the tiles
your feet have not yet regarded
I am the stream
past which you will never step
the woman you can not deal with
I am the mouth
of your scorn.

The isolation of these plainly worded phrases enforces a feeling of deliberateness and thoughtfulness. Free verse in general tends to fewer slack syllables than prose because poetry tends to seek a sense of concentration. In this poem, the scant two punctuation marks, both periods, indicate structure: the first two antithetical lines establish a general time, while the rest develop three parallel metaphors: "I am scarred ...," "I am the stream ...," "I am the mouth." The suppressed punctuation also generates functional ambiguities: "without you" can be taken to complete the previous line or begin the following, as can the phrase "a woman." The shorter three- or four-syllable lines, contrasting with lines just slightly longer, first isolate key phrases ("without you ... a woman") and then bring the threefold parallel structure to closure ("I am the stream ... I am the mouth/ of your scorn"). From a prosodic standpoint, such technique is uncomplicated but often highly effective.

The poet who most vigorously explored the effects of breaking phrases across the line ends was William Carlos Williams. In one celebrated poem, Williams captures the cat's adroitness:

> As the cat
> climbed over
> the top of
>
> the jamcloset
> first the right
> forefoot
>
> carefully
> then the hind
> stepped down
>
> into the pit of
> the empty
> flowerpot

Williams entitles this poem "Poem," as if to dare anyone to say that, with its visibly regular stanzas and trim lines (ranging from two to five syllables, one or two accents per line) justified to the left margin, it could be anything else. But on inspection, one observes not only the absence of meter, but an apparent irrationality of lineation. The line ends—and the stanza breaks as well—cut across phrase boundaries, separating adjective from noun, preposition from object. The syntax of the single complete (but unpunctuated) sentence remains the motor that propels the rhythm forward. The breaks after "climbed over" and "the top of" suggest a sense of effort; the isolation of the words "forefoot" and "carefully," each with a line to itself separated by stanza break, suggests the deliberateness of the movement; the break after "down" suggests downwardness, as the eye is urged forward across the blank space on the page. Such prosodic effects are possible partly because we assume, by convention, that the sound must seem an echo to the sense, and partly because we have learned the effects of enjambment from metered poetry.

Quite apart from imitative effects, however, the apparently arbitrary lineation of free verse retains the feel for movement created by enjambment and caesura in good blank verse. Here is the start of Christopher Middleton's "The Child at the Piano":

> The child at the piano
> plinking, planking, plonks.
> I stare and stare. Twigs
> angle the air with green outside.
>
> Handfuls of notes, all happening at once,
> but tunes do not occur; on their backs
> round they whizz like stunned wasps; contour
> would crush that kind of mass.
>
> Telescoping flukes and faults, their
> tenuous terrain dislocates
> no spheres I know of. Her index rebounding
> off high C beckons no hell boulder up.

Inspection for some kind of metrical system yields no result: the fifth line is potential iambic pentameter, but it is the only such line in the poem, and probably reads better with four beats; suggestions of metricality are otherwise avoided; there is no regular accent; syllable count ranges widely from five to eleven per line, accentual count from two to four. This is free verse, no doubt about it. Yet there are consistent, though unrhymed, quatrains, each end-stopped, setting up a rough rhythmic framework. The first two lines coincide with syntactic units, but in line three, caesura and enjambment isolate the image "twigs" at the line end, mysteriously. The enjambments in stanza two begin earlier, and become yet more radical in stanza three, severing "their/ tenuous terrain" mid-phrase. Stanza four, however, restores the coincidence of line and phrase, which is disturbed again in the final stanza before returning for closure in the last line:

> The heroics, fatuous, ordain yet
> this act's assumption of her whole element.
> Boughs of sound swoop through the room,
> happily, for her to swing from.
>
> So I call my thought's bluff. My thumb
> struts down the keys too, pings
> to her plonks, on both white and black notes,
> while the green air outside lets us be.

No two of the five stanzas is identical in its syntactic fluidity. There is no recourse to devices of syntactic parallelism or repetition to suggest structure; instead, the poet achieves variety of movement within the quatrain. Other prosodic effects work here as well: assonance, alliteration, and delicate internal rhymes ("stare"/"air," "terrain"/"ordain") and near rhymes ("plonks"/"once," "room"/"thumb"). The poem develops arboreal and geological imagery in a fairly complex way, with allusion to the music of the spheres in stanza three, and verbal recollections for closure at the end. From a strictly metrical standpoint, however, the poem illustrates the effectiveness of the ordinary printed free verse line and stanza.

But these effects, some have complained, are merely visual, and lose the auditory charm of metered poetry. To an extent this is true: free verse depends on typographic conventions for its existence. Yet one may recall that Dr. Johnson raised the same objection against the blank verse of *Paradise Lost*, calling it "verse only to the eye."[8] Milton's unrhymed lines nonetheless have a true—and perceptible—auditory structure, while Williams' and Middleton's lines do not. Their line ends are unpredictable and arbitrary; yet on the printed page, they do become meaningful. Free verse depends on typography, and thus marks a weakening of ear dominance in the art of poetry. It is, as some have called it, a "visual prosody." On the other hand, its auditory effects frequently demand an even more perceptive ear than metered verse.

Yet this statement needs to be qualified. Another Williams example illustrates how arbitrary yet calculated line breaks do in fact interact with auditory sense:

To a Poor Old Woman

munching a plum on
the street a paper bag
of them in her hand

They taste good to her
They taste good
to her. They taste
good to her

Here the line breaks suggest three different inflections for the same unadorned statement. The first is a simple declaration: "They taste good to her." The second and third throw different emphases across the line ends: "They taste good/ *to her*. They taste/ *good* to her." The same words seem to have three contrasting intonations, three different shades of meaning. The line breaks indeed have auditory as well as visual effect, entering into the sense of the poem in a subtle way, just as they do in the hesitations and innuendoes of Veronica Forrest-Thomson's "poem" about the BBC.

---

[8] Johnson, "Life of Milton."

Many writers of free verse use the visual design of the page as Williams and Middleton do in these last examples, with a column of lines more or less equal in length surrounded by space. This establishes a kind of prosody, in that the line-units inevitably sound more or less equivalent, while ignoring any regularity of stressed and unstressed syllables. It is often a valuable prosodic observation to define a work's outer limits—how many and how few syllables and accents appear per line. Within this frame, a short line may project a feeling of deliberateness, and a longer line a feeling of weight or hurry, while a sudden change of line length may signal a change of direction.

In Williams' baseball poem from *Spring and All* (sometimes titled "At the Ball Game"), for example, the first six two-line stanzas, ranging in syllable count from three to eight per line, deal positively with the watching crowd; a two-syllable line, however, marks a change of emphasis, a turn in the poetic tone:

> for this
> to be warned against

Six couplets later, further two-syllable lines switch the poem's direction back, and the final lines pit longer against shorter lines:

> This is
> the power of their faces
>
> It is summer, it is the solstice
> the crowd is
>
> cheering, the crowd is laughing
> in detail
>
> permanently, seriously
> without thought

An extreme example is A.R. Ammons' witty *Tape for the Turn of the Year*, which was composed on a roll of adding-machine tape, the poet writing daily between December and January. The long, thin poem that resulted is largely a product of peculiar printing constraint; it maintains a sort of aural regularity or predictability arising out of the finite number of alphabetic characters per line:

> I wish I had a great
> story to tell: the
> words then
> could be quiet, as I'm
> trying to make them now—

immersed in the play
of events: but
I can't tell a great
story: if I were
Odysseus, I couldn't
survive
pulling away from
Lestrygonia, 11 of
12 ships lost
with 11 crews: I couldn't
pull away with
the joy of one
escaped with his life:

Like Williams, Ammons allows himself free enjambment cutting across syntax, with occasional very short lines that seem to add prosodic emphasis: "words then," "survive." In this type of writing, as Stephen Cushman has observed, "the end-stopped line is an endangered species" that provides "a moment of rest, relief, and stability."[9] In this poem, however, Ammons disrupts stability by avoiding periods altogether, relying wholly on colons. One can sometimes gauge such verse as well by measuring the syllabic limits within which a poem restrains itself—a range of, say, two to a maximum of seven syllables. Such measurement is rough, of course, but it can provide a scale against which a given line can be described as longer or shorter than the norm. Even this rough measure, however, is stretched here by Ammons' use of number syllables: "Lestrygonia, 11 of" crushes together nine syllables in one visually short line.

The Williams and Middleton examples, however, are still printed in lines grouped into recognizable stanzas. Furthermore, they are constituted of grammatical sentences with a drive to completion that provides forward momentum. Some types of free verse, however, abandon both syntactic and stanzaic coherence, isolating words and phrases in fragmented, discontinuous lines:

So the distances are Galatea
                              and one does fall in love and desires
    mastery

        old Zeus—young Augustus

So Love knows no distance, no place
                              is that far away or heat changes
    into signals, and control

---

[9] Pp. 44–45.

old Zeus—young Augustus

Death is a loving matter, then, a horror
                         we cannot bide, and avoid
by greedy life

          we think all living things are precious
          —Pygmalions

                         a German inventor in Key West
who had a Cuban girl, and kept her, after her death
in his bed
                         after her family retrieved her
he stole the body again from the vault

Torso on torso in either direction,
          young Augustus
                         out via nothing where messages
are
          or in, down La Cluny's steps to the old man sitting
a god throned on torsoes,

          old Zeus

In such dispersed or "open" verse, as Marjorie Perloff contends, "the *page* rather than the foot or line or stanza becomes the unit of measure."[10] The typography isolates verbal fragments for scrutiny, while the fragmented syntax obstructs continuities and thereby weakens the feeling of enjambment. It suggests concentrated attention of every atom of meaning and sound.

This passage, the first half of a short poem by Charles Olson, though seemingly chaotic at first sight, still yields some formal properties on examination. Several lines are broken at a mid-page margin and continued without spacing; in each case the syntax seems continuous as well. Much open verse that seems highly dispersed on the page is actually governed by a system of multiple margins. There is a kind of refrain ("old Zeus—young Augustus"), spaced consistently even while it is varied. There are moments that carry the force of enjambment, though ambiguously: "and desires/ mastery" at the beginning, and "where messages/ are" near the end. The isolation of "are" in one line emphasizes the

---

[10] "To Give a Design: Williams and the Visualization of Poetry," in Carroll F. Terrell, ed., *William Carlos Williams: Man and Poet* (Orono: National Poetry Foundation, 1983), 159–86. For an extension of this view, see Henry M. Sayre, *The Visual Text of William Carlos Williams* (Urbana: Univ. of Illinois Press, 1983). Valuable for radically "open forms" is bpNichol and Frank Davey, "The Prosody of Open Verse," *Open Letter,* 5th series, 2 (1982), 5–13.

poem's theme of mortal existence. These are just a few places in a complex passage where the poet's formal strategies of spacing and lineation can be felt to work meaningfully.

At the same time, one recognizes that line and enjambment seem to play a lesser role in this example than in the others. And Perloff's claim that the page is the unit of measure is not strictly true, since the page is not a formal boundary, and this passage can be broken over the page at any point. (More recent poets sometimes go farther and insist on the printed page as a unit, while others deliberately violate the conventions of the printed book, requiring the reader to skip around, read from right to left—thus creating dilemmas for anthologists.)

But the real issue here, I think, is syntactic continuity. When the forward thrust of syntax is frustrated, line and enjambment begin to lose significance. Williams, so often the boldest innovator of his generation, writes in "The Locust Tree in Flower," a poem emblematic of the possibilities of syntactic disruption:

> Among
> of
> green
>
> stiff
> old
> bright
>
> broken
> branch
> come
>
> white
> sweet
> May
>
> again

This at first appears wholly unintelligible; but a little effort forces meaning out of it. Yet, without syntactic continuity, there is little sense talking about "enjambment" or "end-stopping." Here, the isolation of each word forces the reader to locate the syntactic gaps and construe meaning across them: "among [something—a noun, because 'among' is a preposition] of [something], [something is—because there has to be a noun—] green; stiff, old [slightly negative adjectives, but nonetheless] bright; [despite the] broken branch, [some things, plural] come [like] white sweet May, again." The statement about the renewal of the seasonal cycle is rather banal, but poetically it is less significant than the verbal enactment of syntax retaining a degree of intelligibility and vitality despite severe mutilation, mimesis of life winning out in the face of adversity. Yet, despite the presence of an implied syntactic momentum, this poem seems not so much made of "lines" as of words arranged in relationship to each other.

This constructivist approach to writing poetry has developed in too many various directions during recent decades to be charted here. But here is an example, a short fragment from the conclusion of John Cage's "Anarchy":

Before

the groUnd

hypnotiC

maKe life

Manhattan the age for

real socIal wealth

away aNd it

for ultra high voltageS global

libertTy

sociEty

pRoblem

liberty oF each

by virtUe of

deepLy with

buwaLda for daring to

brutE

laws of ouR own individual nature

The one coherent strand in all this is the acrostic, highlighted in capital letters, on the name of the architect and philosopher Buckminster Fuller, whose work is perhaps being used or commented on.[11] As one "reads," the initial sense quickly dissolves into near nonsense. One can only read it like Williams' "Locust Tree in Flower," by filling in the apparent blanks: "hypnotic" has something to do with making "life;" the scene may be Manhattan, certainly a source of hypnotic vital energies; the sociological diction suggests a contemplation of "wealth" and its relation to abstract ideals like "liberty" and "society," and "individual nature" (in a political context conditioned by the work's title). The proper name "buwalda" (if it is a name), coupled with "daring" and "brute," interject a disturbing note amid the tone of social idealism. Something like stanza breaks, falling without regard to Fuller's name, seems to group lines together. An equivocal meaning does emerge.

---

[11] Cage called this form the "mesostic," an acrostic line ("stich") centred in the middle of the page. The poem appears in R. Fleming and W. Duckworth, eds., *John Cage at Seventy Five* (Lewisburg: Bucknell Univ. Press, 1989). I am indebted for this example to Michael O'Driscoll, *The Truth in Pointing: Whitman, Pound, Cage and Text as Index* (Ph.D. diss., Univ. of Western Ontario, 1996), pp. 276–80.

Cage, however, also provides information about how he arrived at his text, by culling some thirty quotations from various anarchist writings (Emma Goldman's autobiography, Paul Berman's *Quotations from the Anarchists*) and then subjecting them to a number of chance procedures based on the Chinese *I Ching* and applied by computer:

> How many and which of the thirty quotations were used as a source for each of the twenty mesostics was answered by IC (a program by Andrew Culver simulating the coin oracle of the *I Ching*). Which of the thirty quotations, together with the fourteen names (authors, book titles, graffiti) was to be used as the string upon which each mesostic was written was also determined by IC ...[12]

Cage's aleatoric procedures themselves become part of his meaning. He adopted them originally in order to suppress his own personal involvement in his texts, and in so doing, he succeeds as well in disrupting the conventions of reading— reading for meaning, reading from left to right on the page, reading for a personal "voice" constructed from the text. In so doing, Cage's text also strips the poetic line of syntactic pressure, renders it static rather than dynamic, and mutes the conventional sensitivities of line end and enjambment.

At the farthest extreme of fragmentation, is it possible for the line ends to cut across word boundaries? To isolate individual phonemes? That has been tried, too, with exceptional inventiveness by E.E. Cummings:

> l(a
>
> le
> af
> fa
>
> ll
>
> s)
> one
> l
>
> iness

Cummings' poetry ranges through an extraordinary number of verse forms, from perfectly regular sonnets to the most radical experiments in typography. In the mode characteristic of him here, he freely breaks the poetic "line" into

---

[12] Fleming and Duckworth, p. 122.

its component phonemes or graphemes: the effect is to release surprising discoveries among the accidents of the printed language, but at the same time calling into question the concept of the poetic line. The haiku-like statement of this poem:

> a leaf falls:
> loneliness—

seems neither fresh nor memorable. But as printed, Cummings detects such emblems of loneliness as the letter *l* standing by itself, the French definite article "le," the word "one," and the neologism "i-ness." The "af/fa" collocation may be related to the waver of the falling leaf. Language under the microscope yields many surprises. In such a poem, the effect of "line" is questionable: does the rhythm move forward, with a feeling of enjambment, as we wait to complete each word? Or do we regard the entire text as a construction, an arrangement of letters on a blank page (which still retains the convention of left-to-right reading)? The poem remains just barely pronounceable, but its interest is overwhelmingly in the typographic display.

Another famous Cummings poem is truly unpronounceable:

```
                                 r-p-o-p-h-e-s-s-a-g-r
              who
     a)s w(e loo)k
     upnowgath
              PPEGORHRASS
                                        eringint(o-
     aThe):l
           eA
              !p:
     S                                                   a
                           (r
     rIvInG                            .gRrEaPsPhOs)
                                             to
     rea(be)rran(com)gi(e)ngly
     ,grasshopper;
```

The point of such writing, which appears so bewildering at first sight, is simple, once the main point is deciphered. Cummings has forced language to enact the gradual coming into visual awareness of the startling blur, the moment just before, and the moment just when we come to identify it as a grasshopper; he also forces readers to look at printed language in a new way.

This is truly composition by typewriter (or typesetter). The effects depend on the visual conventions of print—the alphabet, punctuation, spacing, the habituated movement of the eye—and the result is scarcely a "poem" in the auditory sense. When poetry becomes unpronounceable and purely typographical, it moves in the direction of visual art and becomes *concrete poetry;* on the other hand, when it becomes pure vocal sound, unintelligible and virtually unnotatable, it moves in the direction of music and becomes *sound poetry*. Both of these types are discussed below.

Numbers: Metrical Presences in Free Verse

According to T.S. Eliot, "the ghost of some simple meter should lurk behind the arras in even the 'freest' verse; to advance menacingly as we doze, and withdraw as we rouse."[13] Eliot's comment points to another way of thinking about formal effects in free verse. It may be that metrical lines and fragments of lines appear and disappear in a passage that otherwise conforms to no set meter; or a passage may consist of metrical lines loosened up to the point of being unrecognizable, and then tightened again. Such effects allow the poet the freedom of free verse, while preserving the allusions to the poetic tradition found in meters and forms. The cadence of iambic pentameter is so familiar that it often supplies a base from which a poet may range and finally return.

When "The Love Song of J. Alfred Prufrock" appeared in 1915, it seemed outrageously modern, both in feeling and form; yet it is easy now to hear the iambic pentameters drift in and out of the texture (the lines marked with an asterisk):

> Let us go then, you and I,
> When the evening is spread out against the sky
> Like a patient etherised upon a table;   *
> Let us go, through certain half-deserted streets,   *
> The muttering retreats
> Of restless nights in one-night cheap hotels   *
> And sawdust restaurants with oyster-shells: *
> Streets that follow like a tedious argument
> Of insidious intent
> To lead you to an overwhelming question ...   *
>
> In the room the women come and go
> Talking of Michaelangelo.

This begins, as I hear it, with a firm trochaic tetrameter, and the second, which *could* be heard as iambic pentameter, is more likely to be heard as another four-beat accentual line. Line 3, however, asserts iambic pentameter more insistently. In all but one instance, the marked iambic pentameter lines—reinforced by ever-

---

[13] "Reflections on *Vers Libre*," in *To Criticize the Critic*, p. 187.

present but unpredictable rhyme—participate in a feeling of syntactic closure, as if the meter brings the wandering rhythms home to rest. The same is true of the poem as a whole, the last twenty lines being almost regular pentameters. But the appearances and disappearances of scannable pentameter lines are, like the rhymes, unpredictable. Elsewhere, the meter stretches to fourteeners, before contracting to the pentameter base:

> The yellow fog that rubs its back upon the window panes,
> The yellow smoke that rubs its muzzle on the window panes,
> Licked its tongue into the corners of the evening,
> Lingered upon the pools that stand in drains ...

One famous line, which scans as iambic hexameter, underscores the humour by seeming to lurch on too long:

> There will be time, there will be time
> To prepare a face to meet the faces that you meet

Such effects are clearly metrical, though they occur in a poem often said to be written in "free verse," that is, without meter. Charles Hartman aptly describes such writing not as *vers libre* but as *vers libéré*, not "free" verse but "freed up" verse.[14]

Some poems seem to hover on the brink of iambic pentameter while at the same time studiously avoiding it. An example is W.S. Merwin's "Odysseus":

> Always the setting forth was the same,
> Same sea, same dangers waiting for him
> As though he had got nowhere but older.
> Behind him on the receding shore
> The identical reproaches, and somewhere
> Out before him, the unravelling patience
> He was wedded to. There were the islands
> Each with its woman and twining welcome
> To be navigated, and one to call "home."

Such meter might seem at first syllabic, with a nine-syllable line: but this breaks down at line five. Or it might seem like an accentual four-beat line: but lines four and five don't quite fit. Yet throughout, the visual regularity and auditory presence of blank verse tease without becoming realised. The effect of such a metric is difficult to characterize: it is as though the poet holds out an ideal of order and refinement while at the same time rudely withholding it. One suspects

---

[14] P. 111.

that he wrote the lines in regular meter and deliberately roughed them up. But this example suggests, too, that in free verse where the presence of traditional pentameter lingers, the destabilizing evasions are as significant as the relaxations into it. An unmistakable iambic pentameter appearing in such a context would bring with it a sense of relaxation and finality.

As well as appearing and disappearing in whole lines, iambic pentameter can be disguised by being broken over the line endings. The following stanza by Ezra Pound is "free" only in its lineation; the iambic pentameter is otherwise quite regular (taking the marked pairs as single lines):

> | Tell her that sheds
> | Such treasure in the air,
>   Recking naught else but that her graces give
> | Life to the moment,
> | I would bid them live
>   As roses might, in magic amber laid,
>   Red overwrought with orange and all made
> | One substance and one colour
> | Braving time.

Sometimes a line will begin as iambic pentameter and continue with an added-on fragment, like these examples from Eliot's "Gerontion":

$$\acute{}\,(\breve{})\,\breve{}\,|\quad\breve{}\quad\acute{}\,|\,\breve{}\quad\acute{}\,|\,\breve{}\quad\acute{}\,|\,\breve{}\,\breve{}$$

History has many cunning passages, contrived corridors

$$\breve{}\quad\acute{}\,|\,\breve{}\,\breve{}\,\acute{}\,|\,\breve{}\quad\acute{}\,|\,\breve{}\quad\acute{}\,|\quad\acute{}\,(\breve{})$$

In memory only, reconsidered passion. Gives too soon

$$\breve{}\quad\acute{}\,|\,\breve{}\quad\acute{}\,|\,\breve{}\quad\acute{}\,|\,\breve{}\,\acute{}\quad|\,\breve{}\quad\acute{}$$

In fractured atoms. Gull against the wind, in the windy straits

Such lines resemble what Annie Finch has termed "embedded pentameters" in her analysis of Whitman's versification.[15] Finch in fact argues for a greater iambic pentameter presence in Whitman than most readers suspect, noting his frequent practice of beginning a poem with the familiar literary cadence, like "Song of Myself":

$$\breve{}\,\acute{}\,|\,\breve{}\,\acute{}\,|\quad\breve{}\,\breve{}\quad|\,\breve{}\quad\acute{}\quad|\,\breve{}\,\breve{}$$

I celebrate myself, and sing myself

---

[15] *The Ghost of Meter: Culture and Prosody in American Free Verse* (Ann Arbor: Univ. of Michigan Press, 1993), chapter 3. Finch also mounts a thematic argument based on her analysis.

Or so ending a poem, like "When I Heard the Learn'd Astronomer":

> Till rising and gliding out I wander'd off by myself,
> In the mystical moist night-air, and from time to time
>
> �‿   ´|�‿ ´|�‿ ´|�‿   `| ˿ ˊ
> Look'd up in perfect silence at the stars.

Elsewhere, Whitman uses "embedded pentameters," extending the basic pentameter into his characteristic long-breathed line:

> ˿   ´|˿   ´|˿   ´ |˿ ´ |˿ ˊ
> You distant, dim unknown—or young or old—countless,
>   unspecified, readers belov'd,
>
>   ˿   ´|˿ ´ |˿ ´ ˊ|
> We never met, and ne'er shall meet—and yet our souls embrace,
>
>   ˊ   ´ |˿ ˊ
>   long, close and long.
>
>
>   ˊ ˿| ˿ ´ | ˿ ´|˿ ´|˿   ´
>   Warble me now for joy of lilac-time, (returning in reminiscence,)
>
>   ˊ   ˿|˿ ´ |˿ ´ |˿ ´|˿   ˊ
>   Sort me O tongue and lips for Nature's sake, souvenirs of earliest
>   summer.

One might object that such "discoveries" can be arbitrary. If one goes looking for iambic pentameters—anywhere—one is sure to find them. The normal alternation of stressed and unstressed syllables in the English language generates them at random. Finch in fact discerns more pentameter in her examples than my ear will easily accept. She hears the above example this way:

>   ˿   ´|˿   ´|˿   ´ |˿ ´ |˿ ´ ‖ ´   ˿ |
>   You distant, dim unknown—or young or old—countless,
>   ˿   ´|˿` | ´ ˿ |˿ ´
>   unspecified, readers belov'd,

As with all metrical analysis, the analyst must employ great tact, recognize the many different ways a given line may be pronounced, and resist the temptation to erect interpretations on dogmatic scansions. Readers will choose for themselves whether to prefer my way of hearing this line (with only four stresses after the dash) or Finch's (as a second embedded pentameter). In free verse particularly, scansion tends to be suspicious, and critical analyses that rest on scansions of free verse are open to the charge of marking (and pronouncing) the verse in the way best suited to the critic's argument. Such scansions are wholly the products of the analyist's ear, with no corroborating support from a metrical frame. Poets are demonstrably *not* thinking in traditional metrical structures, and often seeking deliberately to avoid them; there is no question of expectancy or predictability, no "counterpoint" of verbal rhythm against a metrical paradigm.

But the principle remains, I think, that the conventions of verse expect rhythm to be meaningful, and poets often, whether consciously or unconsciously, return to the familiar traditional cadences, iambic pentameter principal among them. In each of these examples, the embedded pentameter coincides with a phrase boundary, and each occupies a strategic position in the overall structure of the poem. In such cases, scansion—used with considerable circumspection— may reveal meaningful rhythmic patterns in free verse.

Let us revisit Audre Lorde's "A Small Slaughter." The poem begins with a four-beat line that extends itself into something like iambic pentameters:

Day breaks without thanks or caution

past a night without satisfaction or pain.

My words are blind children I have armed

against the casual insolence of morning

without you/ I am scarred and marketed

like a streetcorner in Harlem/ a woman

whose face in the tiles/ your feet have not yet regarded

The poem closes by retracting to trimeter:

I am the stream/ past which you will never step

the woman you can not deal with

I am the mouth/ of your scorn.

Lorde's poem turns out to be closer to metricality than one may have originally suspected.

The following poem by Don McKay looks like very free verse indeed; yet a subtle iambic pentameter undertone persists, embedded in disrupting lineation but still audible despite efforts to disguise it:

Softball

grows along the fringe of industry and corn.
You come upon it out of thick
summer darkness, floodlights
focussing a neighbourhood or township: way to
fire, way to mix, way to hum.
Everything trim,
unlike life: Frost Fence, straight
basepaths of lime, warm-up jackets worn by
wives and girl friends in the bleachers
match the uniforms performing on the field.

Half-tons stare blindly from the sidelines.
Overhead
unnoticed nighthawks flash past the floodlights effortlessly
catching flies: way to
dip, pick, snag that sucker,
way to be.

Down here everyone is casual and tense,
tethered to a base.
Each has a motive, none
an alibi
The body is about to be discovered.

He peers in for the sign, perfect order
a diamond in the pitcher's mind.
Chance will be fate, all
will be out. Someone
will be called to arabesque or glide
                                    someone
muscular and shy

will become the momentary genius of the infield.

The opening line embeds an iambic pentameter prepositional phrase, with a disguising initial stress:

˘ ´ | ˘ ´ | ˘ ´ | ˘ ` | ˘   ´
grows along the fringe of industry and corn.

This rhythm is matched exactly (with a decorative internal rhyme) in the final line of the stanza:

˘ ´ | ˘ ´ | ˘ ´ | ˘   ` | ˘ ´
match the uniforms performing on the field.

This kind of scansion, admittedly, would not be acceptable in a metrical poem: the accented initial syllable would turn the entire line backward into a trochaic pulse. The claim made by this scansion, however, is that the familiar iambic pentameter cadence lingers within the otherwise free rhythms of this poem as a point of reference, at times a point of rest. The third stanza again uses a near pentameter to open, and a perfect pentameter for a feeling of closure:

´   ˘ | ´ ˘˘ | ˘ ´| ˘ ` | ˘   ´
Down here everyone is casual and tense,

˘ ´| ˘ ` | ˘  ´ | ˘  ` | ˘ ´ (˘)
The body is about to be discovered.

And the end of the poem again comes to rest on a noun phrase with the familiar cadence:

˘   ´ | ˘ ´| ˘ ´| ˘ ` | ˘ ˘ ´ (˘)
will become the momentary genius of the infield.

Elsewhere, pentameters emerge over the line breaks:

´   ˘ | ˘ ´| ˘   ´ | ˘ ´| ˘ ´
Each has a motive, none/ an alibi

Perhaps the most striking metrical effect in the poem mimes the swooping nighthawks, in a pentameter line stretched with extra slack syllables over enjambment and alighting on a slyly punning phrase:

˘   ´| ˘   ´ | ˘   ´ | ˘   ˘ ´ | ˘   ´ (˘   ˘ ˘)
unnoticed nighthawks flash past the floodlights effortlessly→
catching flies

McKay's poem also braces itself with syntactic parallelism (which is also disrupted by the lineation): "way to/ fire, way to mix, way to hum," "Chance will be fate, all/ will be out." But although it remains free verse, unpredictable from line to line and stanza to stanza, the iambic pentameter presence emerges at key points to provide structural support.

Iambic pentameter is not the only possible base for embedded meters or *vers libéré*. The symmetrical ballad stanza—or iambic tetrameter or four-beat accentual line—frequently appears, as in the very different examples from Ezra Pound's "Mauberley," below, or David Dabydeen's "Coolie Son (The Toilet Attendant Writes Home)," in which insistent but unpredictable rhyming combines with Caribbean dialect to create the voice of a homesick *emigré*. The contrast repays study. Metrically, Dabydeen's poem is a free handling of the fully end-stopped four-beat accentual line, present but not consistent in every line, creating a folk-like *vers libéré*:

> Taana boy, how do you do?
> How Shanti stay? And Sukhoo?
> Mosquito still a-bite all-you?
> Juncha dead true-true?
> Mala bruk-foot set?
> Food deh foh eat yet?
>
> Englan nice, snow an dem ting,
> A land dey say fit for a king,
> Iceapple plenty on de tree and bird a-sing—
> Is de beginning of what dey call 'The Spring.'
>
> And I eating enough for all-we
> And reading book bad-bad.
>
> But is what make Matam wife fall sick
> And Sonnel cow suck dry wid tick?
>
> Soon, I go turn lawya or dacta,
> But, just now, passage money run out
> So i tek lil wuk—
> I is a Deputy Sanitary Inspecta,
> Big-big office, boy! Tie roun me neck!
> Brand new uniform, one big bunch keys!
> If Ma can see me now how she go please ...

Even here, Dabydeen alights on a line of iambic pentameter for closure; but the four-beat line remains the norm through most of the poem, at times stretching, at times (for the metrical swerve, "So i tek lil wuk") contracting.

Pound's "Hugh Selwyn Mauberley," through much of the sequence, employs a loosely handled quatrain, usually but not consistently rhymed *xaxa*. Metrically, the base is a four-beat accentual line, a version of the common ballad quatrain, clearest in the second stanza here. But the contrast with David Dabydeen's example is striking: Dabydeen abandons the quatrain but preserves end-stopped lines, while Pound preserves the quatrain but departs from the four-beat measure freely, stretching or compressing, breaking from metricality into prose looseness, and gracefully draping syntax over the line lengths:

> Among the pickled fetuses and bottled bones,
> Engaged in perfecting the catalogue,
> I found the last scion of the
> Senatorial families of Strasbourg, Monsieur Verog.
>
> For two hours he talked of Gallifet;
> Of Dowson; of the Rhymer's Club;
> Told me how Johnson (Lionel) died
> By falling from a high stool in a pub ...
>
> But showed no trace of alcohol
> At the autopsy, privately performed—
> Tissue preserved—the pure mind
> Arose toward Newman as the whiskey warmed.
>
> Dowson found harlots cheaper than hotels;
> Headlam for uplift; Image impartially imbued
> With raptures for Bacchus, Terpsichore and the Church.
> So spoke the author of "The Dorian Mood."

Pound frequently writes a unique form of *vers libéré* in which the referent is not an English meter but the classical meters of Greek or Latin. In his letters, Pound recommended that aspiring young poets practice writing sapphic stanzas, to sharpen their ears for English quantity, and in a poem called "Apparuit" (see Chapter 2, pp. 68–69) he displays his own skill in this vein. There is evidence that Pound believed in the perceptibility of English quantities, but in general, his metric works with stress substituted for quantity. In a short poem called "The Return," he plays variations on the classical choriamb (´ ˇ ˇ ´) and adonic (´ ˇ ˇ ´ ˇ) within otherwise non-metrical lines:

> See they return; ah, see the tentative
>   Movements, and the slow feet,
>   The trouble in the pace and the uncertain
>   Wavering!
>
> See, they return, one, and by one
> With fear, as half-awakened;
> As if the snow should hesitate

And murmur in the wind,
      and half turn back;
These were the "Wing'd-with-Awe,"
    Inviolable.

Gods of the wingèd shoe!
With them the silver hounds,
      sniffing the trace of air!

Haie! Haie!
   These were the swift to harry;
These the keen-scented;
These were the souls of blood.

Slow on the leash,
      pallid the leash-men!

This poem begins indeed with "tentative movements" and spondaic "slow feet," but the rhythm gradually begins to coalesce into choriambs ("See, they return, one, and by one"), and crescendo to four metrically identical lines ("These were the 'Wing'd-with-Awe'" ... "Gods of the wingèd shoe" ...), and then trail off, ending with bare choriamb and adonic. The rhythm is free, but it retains a strong metrical feel with its many references to similar groupings of syllables.

Similar principles operate in the many lyrical passages of Pound's *Cantos*:

Floating, each on invisible raft,
On the high current, invisible fluid,
Bourne over the plain, recumbent,
The right arm cast back,
    the right wrist for a pillow,
The left hand like a calyx,
Thumb held against finger, the third,
The first fingers petal'd up, the hand as a lamp,
A calyx.
    From toe to head
The purple, blue-pale smoke, as of incense;
Wrapped each in burnous, smoke as the olibanum's,
Swift, as if joyous.
Wrapped, floating; and the blue-pale smoke of the incense
Swift to rise, then lazily in the wind
    as Aeolus over bean-field,
As hay in the sun, the olibanum, saffron,
As myrrh without styrax;
Each man on his cloth, as on raft, on
    The high invisible current ...

The adonic patterns (hallmark of the classical dactylic hexameter and sapphic stanza, and also a Poundian metrical fingerprint) echo through this passage, endowing the disjunctive phrases of Pound's lotos-eaters with repetitive langour: "invisible fluid," "wrist for a pillow," "hand like a calyx," "held against finger." Notice how the adonic phrase "smoke, as of incense" is stretched to "smoke as the olibanum's,/ Swift, as if joyous," with the adonic displaced to the shorter line. Pound rings variations on his base rhythm, and the lines rarely repeat the same pattern, but the passage feels strongly rhythmical throughout.

The varieties of verse in Pound's *Cantos* are many: they range from occasional metrical rhymed stanzas through various types of accentual and free verse to loose prose documents, and the juxtapositions of one kind of verbal rhythm with another become, in a fascinating way, a measure of decorum within the poem, indeed part of its meaning. Pound's methods—his use of quoted documents, his so-called "ideogrammic method"—have created the genre of the modernist documentary poem, imitated by many subsequent poets; but none, I think, has been able to capture the singular pulse of his free verse rhythms.[16]

Aside from metrical references, free verse can also call on rhyme as a structuring device. Free verse and rhyme are sometimes thought to be mutually exclusive, and many poets avoid rhyme for the same reason they avoid meter—because they want their work to seem "natural" and not "artificial." Yet, as the examples from Dabydeen and Pound's "Mauberley" demonstrate, rhyme is available to free verse poets, and many use it with great effectiveness, sometimes conspicuously and sometimes subtly, sometimes sporadically and sometimes in more or less regular patterns. In every case, it serves to raise awareness of the sensitive line ends, and it may contribute powerfully to a feeling of closure.

F.T. Prince's "Soldiers Bathing" is composed in open couplets, in verse that begins with an iambic pentameter base but departs from it freely (a variety of *vers libéré*):

> He plays with death and animality;
> And reading in the shadows of his pallid flesh, I see
> The idea of Michaelangelo's cartoon
> Of soldiers bathing, breaking off before they were half done
> At some sortie of the enemy, an episode
> Of the Pisan wars with Florence. I remember how he showed
> Their muscular limbs that clamber from the water,
> And heads that turn across the shoulder, eager for the slaughter,
> Forgetful of their bodies that are bare,
> And hot to buckle on and use the weapons lying there.

---

[16] See my article "The Metrical Contract of *The Cantos*," *Journal of Modern Literature* 15 (1988), 55–72; as well as James A. Powell, "The Light of Vers Libre," *Paideuma* 8 (1979), 3–34; and Ellen Keck Stauder, "Crystal Waves Weaving Together: Visual Notation and the Phrasal Music of the Rock-Drill Cantos," *Paideuma* 26 (1997), 93–110.

In Sylvia Plath's "Lady Lazarus," sporadic rhyme builds a crescendo of intensity toward the ending:

> I am your opus,
> I am your valuable,
> The pure gold baby
>
> That melts to a shriek.
> I turn and burn.
> Do not think I underestimate your great concern.
>
> Ash, ash—
> You poke and stir.
> Flesh, bone, there is nothing there—
>
> A cake of soap,
> A wedding ring,
> A gold filling.
>
> Herr God, Herr Lucifer
> Beware
> Beware.
>
> Out of the ash
> I rise with my red hair
> And I eat men like air.

The feeling of closure here is underlined by the coincidence of rhyme with a re-asserted metrical base: the last stanzas in fact constitute a perfect but concealed heroic couplet, with a rhyming iambic trimeter line to close:

> Herr God, Herr Lucifer/ Beware/ Beware.
> Out of the ash/ I rise with my red hair
> And I eat men like air.

Plath's ragged lineation, however, disrupts the conventionality, the sense of neatness and control—not to mention the historical associations—of the heroic couplet, which would be wholly out of place here, and releases the internal pauses, with their suggestions of hesitation and emphasis.

Robert Lowell organizes the six-line stanzas of "Skunk Hour" with rhyme (sometimes exact, sometimes faint), three paired lines in each stanza but with varying rhyme schemes from one stanza to another.

> A car radio bleats,
> "Love, O careless Love ..." I hear

my ill-spirit sob in each blood cell,
as if my hand were at its throat ...
I myself am hell;
nobody's here—

only skunks, that search
in the moonlight for a bite to eat.
They march on their soles up Main Street:
white stripes, moonstruck eyes' red fire
under the chalk-dry and spar spire
of the Trinitarian Church.

I stand on top
of our back steps and breathe the rich air—
a mother skunk with her column of kittens swills the garbage pail.
She jabs her wedge-head in a cup
of sour cream, drops her ostrich tail,
and will not scare.

Rhyme confers a degree of control on the free-verse lines, which vary widely in length and refuse to fall into any metrical pattern, and brings each stanza to firm closure.

Figures: Syntactic Patterning in Free Verse

As we have already noticed, a major structuring element in non-metrical verse is syntax: meter removed, syntax remains. This kind of organization is different from the auditory patterning of stressed and slack syllables, or the typographical set-up of lines and stanzas: it is semantic. Inherently it is more closely bound up with the meaning of the lines than abstract meter or stanza. Of course, syntactic organization, as I have tried to emphasize, also plays an important role in metered verse, from the forceful enjambments of Milton to the tightly coiled wit of Pope's couplets to the polished symmetries of countless lyric stanzas. But in some kinds of free verse, syntactic patterning gains even greater structural prominence.

Syntactic prosody has been present to the English ear for as long as there have been translations of the Hebrew Bible, because the prosody of Old Testament poetry is founded on syntactic parallelism. Here is the opening of Psalm 22, in the King James version:

(1) My God, my God, why hast thou forsaken me?
         why art thou so far from helping me, and from the words of
         my roaring?
(2) O my God, I cry in the daytime, but thou hearest not;
         and in the night season, and am not silent.

(3) But thou art holy,
      O thou that inhabitest the praises of Israel.
(4) Our fathers trusted in thee:
      they trusted, and thou didst deliver them.
(5) They cried unto thee, and were delivered;
      they trusted in thee, and were not confounded.
(6) But I am a worm, and no man;
      a reproach of men, and despised of the people.
(7) All they that see me laugh me to scorn:
      they shoot out the lip, they shake the head, saying,
(8) He trusted on the Lord that he would deliver him:
      let him deliver him, seeing that he delighted in him.

This profound expression of despair employs the same twofold patterning found in other psalms of comfort or exultation: two closely related statements with a central caesura, in an antiphonal or "question-and-answer" pattern. Some scholars see four types of relational patterns in such verse: (1) synonymous, in which the answering statement rewords the meaning of the first; (2) parallel, in which synonymous meanings are parallel in syntax; (3) antithetical, in which contrasted meanings are parallel in syntax; and (4) climactic, in which the second statement is the completion or culmination of the first. In these few lines, we can identify the first as synonymous, the second as antithetical, the third as synonymous, the fourth as climactic, the fifth as parallel. The first half of verse six includes a subsidiary antithesis, the answering half a subsidiary parallelism; verse seven uses a transitional word building into the next. Further analysis of the psalms would reveal great suppleness and variety in these basic patterns.

It is hardly surprising that such assertive rhythms, prevalent for so many centuries in English-speaking cultures, have had an immeasurable influence on writing, in both prose and poetry. And when Walt Whitman staked his career on a new kind of "poetry," a kind that was neither prosaic nor yet recognizable as verse, it is not surprising that its principal model was the Hebrew psalms.

      I celebrate myself, and sing myself,
      And what I assume, you shall assume,
      For every atom belonging to me as good belongs to you.

      I loafe and invite my soul.
      I lean and loafe at my ease observing a spear of summer grass ...

      Creeds and schools in abeyance,
      Retiring back awhile sufficed at what they are, but never forgotten,
      I harbor for good or bad, I permit to speak at every hazard,
      Nature without check with original energy.

Though not as obviously in statement-response form as the passage from the psalms, this typical passage yields to the same kind of analysis: three lines of antithesis, two lines parallel to each other, followed by a sequence of more complex antithetical structures.

Whitman is famous, of course, for his extended catalogues, and one does not look far in his work for cumulative (sometimes tedious) anaphora:

> And I know that the hand of God is the promise of my own,
> And I know that the spirit of God is the brother of my own,
> And that all the men ever born are also my brothers, and the women
>   my sisters and lovers,
> And that a kelson of the creation is love,
> And limitless are leaves stiff or drooping in the fields,
> And brown ants in the little wells beneath them,
> And mossy scabs of the worm fence, heap'd stones, elder, mullein
>   and pokeweed.

Epistrophe, less frequent, is more subtle:

> There was never any more inception than there is now,
> Nor any more youth or age than there is now,
> And will never be any more perfection than there is now,
> Nor any more heaven or hell than there is now.
> Urge and urge and urge,
> Always the procreant urge of the world.

But many passages reveal more various and intricate techniques of patterning:

> When lilacs last in the dooryard bloom'd,
> And the great star early droop'd in the western sky in the night,
> I mourn'd, and yet shall mourn with ever-returning spring.

> Ever-returning spring, trinity sure to me you bring,
> Lilac blooming perennial and drooping star in the west,
> And thought of him I love.

Here, the first two lines are parallel, while the third is poised on antithesis of past and future time. The transitional repeated phrase "ever-returning spring" (anadiplosis) links the first stanza to the next, a line marked by internal rhyme ("spring"/"bring") that hints at parallelism between "spring" and "trinity." The next line sets "blooming" against the antithetical "drooping" in a significant paradox (it seems more plausible to consider flowers as transient and stars permanent), and culminates in the assertion of elegiac meditation. I should note that this emphasis on syntactic patterning does not rule out other approaches, like the analysis of "embedded meters" or, as here, a play of four-beat against predominantly three-beat phrases. But here, syntactic patterning is clearly the most conspicuous feature.

Another passage shows Whitman's rarely employed skill in shaping shorter lines:

> Shine! shine! shine!
> Pour down your warmth, great sun!
> While we bask, we two together.
>
> Two together!
> Winds blow south, or winds blow north,
> Day come white, or night come black,
> Home, or rivers and mountains from home,
> Singing all time, minding all time,
> While we two keep together.

Taken out of context from the more typically Whitmanic longer lines of "Out of the Cradle Endlessly Rocking," this inset lyric loses the advantage of contrast. But it is a good illustration of lyric free verse that gains richness largely through free patterning. The two stanzas are allied by the repeated "two together" (anadiplosis and epistrophe). The parallel commands in the opening lines ("Shine ...," "Pour down ...") open out in the second stanza into hortatory phrases that play variations on parallel relationships: "Winds blow south, or winds blow north" (anaphora plus antithesis, with an allusion to Ecclesiastes); "Day come white, or night come black" (antithesis with internal rhyme, suggesting an auditory chiasmus); "Home, or rivers and mountains from home" (epanalepsis, with surprisingly displaced caesura); "Singing all time, minding all time" (parallelism plus epistrophe). Such formal inventiveness foreshadows many later developments in free verse technique.

The opening of Pound's "The River Merchant's Wife: A Letter" displays a skill in varying syntactic units, chiefly the bare independent clause and the participial phrase:

> While my hair was still cut straight across my forehead
> I played about the front gate, pulling flowers.
> You came by on bamboo stilts, playing horse,
> You walked about my seat, playing with blue plums.
> And we went on living in the village of Chokan:
> Two small people, without dislike or suspicion.
>
> At fourteen I married My Lord you.
> I never laughed, being bashful.
> Lowering my head, I looked at the wall.
> Called to, a thousand times, I never looked back.

The four parallel participial phrases in the first stanza, which suggest an ongoing process, accumulate, the fourth subtly differentiated from the first three. In the second, the pattern is first repeated ("being bashful"), then turned around, participle coming first, then altered to past participle. Meanwhile, as the poem continues, the independent clauses progress, diminuendo, from the confident opening stanzas, "At fourteen I married," to "At fifteen I stopped scowling ... At sixteen you departed," until two appear in a single line: "They hurt me. I grow older." This short, plangent line sets up a distinctive and complex conditional syntax, the plea that ends the poem. This syntactic drama is not the whole of the prosodic structure of Pound's poem, but it is a force that helps bind it together.

Hilda Doolittle's famous imagist exemplum "Oread" shows how syntactic parallelism can be enriched with rhyme and other sound effects, creating a unique free-form miniature:

> Whirl up, sea—
> Whirl your pointed pines,
> splash your great pines
> on our rocks,
> hurl your green over us,
> cover us with your pools of fir.

The opening anaphora ("Whirl ... Whirl ...") is followed by epistrophe ("pines ... pines"), with the phrase "great pines" echoed by alliteration in "green ... pools;" the initial "whirl," repeated, becomes the rhyming parallel "hurl," which then culminates in the final assonantal word "fir;" the phrase "over us" turns round the line end to become, with rhyme, "cover us." These effects all contribute to a sense of formal inevitability in a poem formally free and unlike any other.

Verse satire in the mode of Dryden and Pope is associated both with the constraints of the heroic couplet and with the power of antithetical rhetoric. F.R. Scott, writing about a specific political leader, shows he can deploy syntactic patterning for both metrical solidity and satirical point even in free verse, in a political portrait that, like those of Dryden and Pope, remains historically specific[17] and yet transcends the particulars of its historical time and place:

> He blunted us.
>
> We had no shape
> Because he never took sides,

---

[17] The object of Scott's satire is William Lyon MacKenzie King, prime minister of Canada from 1921 to 1948 (with two interruptions).

And no sides
Because he never allowed them to take shape.

He skilfully avoided what was wrong
Without saying what was right,
And never let his on the one hand
Know what his on the other hand was doing ...

He seemed to be in the centre
Because we had no centre,
No vision
To pierce the smoke-screen of his politics.

Truly he will be remembered
Wherever men honour ingenuity,
Ambiguity, inactivity, and political longevity.

Let us raise up a temple
To mediocrity,
Do nothing by halves
Which can be done by quarters.

The rhetorical schemes wittily echo the commonplaces of political rhetoric, while at the same time structuring the free stanzas. Besides simple antithesis, Scott deploys elaborate antimetabole (shape/sides, sides/shape); anthimeria, substituting prepositional phrase for noun ("his on the one hand"); epistrophe ("He seemed to be in the centre/ Because we had no centre"); and climax—or bathos ("Wherever men honour ingenuity,/ Ambiguity, inactivity, and political longevity," "Let us raise up a temple/ To mediocrity"). While Scott's poem relies heavily on figures of parallelism, it draws on many of the other rhetorical schemes to energize its language.

Anne Wilkinson's "Lens," too, relies heavily on syntactic parallelism, but on more intricate patterning devices as well, as its compressed language extends a highly metaphorical equation between the poet's eye and the lens of a camera. The lines range freely from two or three to four accents. Here is the opening:

The poet's daily chore
Is my long duty;
To keep and cherish my good lens
For love and war
And wasps about the lilies
And mutiny within.

The opening antithesis between "daily" and "long" turns a single "chore" into constant "duty," while the common love-versus-war contrast generates the curiously metonymic external and outwardly aggressive "wasps" plus the inward self-directed "mutiny." One begins to notice the sporadic rhyming ("chore"/ "war") as well as several threads of assonance and alliteration.

> My woman's eye is weak
> And veiled with milk;
> My working eye is muscled
> With a curious tension,
> Stretched and open
> As the eyes of children;
> Trusting in its vision
> Even should it see
> The holy holy spirit gambol
> Counterheadwise
> Lithe and warm as any animal.

The antithesis between the "woman's eye" ("veiled with milk," metonymy for femaleness) and the "working eye" suggests that the poet achieves a superhuman state in the act of creation, but a state comparable to the innocent "vision" (in both the common and the mystical senses) of children. The oppositions are sustained in the contrast between "trusting" and gamboling (with a pun on "gambling"), and between "spirit" and "animal" (itself derived from *anima*, Latin for spirit, a *double entendre* that collapses the opposition).

> My woman's iris circles
> A blind pupil;
> The poet's eye is crystal,
> Polished to accept the negative,
> The contradictions in a proof
> And the accidental
> Candour of the shadows ...

Again, the contrast between the mere human eye and the poet's is sustained by syntactic antithesis and a climactic series of *double entendres*: the "blind pupil" is both the physical eye and synecdoche for the blind self; "negative" and "proof" carry both their common and their photographic meanings; "candour" is both "frankness" and "whiteness" (from the Latin *candor*) as in the reversed image of the photographic negative. The meditation continues in this way, the patterned syntax a bracing sinew running through the taut lines of Wilkinson's poem.

Still, the rhetoric of parallelism, antithesis, and climax is somewhat restrictive, even though it accounts for the patterning of a surprisingly large number of poems. Other rhetorical schemes enter into syntactic prosody, and it is sometimes hard to say where strictly prosodic concerns merge into rhetorical ones.

William Carlos Williams' poem from *Spring and All* beginning "The rose is obsolete" is a *tour de force* of syntactic dislocation:

> The rose is obsolete
> but each petal ends in
> an edge, the double facet
> cementing the grooved
> columns of air—The edge
> cuts without cutting
> meets—nothing—renews
> itself in metal or porcelain
>
> whither? It ends—
>
> But if it ends
> the start is begun
> so that to engage roses
> becomes a geometry
> Sharper, neater, more cutting
> figured in majolica
> the broken plate
> glazed with a rose
>
> Somewhere the sense
> makes copper roses
> steel roses
>
> The rose carried weight of love
> but love is at an end—of roses
> It is at the edge of the
> petal that love waits
>
> Crisp, worked to defeat
> laboredness—fragile
> plucked, moist, half-raised
> cold, precise, touching
>
> What
>
> The place between the petal's
> edge and the
>
> From the petal's edge a line starts
> that being of steel

> infinitely fine, infinitely
> rigid penetrates
> the Milky Way
> without contact—lifting
> from it—neither hanging
> nor pushing—
>
> The fragility of the flower
> unbruised
> penetrates space

The lines carry generally two or three accents, dropping to a minimum of one ("What") and rising to a maximum of four, in the line that initiates the final summary ("From the petal's edge a line starts"). But the poem's vitality lies in the many surprises of word-play and syntax-play. The entire poem hangs by a rejection of poetic cliché, immediately qualified: "The rose is obsolete/ but ..." In the ensuing meditation, the rose becomes not the hackneyed symbol of love poetry but a natural object whose thingness defines itself in space, like a piece of sculpture. In the assonantal sequence "obsolete ... each ... ends ... edge ... air"—what Alexander Pope called "open vowels"—the vowel sound intersects silence with a glottal pop, just as the petal's edge cuts itself into space. It "cuts without cutting" (paradox, polyptoton); "meets—nothing—renews" (further paradox): "whither?" asks the poet, and we suspect a pun on "wither," giving one reason why "It ends—." And the syntax turns back upon itself (anacoluthon) with new promise: "But if it ends/ the start is begun ..." The syntax rushes forward without connective (asyndeton), culminating in epistrophe:

> so that to engage roses
> becomes a geometry
> Sharper, neater, more cutting
> figured in majolica
> the broken plate
> glazed with a rose
>
> Somewhere the sense
> makes copper roses
> steel roses

Here, midway in the poem, Williams introduces the conventional symbolic referent of roses; but "The rose carried weight of love" is an ambiguous phrase: is "carried" a verb? or is it part of an unhyphenated compound, "rose-carried"? In either case, the syntax veers in another direction (anacoluthon again) to declare "but love is at an end ... [gasp of despair] ... of roses," and we return to the contemplation of edges, boundaries of intersection, objects in relationship:

> It is at the edge of the
> petal that love waits

And "waits" echoes the "rose carried weight" from a few lines before. After another burst of disconnected phrases, the poem is reduced to two unfinished statements (aposiopesis), the first an expression of questioning in general, the second a dramatic syntactic mimesis of the petal's encounter with empty space:

> What

> The place between the petal's
> edge and the

At this point, the poem recovers its poise for a final summary, an extended series of finite statements of paradox, expanding from the original "cuts without cutting" to a cosmic plane:

> The fragility of the flower
> unbruised
> penetrates space

The prosodic life of a poem like this resides in the inventiveness of its syntax, a force that in this case goes beyond the usual formal patterning of parallelism, antithesis, and climax.

The Margins of Genre

Shaped Poetry, Concrete Poetry, Sound Poetry

All poetry in one way or another spotlights the physical properties of the language medium, whether the idealized rhythm and the accidents of rhyme and word sounds that constitute traditional metrical prosody, or, as the history of free verse demonstrates, the arbitrary visual and typographic signs that constitute the printed language. At the outer extremes, certain types of poetry merge from verbal into visual art, or from verbal art into music. These extreme types have always been minor traditions within the history of poetry, and Barbara Herrnstein Smith has wisely warned against the dangers of expecting extreme, or marginal, or hybrid forms to tell us much about the character of any particular genre.[18]

---

[18] See *On the Margins of Discourse: The Relation of Literature to Language* (Chicago: Univ. of Chicago Press, 1978).

All of these types seem to have stronger traditions in languages other than English. Yet English versions exist, and they reward critical attention.

The oldest of these, the shaped poem, has a history that extends to classical antiquity, a form not unrelated to the practice of calligraphy in the non-alphabetic, pre-print cultures of Asia. There are Greek shaped poems dating probably from about the third century B.C., and the first English imitation of them, called "A Pair of Wings," was written in the early sixteenth century by Stephen Hawes, who had seen similar experiments in France.[19] But the most familiar examples by far are by George Herbert, in "The Altar" and "Easter Wings." Here is the first of the two stanzas of the latter:

> Lord, who createdst man in wealth and store,
> Though foolishly he lost the same,
> Decaying more and more,
> Till he became
> Most poor:
> With thee
> O let me rise
> As larks, harmoniously,
> And sing this day thy victories:
> Then shall the fall further the flight in me.

Most shaped poems favour simple geometrical outlines: wings, diamonds, hour-glasses, eggs, and the like. Aside from the obvious visual impact of such writing, two other points need to be observed. First, the lines are still metrical, though controlled to create the visual shape. Secondly, the meter clearly reflects the meaning, here dwindling from a state of "wealth and store," becoming "most poor," until taking further flight.

It is debatable whether Herbert intended high seriousness or amusement or a mixture of both in these poems, but there is no doubt that Herbert's reputation suffered at the hands of sober Enlightenment critics of the next century because of this sort of trifling. In this century, however, interest in shaped poems has revived. While most of these poems are untypical within a poet's work as a whole, a few poets have attempted larger collections: The Polish-born French writer Guillaume Apollinaire produced a large number of hand-written "calligrammes," and more recently the American poets May Swenson and John Hollander have produced collections of shaped poems.

Dylan Thomas' "Vision and Prayer" revisits the themes of George Herbert using a syllabic meter, increasing or decreasing one syllable per line:

---

[19] See R.T. Davies, ed., *Medieval English Lyrics: A Critical Anthology*, poem 152 (London: Faber, 1963).

Who
Are you
Who is born
In the next room
So loud to my own
That I can hear the womb
Opening and the dark run
Over the ghost and the dropped son
Behind the wall thin as a wren's bone?
In the birth bloody room unknown
To the burn and turn of time
And the heart print of man
Bows no baptism
But dark alone
Blessing on
The wild
Child

I
Must lie
Still as stone
By the wren bone
Wall hearing the moan
Of the mother hidden
And the shadowed head of pain
Casting to-morrow like a thorn
And the midwives of miracle sing
Until the turbulent new born
Burns me his name and his flame
And the winged wall is torn
By his torrid crown
And the dark thrown
From his loin
To bright
light

E.E. Cummings' elaborate typographic play turns to a serious subject in the
following, an elegy written on the death of a friend, the critic Paul Rosenfeld:

o

the round
little man we
loved so isn't

no!w

a gay of a
brave and
a true of a

who have

r
olle
d i

nt

o
n
o

w(he)re

Study of the typographic effects here reveals expressions of shock ("no!," "o no"—dropping rapidly down the page), of negation ("nt"), of possible hope for continued existence (the parenthetical "he" at the end). But the poem's status as a shaped poem is not likely to reveal itself until the reader turns the page upon its side.

The distinction between a "shaped poem" and a "visual" or "concrete" poem is not always obvious, and the terminology is not consistent in critical usage.[20] Both types concentrate on the physical material of language. But there is no question that the shaped poems presented here need to be read like any other poem. A visual poem, on the other hand, is "an object to be perceived rather than read."[21] Demands of reading remain, since the material is (most often) printed language, but reading is secondary to the total visual effect. Most shaped poems are reproduceable, like texts, but certain kinds are one-of-a-kind objects, like paintings. In either case, the page asks to be looked at like a picture:

---

[20] The entry in Alex Preminger's *Princeton Encyclopedia of Poetry and Poetics* is under "pattern poetry."

[21] Mary Ellen Solt, *Concrete Poetry: A World View* (Bloomington: Indiana Univ. Press, 1969), p. 7.

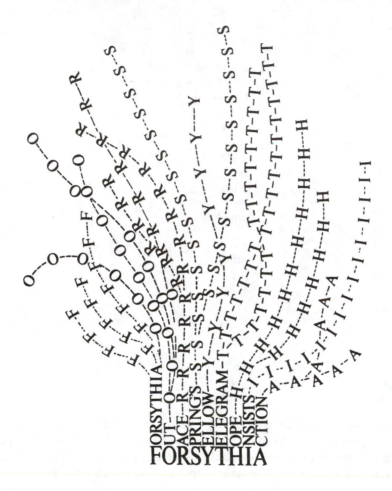

Mary Ellen Solt's "Forsythia" is created from the letters that form the title, plus their equivalents in Morse code. This kind of work, which seems a radical extension of the shaped poem tradition, was practiced early in this century, mainly by poets in languages other than English.[22] It roughly coincides with the practice of painters (like Picasso or Andy Warhol) who include words or lettering in their paintings. Interest revived in visual poetry during the 1950s and 1960s; there is now a substantial body of this work in English which varies widely in appearance. Some depend on particular kinds of typography. Some disperse legible words across the page, others simply letters. There are recognized subgenres: the "serial poem" is a series of visual poems manipulating the material in different ways. Here are just two sections of Emmett Williams' *"Sweethearts"*:

---

[22] See Willard Bohn, *The Aesthetics of Visual Poetry 1914–1928* (Chicago: Univ. of Chicago Press, 1986).

The entire sequence is made up of the eleven letters in the key word, seven different letters in all. According to the author, "The position of each letter on the page is determined by its place in the word *sweethearts*. [N]o single poem can be more than 11 letters wide or 11 letters deep."[23] This remarkable construction is actually an animator's flip-book, read by flipping the pages from back to front "fast enough to achieve a primitive cinematic effect."

Another subgenre, the "process poem," is a text, like John Cage's mesostics (see above), created by applying certain procedures to a set of words or a preexisting text. The "semiotic poem" is a visual poem made up purely of printed signs, not even words—like "Estrangement," by Václav Havel:[24]

---

[23] Mary Ellen Solt, p. 51.

[24] In Havel's native Czech, *já* is the first person pronoun, "I."

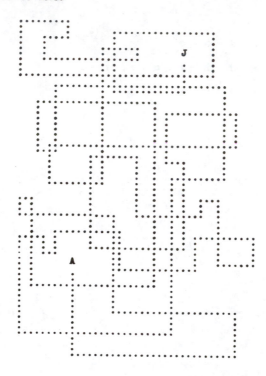

The reading process could hardly be further minimized. Some commentators distinguish concrete poems as either "clean" or "dirty"—the clean using only printed words or letters, the dirty introducing pictorial or collage elements.

If the visual poem is intended to be seen like a painting, "the sound poem is composed to be listened to like music."[25] Such poems may be printed, but like a musical score, the work does not truly exist until it is realized in performance. Sound poetry thus hovers at the intersection of poetry, music, and theater. Like visual poetry, sound poetry emerged early in the twentieth century with certain performance pieces by the Italian futurist F.T. Marinetti, who celebrated the advances of modern technology; and it revived after 1945. Here is part of Earle Birney's "trawna tuh bellvul by knayjin psifik," a *jeu d'esprit* that combines train sounds with a mid-continental slur:

> Awwwwww *bord*! ... Aw bord .... Bore .... *Bord*!

> Uhm hunhun Uhm Ay du dun   *Day* duh dun
> *day* duh duh *day* duh duh
> WACKITY duh duh WACKITY CLAG CLANG duh duh
> WANGDITTY KLONG

---

[25] Mary Ellen Solt, p. 7.

duh DUB de dub deDUB de dub de DRUB de DRUB
de WANGITY WACKLEDEE GELACK GELACK
DUB de dub de DUB de dub de didee
Dub de Didee   Dub de Didee de didee de dee
past the Guild and blast the mills
and whatta lotta whatta lotta lotta autos lotta autos
o good grayshun land of goshen autos waitin
autos banded by the station for the Go train
on we rush   skirting the bluffs   swirling the roughs
starling the puffs   the smelling the luffs
the luff the lufflee flowers the weeds the flowers ...

Such a text clearly benefits from an expert performance. Like visual poetry, sound poetry has emerged during the same period when composers have taken interest in musicalizing verbal texts: Arnold Schoenberg's *Sprechstimme*, a sort of half speech, half singing to indefinite pitches is a manifestation of this interest. Ernst Toch's witty *Geographical Fugue* is a spoken text for four-part choir that mimics the procedures of musical fugue. Cathy Berberian's *Stripsody* is a collage of phrases and images clipped from comic strips, performed by solo voice. R. Murray Schafer's *Hear Me Out* is a dramatic text for four solo voices constructed from clichés of common speech. Some poets (Robert Bringhurst is one) have written texts to be delivered by multiple voices simultaneously. Like concrete poems, sound poems can be distinguished as "clean" or "dirty," depending on whether they confine themselves to ordinary words, or incorporate other sound effects as well. In all of these cases, the question where poetry ceases and another genre begins cannot be stated with certainty.

The Prose Poem

If lines are the master convention of free verse, the ultimate oxymoron is the "prose poem," a species of writing in prose intended to be read as a "poem." As with free verse, intention is a key concept, prose poetry being highly self-conscious; but of course an author's intention is always problematic, and the "prose poem" is not susceptible to precise definition. This hybrid genre originated in France, where the constraints of French metrics, particularly the rules governing the French alexandrine, coupled with a lack of alternative systems, made the prose poem (like *vers libre*) seem a welcome release, notably in the work of Baudelaire and Rimbaud. In English, the prose poem appears to be simply another available kind of poem imported from abroad, welcome perhaps because of the scarcity of short prose genres (which include anecdote and aphorism). It was not widely practiced in the early twentieth century, though T.S. Eliot with his broad influence helped legitimize it with his single example "Hysteria." Amy Lowell developed a type called "polyphonic prose," incorporating rhyme and other sonic effects, but she had few imitators. The prose poem appeared more often in less established writers like Gertrude Stein, in her enigmatic *Tender Buttons* (if prose poems they are), or William Carlos Williams' *Kora in Hell*.

As most of these examples suggest, the prose poem is often obscure, even impenetrable. Here is a sample from Gertrude Stein, the entire text of a piece called "A Box":

> Out of kindness comes redness and out of rudeness comes rapid same question, out of an eye comes research, out of selection comes painful cattle. So then the order is that a white way of being round is something suggesting a pin and is it disappointing, it is not, it is so rudimentary to be analysed and see a fine substance strangely, it is so earnest to have a green point not to red but to point again.

In this particular example, I can make certain observations: the modulation from "redness" to "rudeness" to "rudimentary," for example, or the covert puns on "pin" and "disappointing" that lead to "green point" and "to point again," or "out of an eye [I] comes research." But I cannot say what it "means." It is not surprising that theories about the prose poem as a genre tend to be phrased in psychological terms, and the prose poem has been favoured by writers influenced by psychologically oriented movements like surrealism.

The few critics in English to have theorized the prose poem have, like early defenders of *vers libre*, emphasized the genre's liberation from formal constraints. According to Michael Benedikt, "The attention to the unconscious, and to its particular logic, unfettered by the relatively formalistic interruptions of the line break, remains the most immediately apparent property of the prose poem."[26] One may not immediately think of the free verse line break as a "formalistic interruption," but this chapter has shown otherwise. The printed format of the poems, the insistence on the meaning of line ends, the aura of "poem," still needs to be questioned.

This ideal of maximum spontaneity, pure improvisation—whether real or feigned—seems to imply a direct presentation of lyric subjectivity in an intense, autonomous text; yet the prose itself, the medium of the novel and of expository non-fiction, subverts this effort. This is the direction Jonathan Monroe pursues in *A Poverty of Objects*: the prose poem rejects poetry's "dream of itself as a pure *other* set apart in sublime isolation;" instead, "because it gestures toward opening up literature to prosaic speech, themes, and subject matter previously considered unworthy of aesthetic attention, the prose poem serves to legitimate and, at the same time, undermine literary culture." The genre, Monroe speculates,

---

[26] Benedikt, ed., *The Prose Poem: An International Anthology* (New York: Dell, 1976), p. 48.

perhaps appears at historical moments "when the lyric and the lyrical self seem most sublimely autonomous, detached, set apart from reality."[27]

This paradoxical genre is flagrantly transgressive. The relation of free verse to prose poem is one of complementary opposition: if one function of free verse is to undo and make visible the conventions of verse, preserving only the lineation, so one function, at least, of the prose poem is to undo and make visible the conventions of prose, preserving only the justified margins. The conventions of prose, at least as they are found in ordinary narrative or expository prose, uphold ideals of transparency, conciseness, and linearity. But the most characteristic poems present "prose" which is not transparent but opaque—non-sequential, non-rational, non-referential. If the traditional categories of prose composition are narrative, description, exposition, and argumentation, then the prose poem typically avoids or subverts those categories. For this reason, I would categorize as prose poems the Stein example above, or the following piece by Rosemarie Waldrop—but not, say, the brief interchapters of Ernest Hemingway's *In Our Time*, which are purely narrative or descriptive:

> Although you are thin you always seemed to be in front of my eyes, putting back in the body the roads my thoughts might have taken. As if forward and backward meant no more than right and left, and the earth could just as easily reverse its spin. So that we made each other the present of a stage where time would not pass, and only space would age, encompassing all 200,000 dramatic situations, but over the rest of the proceedings, the increase of entropy and unemployment. Meanwhile we juggled details of our feelings into an exaggeration which took the place of explanation, and consequences remained in the kind of repose that, like a dancer's, always holds the leap toward inside turning out.

Like most prose poems, this reads far more readily than the Stein example: it presents an account of a very novelistic subject, an intimate relationship. Yet besides alluding to a well-known poem (Frost's "The Road Not Taken"), the language subverts the rationality of ordinary prose: why, one asks, does being "thin" contrast with seeming "to be in front of my eyes"? How does "so that" follow from the preceding statement? Given that time "would not pass," does it follow that "only space would age"? The narrating voice may begin simply enough—"Meanwhile we juggled details of our feelings"—but the continuation bewilders, and the final simile is impossible to visualize. This mimics the transparent prose of realistic narrative, but could never be mistaken for it.

Still, there is a growing body of short prose compositions without definite genre, writings that could just as easily be called "postcard stories" as "prose

---

[27] Jonathan Monroe, *A Poverty of Objects: The Prose Poem and the Politics of Genre* (Ithaca: Cornell Univ. Press, 1987), pp. 19–22, 28.

poems." As with categories of free verse, types of short prose writings are without limit and escape definition.

Free verse and prose poetry together, then, wholly dependent as they are on print, mark the farthest remove of poetry from any pretension to speech or song towards the direction of pure writing. Ultimately, when the boundary separating poetry and prose is erased, writers are left to compose in a nameless genre, or to borrow Samuel Beckett's phrase, texts for nothing.

Appendix 1

The Terminology of Rhyming

These terms occur frequently in critical writing, but not with notable consistency. It may be tempting, merely by listing the terms here, to get overly scrupulous about fine distinctions between, say, "identical" and "rich" rhyme, or "broken" as opposed to "linked" rhyme—distinctions that rarely find practical sanction in critical usage. Nonetheless, it may be useful to consider the various terms that do appear in criticism. Even more, it may be useful to bring together a table of rhyme inventions available in the English language. Our language is often said to be poor in rhyme, as opposed to, say, Italian, but this array of terms may raise awareness of the potential variety.[1]

Rhymes Defined by Nature of Similarity

perfect rhyme, full rhyme, true rhyme: These terms refer to the immediately recognizable norm: *true/blue, mountain/fountain.*

imperfect rhyme, slant rhyme, half rhyme, approximate rhyme, near rhyme, off rhyme, oblique rhyme: These are all general terms referring to rhymes that are close but not exact: *lap/shape, glorious/nefarious.*

eye rhyme: This refers to rhymes based on similarity of spelling rather than sound. Often these are highly conventional, and reflect historical changes in pronunciation: *love/move/prove, why/envý.*

identical rhyme: A word rhymes with itself, as in Emily Dickinson's "Because I Could not Stop for Death":

We paused before a House that seemed
A Swelling of the Ground—

---

[1] This list is adapted from Joseph Malof's *Manual of English Meters* (Bloomington: Indiana Univ. Press, 1970).

The Roof was scarcely visible—
The Cornice—in the Ground—

rich rhyme (from French *rime riche*): A word rhymes with its homonym: *blue/blew, guessed/guest.*

assonant rhyme: Rhyming with similar vowels, different consonants: *dip/limp, man/prank.*

consonant rhyme: Rhyming with similar consonants, different vowels: *limp/lump, bit/bet.*

scarce rhyme: Rhyming on words with limited rhyming alternatives: *whisp/lisp, motionless/oceanless.*

macaronic rhyme: Macaronic verse uses more than one language, as in medieval lyrics with Latin refrains. Macaronic rhyme is also bilingual: *glory/pro patria mori, Τροιη/lee-way, sure/Kreatur, queasy/civilisé.*

Rhymes Defined by Relation to Stress Pattern

one-syllable rhyme, masculine rhyme: The norm, in which rhyme occurs on the final stressed syllables:

One, two,
Buckle my shoe

extra-syllable rhyme, triple rhyme, multiple rhyme, extended rhyme, feminine rhyme: These all refer to rhyming double or triple or multiple extra-syllable endings: *dying/flying, generate/venerate, salubrious/lugubrious.*

light rhyme: Rhyming of a stressed syllable with a secondary stress: *frog/dialog, live/prohibitive.*

wrenched rhyme: Rhyming of a stressed syllable with an unstressed syllable. This often occurs in ballads and folk poetry, often on conventional words like *ladý, countrý.* Here is an example from the anonymous ballad "Sir Patrick Spens":

They had not been a week, a week,
In Norraway but three,
Till lords of Norraway gan to say
   Ye spend all our white moníe

Rhymes Defined by Position

By Position in the Line

end rhyme, terminal rhyme: All rhymes occur at line ends—the standard procedure.

initial rhyme, head rhyme: Alliteration.

internal rhyme: Rhyme that occurs within a line or passage, whether randomly (as below, on "flow" and "grow") or in some kind of pattern:

> A heavenly paradise is that place,
> Wherein all pleasant fruits do flow.
> These cherries grow, which none may buy
> Till "Cherry Ripe!" themselves do cry.

leonine rhyme, medial rhyme: Rhyme that occurs at the caesura and line end within a single line—like a rhymed couplet printed as a single line:

> I bring fresh showers for the thirsting flowers

caesural rhyme, interlaced rhyme: Rhymes that occur at the caesura and line end within a pair of lines—like an *abab* quatrain printed as two lines:

> Sweet is the treading of wine, and sweet the feet of the dove;
> But a goodlier gift is thine than foam of the grapes or love.
> Yea, is not even Apollo, with hair and harp-string of gold,
> A bitter God to follow, a beautiful God to behold?

Or the following unusual example, an *In Memoriam* stanza (*abba*) printed as couplets:

> Upon the mat she lies and leers and on the tawny throat of her
> Flutters the soft and silky fur or ripples to her pointed ears.
>
> Come forth, my lovely seneschal! so somnolent, so statuesque!
> Come forth you exquisite grotesque! half woman and half animal!

By Position in the Stanza or Verse Paragraph

crossed rhyme, alternating rhyme, interlocking rhyme: Rhyming in an *abab* pattern.

intermittent rhyme: Rhyming every other line, as in the standard ballad quatrain: *xaxa.*

envelope rhyme, inserted rhyme: Rhyming *abba* (as in the *In Memoriam* stanza).

irregular rhyme: Rhyming that follows no fixed pattern (as in the pseudopindaric or irregular ode).

sporadic rhyme, occasional rhyme: Rhyming that occurs unpredictably in a poem with mostly unrhymed lines.

thorn line: A line left without rhyme in a generally rhymed passage. (There are ten thorn lines among the 193 lines in Milton's irregularly rhymed *Lycidas.*)

Rhyme across Word Boundaries

broken rhyme: Rhyme using more than one word:

> But—Oh! ye lords of ladies intellectual,
> Inform us truly, have they not hen-peck'd you all?

Or rhyme in which one word is broken over the line end:

> I caught this morning morning's minion, king-
> dom of daylight's dauphin, dapple-dawn-drawn Falcon, in his riding
> Of the rolling level underneath him steady air, and striding
> High there, how he rung upon the rein of a wimpling wing ...

linked rhyme: Rhyme that depends on completing the rhyme sound by enjambment over the line end:

> But what black Boreas wrecked her? he
> Came equipped, deadly-electric,

apocopated rhyme: Rhyming a line end with a penultimate syllable:

> A poem should be wordless
> As the flight of birds.

Appendix 2

Sample Scansions, with Commentary

William Shakespeare, "Sonnet 94"

    ´   ˘ | ˘   ´ | ˘ ´ ‖˘   ´ | ˘   ´
They that have pow'r to hurt and will do none,

    ˘   ´| ˘ ´| ˘   ´ | ˘   ´ | ˘   ´
That do not do the thing they most do show,

    ˘ ‖ ´| ˘   ´| ˘ ‖´ | ˘   ´ |˘   ´
Who, moving others, are themselves as stone,

    ˘   ´|˘ ‖ ´ ‖˘   `| ˘   ´| ´
Unmovèd, cold, and to temptation slow;

    ˘   ´ |˘ ´| ˘ ´|˘   ´ | ´ (˘)
They rightly do inherit heaven's graces   5

    ˘   ´|˘   ´|˘   ´|˘   `|˘   ´
And husband nature's riches from expense;

    ´ ˘ | ˘ ´ |˘   ´ |˘ `| ˘   ´ (˘)
They are the lords and owners of their faces,

    ´   ˘ | ˘   ´|˘ `| ˘   ´|˘ `
Others but stewards of their excellence.

    ˘ ´ | ˘   ´ |˘ `| ˘ ´ | ˘   ´
The summer's flow'r is to the summer sweet,

    ˘   ´|˘ ´ |˘ ´|˘ ´ |˘   ´
Though to itself it only live and die;   10

˘ ´ | ˘   ´ | ˘   ´ |˘ ´ |˘   ´
But if that flow'r with base infection meet,

˘   ´|˘   ´ |˘   ´ | ˘   ´ | ˘˘
The basest weed outbraves his dignity:

˘   ´ |˘   ´ | ˘   ´ |˘   `| ˘   ´
For sweetest things turn sourest by their deeds;

´˘ | ˘   ´|˘   ´ |´   ´ | ˘   ´
Lilies that fester smell far worse than weeds.

Shakespeare's poem is a product of the sonnet fashion introduced from the continent, which swept England in the last decades of the sixteenth century. Iambic pentameter, with its regular alteration of weak and accented syllables, was formalized around the time of Tottel's *Miscellany* (1557), and since then poets had worked within fairly narrow limits of regularity, avoiding frequent metrical variation or radical enjambment. Shakespeare's sonnets were written early in his career and therefore share this cautious treatment of the pentameter line, as do his early plays (though one must remember the different demands of writing for the dramatic voice on stage).

Here metrical variation is limited to three strategic trochaic reversals, plus some use of lightened accent (˘ `), one spondee, and one pair of extra-syllable rhymes. Enjambment is avoided, and even caesura minimized, except for one specific effect. Within such a narrow range of variation, departures from metrical regularity stand out with added sharpness.

This is an English sonnet—three quatrains plus couplet—but inspection reveals that Shakespeare has organized it rhetorically into an octave plus sestet, like an Italian sonnet. The octave is organized on a threefold anaphora on the word "They," twice heightened by initial trochaic reversal avoided elsewhere. The first quatrain itself builds up a threefold parallel pattern of negations, line 1, line 2, then expanded in lines 3–4, with syntactic momentum brought to a halt by multiple caesuras (avoided elsewhere), stretched syllables ("unmovèd," "and tò temptation"), and syntactic inversion, finally to arrive on the word "slow."

In the second quatrain, metrical regularity restores the tempo, and the turn to positive statement (however ironic) is underscored by the light extra-syllable rhymes. In the third and climactic anaphora on "They," however, the trochaic reversal suggests a note of severity—"They are the lords and owners"—rounded off by neat antithesis in line 8.

The third quatrain (or sestet) introduces without preparation a new image by way of illustration; but the link with the preceding is underscored by a most unusual device, the internal rhyme of "flow'r" with "pow'r" in line 1. For two lines, the flower is a thing of beauty; but in the third, with parallel repetition of the word, the flower's vulnerability is heightened by significant alliteration that links "flow'r" to "infection," raises "base" to "basest," and pits "sweetest" against "sourest"—this climactic word culminating the internal rhyme sequence "pow'r … flow'r … flow'r … sourest."

The clinching line of the final couplet pits "Lilies" (heightened by initial trochee) against "weeds." The weight of this line, as I hear it, provokes the only spondee in the poem, on "far worse." Semantic linkage continues its work, tying together "sweetest," "sourest," and "smell"; "fester" and "far"; "worse" and "weeds"; while the couplet rhyme conclusively relates "weeds" to the "deeds" of the individuals under discussion.

Note that although prosodic analysis is a type of interpretation, this analysis does not pretend to be a full interpretation of Shakespeare's poem. It merely outlines the rhetorical, syntactic, and sonic patterns that energize Shakespeare's use of the sonnet form.

John Milton, *Paradise Lost,* I.1–16

Of Man's First Disobedience, and the Fruit→

Of that Forbidden Tree, whose mortal taste→

Brought Death into the World, and all our woe,

With loss of *Eden*, till one greater Man→

Restore us, and regain the blissful Seat,→   5

Sing Heav'nly Muse, that on the secret top→

Of *Oreb* or of *Sinai* didst inspire→

That Shepherd, who first taught the chosen Seed,

In the Beginning how the Heav'ns and Earth→

Rose out of *Chaos*: or if *Sion* Hill→   10

Delight thee more, and *Siloa's* Brook that flow'd→

Fast by the Oracle of God; I thence→

Invoke thy aid to my advent'rous Song,

That with no middle flight intends to soar

Above th'*Aonian* Mount, while it pursues→   15

Things unattempted yet in Prose or Rhyme.

This is the opening of Milton's *Paradise Lost*, the invocation to the Muse traditionally found at the beginning of an epic. Before setting out to write his poem, Milton made two crucial decisions. First, he chose to write in English rather than Latin (which he could easily have done), and thus, though the poem is immensely learned, he defined his audience to include all readers of the English vernacular. Second, he chose to write in blank verse—unrhymed iambic pentameter—a decision rather daring at the time; he appealed in a headnote to his poem not only to the precedent of Greek and Latin poetry, always unrhymed, but also to that of "our best English Tragedies" for the freedom to dispense with "the troublesome and modern bondage of Riming." Such conscious decisions, often ignored by critics, form part of a poet's formal contract with his readership. Had Milton chosen to write his influential epic in rhyming couplets, the subsequent development of English blank verse might have been very different indeed.

Milton's treatment of the iambic pentameter line, however, sounds very different from that of Shakespeare's sonnet. Though both adhere closely to the ten-syllable norm (Milton largely avoiding extra-syllable endings), Shakespeare's lines are controlled by syntactic parallelism and end-stopping within his rhyme scheme; Milton's, however, freed from rhyme, surge forward with continuous enjambment and periodic syntax—that is, sentences that pile up phrases and clauses, ever delaying completion of subject and verb. The most immediate effect of this passage is the impact of the command "Sing Heav'nly Muse," heightened by the periodic delay and enjambment alighting on the first initial trochee of the poem. But the syntax still rushes forward, not reaching full stop until line 10, where "Rose out of Chaos" is again underlined by enjambment plus initial trochee. Even then, the rhetoric forges ahead to the end of the verse paragraph, the final line underscored for a third time with enjambment and trochee.

Within this grand sweep, Milton's fine-tuning is also noteworthy. The very first line, as I scan it here, startles with trochaic reversal in the unlikeliest position: the second foot. This scansion is admittedly an interpretive decision on my part; one could read an accent falling more predictably on the first syllable of disobedience—but with a subtle change of meaning. Such accentuation would imply that Milton's subject is humanity's first *dis*obedience, implying a prior record of obedience not conspicuous in the biblical story. As I scan the line, Milton's subject is humankind's *first* disobedience, the first of a long list, and this reading seems truer to both biblical record and human experience. The accented "first" is thus linked by alliteration to "Fruit" (poised on the line-end)—both the literal fruit in the Garden of Eden and the metaphoric fruit, or consequence, of humankind's first sin. This is a good illustration of the interplay between metrical analysis and interpretation.

These lines set in motion several features typical of Milton's metrical style. Semantic linkage through alliteration continues, with "Tree" and "taste," "World" and "woe," and the series of sibilants "Restore," "Seat," "Sing," "secret," "Sinai," "inspire," "Shepherd," "Seed." The four-syllable "disobedience" typifies Milton's polysyllabic texture, which metrically generates a suppleness in degrees of accentuation. I have chosen to scan the end of this word as a single elided syllable, partly because it is easily pronounced and partly because anapests in Milton are scarce; in this same passage, I have scanned anapests on the words "Siloa's" and "th'Aonian," mainly because further elision sounds forced to my ear, even though elision is what Milton may have intended.

The spondee on "no middle flight" is an interpretive reading on my part: it underlines Milton's vaunting claim to the high style of epic tradition, and the empowerment to treat the grandest of sacred subjects.

Alexander Pope, "An Essay on Criticism," 337–57, 362–73

      ˘   ´ | ˘ ´ | ˘   ´ | ˘ ´| ˘   ´
But most by Numbers judge a Poet's song,

      ˘   ´ | ˘ ´ | ˘   ´ | ˘ ´ | ˘   ´
And smooth or rough, with them, is right or wrong;

      ˘   ˘ | ´   ´ | ˘   ´ | ˘   ´ | ˘   ´
In the Bright Muse tho' thousand charms conspire,

      ˘   ´ | ˘ ´ | ˘   ´ | ˘ ´ | ˘   ´
Her Voice is all these tuneful fools admire;   340

        ˘   ´ | ˘ ´| ˘   ´| ˘ ´ | ˘ ´
Who haunt Parnassus but to please their ear,→

˘ ˊ | ˘ ˊ ‖˘ ˊ | ˊ | ˘ ˘

Not mend their minds; as some to Church repair→

ˊ ˘ | ˘ ˊ | ˘ ‖ ˋ | ˘ ˊ|˘ ˊ

Not for the doctrine, but the music there.

ˊ ˊ| ˘ ˊ|˘ ˋ |˘ ˊ | ˘ ˘

These equal syllables alone require,

˘ ˊ | ˘ ˊ | ˘ ˊ|˘ ˊ|˘ ˊ

Tho' oft the ear the open vowels tire;   345

˘ ˊ| ˘ | ˘ ˊ|˘ ˊ | ˘ ˊ

While expletives their feeble aid do join;

˘   ˊ | ˊ ˊ |ˊ ˊ|˘ | ˊ ˘

And ten low words oft creep in one dull line;

ˊ ˘ | ˊ ˊ | ˘ ˊ |˘ ˊ| ˊ

While they ring round the same unvary'd chimes

˘ ˊ | ˘ ˊ |˘ ˊ|ˊ ˊ|˘   ˊ

With sure returns of still expected rhymes.

˘ ˊ | ˘ ˊ | ˘ ˊ|˘   ˊ|˘ ˊ

Where-e'er you find 'the cooling western breeze,'   350

˘   ˘| ˊ ˊ | ˘   ˊ|˘   ˋ | ˘ ˊ

In the next line, it 'whispers thro' the trees;'

˘ ˊ |˘   ˊ | ˘   ˊ|˘   ˊ | ˘ ˊ

If crystal streams 'with pleasing murmurs creep,'

˘ ˊ |˘   ˊ |˘   ˊ|˘ ˊ | ˘   ˊ

The reader's threaten'd (not in vain) with 'sleep.'

ˊ ˘| ˘   ˊ|˘ ˊ |˘ ˊ|˘   ˊ

Then, at the last and only couplet fraught→

˘ ˊ |˘ ˊ|˘   ˊ | ˘ ˊ|˘   ˊ

With some unmeaning thing they call a thought,   355

˘ ˊ|˘ ˊ|˘ˊ | ˘ ˊ | ˘ ˊ

A needless Alexandrine ends the song,

˘ ˊ |ˊ |ˊ   ˊ ‖ ˊ   ˘ | ˊ   ˊ |˘ ˊ

That, like a wounded snake, drags its slow length along ...

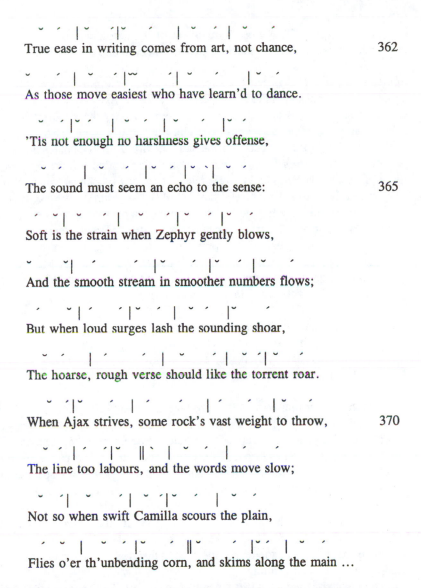

True ease in writing comes from art, not chance,   362

As those move easiest who have learn'd to dance.

'Tis not enough no harshness gives offense,

The sound must seem an echo to the sense: 365

Soft is the strain when Zephyr gently blows,

And the smooth stream in smoother numbers flows;

But when loud surges lash the sounding shoar,

The hoarse, rough verse should like the torrent roar.

When Ajax strives, some rock's vast weight to throw,   370

The line too labours, and the words move slow;

Not so when swift Camilla scours the plain,

Flies o'er th'unbending corn, and skims along the main ...

Sceptics who question whether poets really pay such minute attention to particulars as the analysts claim must read with care Alexander Pope's celebrated passage on versification in his "Essay on Criticism." Here the youthful Pope demonstrates the self-consciousness of the poetic artist, the deliberateness of choice, while at the same time wittily illustrating metrical effects as he describes them. Even while giving these matters due attention, however, Pope, within the larger argument of his poem, scolds the reader who judges more by "numbers" (that is, metrical correctness) than by thought. Versification, as always, is the means, not an end in itself.

This passage exhibits Pope's treatment of the heroic couplet, the dominant non-dramatic verse form of much of the seventeenth and most of the eighteenth centuries. The line is predominantly regular: allowed are trochaic substitutions, lightened accents (˘ `), and occasional spondees or ionic patterns (˘ ˘ ´ ´); avoided are anapests, unless they can be elided. Extra-syllable rhymes are scarce. The couplet is closed, no enjambment, or only the slightest, being the norm. Variety is achieved by ensuring that the caesura, whether or not marked in the scansion, does not occur in the same position for too many lines in succession. Energy arises from syntactic units being coiled within the restricted space of twenty syllables and two rhymes. Occasionally, the poet may allow the couplet to relax into a triplet (see lines 341–43). Sometimes, as here, this seems a convenience, the poet having bitten off more matter than a couplet can chew. Sometimes, however, the triplet occupies a position of rhetorical climax.[2]

Pope begins by illustrating several prosodic faults a poet must avoid. The list is not meant to be exhaustive. First-time readers of this passage may treat it as a kind of quiz: By examining the examples, explain what Pope means by "open vowels," "expletives," and "low words":

> These equal syllables alone require,
> Tho' oft the ear the open vowels tire;
> While expletives their feeble aid do join;
> And ten low words oft creep in one dull line

Open vowels are initial vowels that produce an unattractive glottal pop. Expletives are words like "do" used solely to eke out the meter. (This verb form, which figured regularly in couplet verse before Pope, virtually disappeared after this line focused attention on it.) "Low words" are common monosyllables, which lead not only to lifeless diction but to plodding meter, as Pope's unjustifiable spondaic plod illustrates. Pope's witty remarks on unimaginative rhyming scarcely need comment; but his remarks on the alexandrine do. Pope condemns not the line itself, but the alexandrine not justified by its content. His example, broken in the middle by caesura like most hexameters, is comically debilitated further by trochee and spondee, while the rhythm rises bathetically on a trivial and expendable word, "along."

The next passage introduces a positive ideal that goes beyond mere metrical correctness and euphony: "The sound must seem an echo to the sense." Pope's famous maxim is frequently mistaken for an endorsement of naive mimicry in the abstract realm of metrics, and his examples may reinforce this misunder-

---

[2] In such cases, the third line is often an alexandrine. Good illustration can be found in Dryden's elegy "To the Memory of Mr. Oldham," where the effect occurs twice. Eighteenth-century printers usually bracketed triplets in couplet poetry, a useful device normally omitted by modern editors.

standing. But his intent is clear. The sound must "seem an echo": occasions when sound can truly imitate sense may be rare, but the sound must always seem prosodically appropriate, and this demand calls on the poet's, or the analyst's, deepest instincts and critical tact.

The general statement about "true ease in writing," reinforced by a superb metaphor (lines 362–65), falls into regular iambics. The pair of couplets illustrating softness and harshness, however, contrast partly through metric variation and partly through sound value. Though the "soft" couplet admits an initial trochee and the pyrrhic-spondee rhythm, graceful enough in themselves, the soft effect arises largely from the long vowels and voiced, sustained consonants. The harsh couplet is more agitated metrically, scanned here with initial trochee and two spondees (not lightened with pyrrhic), and the word sounds are cluttered with consonants and overladen with internal rhyme and near rhyme: "surges," "shoar," "hoarse," "verse," "torrent," "roar." The couplet on Ajax achieves slowness and weight most obviously from the excessive spondaic rhythms, but also through the adjacent sibilants, difficult to pronounce without deliberation: "Ajax strives some ..." Camilla's couplet, returning to unimpeded metrical regularity, appears swift by contrast, and her alexandrine—far from dragging like a wounded snake—skims along many elided syllables as well as along the main.

Pope's passage is a self-conscious display of prosodic virtuosity. No one, I think, can study it and believe that Pope was not perfectly aware of what he was doing.

Christina Rossetti

Song

When I am dead, my dearest,

Sing no sad songs for me;

Plant thou no roses at my head,

Nor shady cypress tree:

Be the green grass above me   5

With showers and dewdrops wet:

˘   ´ | ˘   ´ | ˘ ˘ (˘)
And if thou wilt, remember,

˘   ´ | ˘   ´ | ˘ ´
And if thou wilt, forget.

˘   ´ | ˘   ´ | ˘   ´(˘)
I shall not see the shadows,

˘   ´ | ˘   ´ | ˘ ´
I shall not feel the rain;

˘   ´ | ˘   ´ | ˘   ´|
I shall not hear the nightingale→

˘   ´ ‖ ˘   ´| ´
Sing on, as if in pain:

˘   ´ |˘   ´ | ˘   ´(˘)
And dreaming through the twilight

˘   ´ | ˘   ´ | ˘ ´
That doth not rise nor set,

´ ˘|˘   ´ | ˘ ´ (˘)
Haply I may remember,

˘   ´|˘   ´ | ˘ ´
And haply may forget.

10

15

Christina Rossetti's apparently simple "Song" succeeds through its creation of a believably plaintive speaker, its quietly muted diction, and a meticulous control of form. The speaker, presumably female, addresses her mate in the simplest words, *as if* from the grave. Her song-like stanza is an extension of the ballad stanza, a quatrain of short meter followed by a quatrain of iambic trimeter, both rhymed *xaxa*. (The "me" in line 5, incidentally, is *not* a rhyme word, falling as it does on an unaccented extra syllable.) The first of the two stanzas addresses the husband's prospects, the second the wife's. Both stanzas are subdivided in two parts: the first begins with a quatrain of command, then continues with a gentler wish in hortatory subjunctive; the second begins with a firm assertion about the future, then trails off in participial reflection. Both stanzas conclude with a two-line refrain, a varied antithesis on the words "remember" and "forget."

The most emphatic effect in the poem occurs in stanza 2, with the anaphora on "I shall not," a rhetoric of self-denial. The speaker's self-effacing insistence mounts on a threefold climax to the most plangent metrical effect in the poem: the enjambment in the tetrameter (and thus unpaused) line 11—the sole enjambment in the poem—cruelly prolonging the nightingale's singing on, "as if in pain."

The second stanza develops threefold parallel imagery from the first: "shadows" picks up "shady" from line 4; "rain" picks up "showers and dewdrops" from line 5; and the nightingale's song picks up "sing" from line 2. But the speaker, in her acceptance of fate, accepts also its indeterminacy. She serenely closes with paradox ("the twilight/ that does not rise or set") and aporia, the uncertainty of individual consciousness after death.

Wallace Stevens, from "Sunday Morning"

Complacencies of the peignoir, and late→

Coffee and oranges in a sunny chair,

And the green freedom of a cockatoo→

Upon a rug mingle to dissipate→

The holy hush of ancient sacrifice.   5

She dreams a little, and she feels the dark→

Encroachment of that old catastrophe,

As a calm darkens among water-lights.

The pungent oranges and bright, green wings→

Seem things in some procession of the dead,   10

ˊ ˇ |ˇ ˊ | ˊ ˊ|ˇ ‖ ˇ|ˊ ˊ
Winding across wide water, without sound.

ˇ ˊ|ˇ ˇ |ˊ ˊ|ˇ ‖ ˇ|ˊ ˊ
The day is like wide water, without sound,

ˊ ˇ|ˇ ˊ|ˇ ˋ|ˇ ˊ|ˇ ˊ
Stilled for the passing of her dreaming feet

ˊ ˇ| ˇ ˊ ‖ ˇ ˊ|ˇ ˊ|ˇ ˋ
Over the seas, to silent Palestine,

ˇ ˊ|ˇ ˋ|ˇ ˊ |ˇ ˊ|ˇ ˋ
Dominion of the blood and sepulchre.   15

Wallace Stevens' profoundly felt exploration of post-religious nostalgia begins with a blank verse stanza describing a casual Sunday morning scene, the female protagonist in *dishabille*, comfortably relaxing but still feeling vaguely guilty about not being in church. Metrically, her meditation, which is descended from a heritage of philosophic blank verse meditations, likewise begins with hesitant rhythms, metrical irregularities reflecting an oddly frazzled state of mind. Line 1 begins metrically off balance, with its uncertain accentuation and late caesura; the enjambments urge forward; and the most striking feature in what follows, the spondee on "green freedom," underlines, with its oddly transferred epithet, the paradoxical half-way freedom of the caged bird, emblem of the woman's ambivalent mood.

All these wavering rhythms converge on the main verb "mingle," heightened with mid-line trochaic reversal, and finally come to rest on the first fully regular iambic pentameter line in the poem, "The holy hush of ancient sacrifice." The source of the woman's perturbation has surfaced. She is worried by what the periphrastic phrases "ancient sacrifice" and "old catastrophe," thinly disguise: the crucifixion of Jesus, and all it represents. The ensuing simile—"As a calm darkens among water lights"—ineffably captures the sense of mental calm amid jitters, reflected in the very unusual repetition of the ionic foot (the pyrrhic-spondee combination).

The woman collects her thoughts, the worrisome cockatoo reduced by synecdoche to "bright green wings," as her natural world is scaled down to a single thought of mortality. The meter now unfolds with inevitable regularity, and the repetitiveness of lines 11–12 suggests the bleak monotony of hopelessness. Her mind travels (via the metaphoric hypallage "dreaming feet") to a "silent Palestine," a holy land that withholds its answers, and yet remains the site of "the blood and sepulchre," that is, Jesus' violent death and probable end.

Earle Birney

Bushed

He invented a rainbow, but lightning struck it

ˊ ˘ | ˘ ˊ | ˘   ˘ ˊ | ˘   ˋ | ˘   ˊ (˘)
shattered it into the lake-lap of a mountain

˘   ˊ | ˘   ˊ | ˊ   ˘ | ˘ ˊ | ˘ ˋ
so big his mind slowed when he looked at it

Yet he built a shack on the shore

learned to roast porcupine belly and→   5

wore the quills on his hatband

At first he was out with the dawn

ˊ   ˘ | ˘ ˊ | ˘   ˊ | ˘   ˘   ˊ | ˘   ˋ
whether it yellowed bright as wood-columbine

˘   ˘   ˊ | ˘ ˘ | ˊ   ˊ | ˘ ˘ ˊ | ˘ ˘   ˊ
or was only a fuzzed moth in a flannel of storm

But he found the mountain was clearly alive   10

˘   ˊ | ˘ ˘   ˊ | ˘   ˊ | ˊ   ˘ | ˊ   ˊ (˘)
sent messages whizzing down every hot morning

boomed proclamations at noon and spread out→

a white guard of goat

˘ ˊ | ˊ ˘ | ˊ   ˊ | ˊ ˘   ˊ | ˊ   ˊ (˘)
before falling asleep on its feet at sundown

When he tried his eyes on the lake   ospreys→   15

would fall like valkyries

choosing the cut-throat

He took then to waiting

till the night smoke rose from the boil of the sunset

⏑   ⏑ ˊ | ⏑ ˊ | ⏑ ˊ|⏑
But the moon carved unknown totems→   20

ˊ | ⏑ ⏑ ˊ (ˋ)
out of the lakeshore

ˊ ⏑ | ⏑ ˊ | ⏑ ˊ | ⏑ ˊ|⏑ ˊ
owls in the beardusky woods derided him

ˊ   ⏑ | ⏑ ⏑ | ˊ ⏑ˊ| ⏑ ˊ | ⏑ ˊ
moosehorned cedars circled his swamps and tossed→

their antlers up to the stars

ˊ ⏑| ˊ   ⏑ | ⏑ ˊ|⏑ ˊ | ⏑ ˊ
then he knew   though the mountain slept   the winds→   25

were shaping its peak to an arrowhead

poised→

⏑   ˊ | ⏑ ⏑ ˊ|⏑
And now he could only

ˊ| ⏑ ⏑ ˊ|⏑   ˊ
bar himself in and wait

⏑ ⏑ˊ| ˊ ˊ | ⏑ ⏑ ˊ|⏑ ˊ|⏑ ⏑ ˊ
for the great flint to come singing into his heart   30

The title of Earle Birney's "Bushed" is a peculiar Canadianism that means not merely "tired out," as in common North American vernacular, but specifically driven mad by isolation from human contact in the wilderness. The phenomenon, of course, is not exclusively Canadian, as Joseph Conrad's Kurtz amply demonstrates.

The poem appears, from its irregular line lengths, its odd spacing on the page, its suppression of punctuation, to be written in free verse. But on examination, it turns out to be more like "freed up" verse (*vers libéré*), depending to a certain degree on iambic pentameter traces lying beneath the surface. The opening line is apparently non-metrical, but the next two fall into familiar pentameter rhythms, even to the extent of deploying trochaic reversal on the word "slowed," for obvious effect.

Section 2 (lines 4–6) drops pentameter feeling entirely, in favour of parallel syntax ("built ... learned ... wore") to suggest the man's controlled adaptation to his surroundings. In section 3 (lines 7–14), pentameter traces reappear, but sporadically and ambiguously. The last line, for example, might be iambic pentameter, but loses that rhythm if one drops the accent on "before." The traces are only traces. The passage is patterned partly by the time progression: "dawn ... morning ... noon ... sundown." These time references subsequently disappear, leaving the rest of the poem in darkness.

As time disappears, the images of celestial portent multiply. We have already had "rainbow" and "lightning" in the first line (with a hint of Christian symbolism), followed by more mysterious "messages" and "proclamations." Now, in section 4 (lines 15–19), ospreys become "valkyries," figures in Nordic mythology who carry off the souls of dead warriors to Valhalla. Birney not only uses enjambment after "ospreys" to suggest the imminence of their predatory swoop, but spaces the word off from the end of the line. This typographic gesture, not found in traditional metrical verse, is now common in free verse.

In section 5 (lines 20–27), the mythology becomes aboriginal with the word "totem"—now alien and "unknown." At the same time, however, iambic pentameter rhythms begin to accumulate, though Birney disguises them by breaking pentameter lines over two lines, or by setting them up with initial trochaic rhythms. The iambic pentameter presence is not continuous, but persistent enough to establish a sense of menacing inevitability. The section ends with the word "poised," visually isolated like the ospreys and "the winds," earlier. This word can be read as grammatically completing the section; but (especially in the absence of punctuation) the effect is one of upward vocal intonation, a kind of aposiopesis, the syntax suspended, incomplete.

The final section (lines 28–30) asserts the man's final isolation, his self-imprisonment and anticipation of ultimate doom. These lines bring the pentameter presence to the surface, enforcing closure; the last line, with its grave spondee on "great flint," is an overt and unmistakable iambic pentameter. But how well it has been prepared.

Index of Sources

Chapter 1

Chapter 2

Chapter 3

Chapter 4

Appendix 1

Index of
Names and Terms